THE
HOLLOW GLOBE;
OR
THE WORLD'S AGITATOR
AND RECONCILER.

A TREATISE

ON THE PHYSICAL CONFORMATION OF THE EARTH.

Presented through the Organism of

M. L. SHERMAN, M. D.,

And Written by

PROF. WM. F. LYON.

CHICAGO:

RELIGIO-PHILOSOPHICAL PUBLISHING HOUSE.

S. S. JONES, PROPRIETOR.

1871.

CONTENTS.

PREFACE.

This book is addressed to the reasoning intelligence of Humanity,—to all inquiring and reflective minds, everywhere upon the earth.

We earnestly request the reader to suspend his judgment concerning the ideas advanced, until he has carefully perused its pages; when he may be better prepared to form his opinions, and offer his criticisms.

We do not claim that the teachings contained in this work are infallible, neither are they presented in an authoritative manner. But, we do claim, that it contains more original, natural and startling ideas, which are of great interest to civilized humanity, and which seem to be entirely irrefutable, than any book of its size, that has made its appearance in modern times.

We therefore commend it to the careful consideration of the modern thinker, being fully persuaded that its pages contain a large fund of thought which may open to his mind new fields of research, thus tending to enlarge his understanding, and enlighten his intellect. We are also of the opinion that its perusal may save multitudes from many superstitious beliefs and shadowy dogmas, respecting natural phenomena, as well as theological teachings, which have hitherto overclouded their minds.

We are deeply impressed with the thought, and venture to predict, that this book will do very much towards aiding humanity in their toilsome progress, from the darkness of mental slavery, to the broad sunshine of enlightened freedom, for which they have so long struggled, but struggled apparently in vain.

INTRODUCTION.

The central idea contained in the following work and the one that most of these chapters are designed to substantiate is, that this globe is constructed in the form of a hollow sphere, with a shell some thirty to forty miles in thickness, and that the interior surface which is a beautiful world in a more highly developed condition than the exterior, is accessible by a circuitous and spirally formed aperture that may be found in the unexplored open Polar Sea, and this opening affords easy navigation, by a broad and deep channel leading from one surface to the other, and that the largest ships or steamers may sail or steam either way, with as much facility as they can pass through any other winding, or somewhat crooked channel. And we have endeavored to show as clearly as possible, that the physical formation of the globe is such as to be perfectly compatible with an outer and inner world, or two worlds instead of one, and it might be proper to present a brief sketch of the leading circumstances that have induced the production of this book and its presentation to the public.

About the middle of September, 1868, the writer of

this work was standing at his desk in his own place of business, attending to some matter, when a strange gentleman made his appearance in the office, and introduced himself as Dr. M. L. Sherman. I told him to be seated, and in a few moments I would give him my attention. He seemed to scan me very closely, and finally among other things told me, You are the man that I have been searching after; the very man I was to find, and we have a large amount of business that we must transact together, but I am not fully prepared to state the nature of that business, for I do not seem to understand it myself. I replied very well, if it is to be so, I trust it will be satisfactory, or something to that effect, but his announcement did not make a vivid impression upon my mind, as in my experience I had heard things of a similar nature previously. However, the Doctor and myself formed an intimacy which has not been interrupted since, only by my absence of about seven months in the Eastern States, that occurred soon after our first introduction; and I have found him to be a very remarkable and peculiar personage, whose day and hour to be widely known to the world, has probably not yet fully come.

The numerous remarkable experiences of his life, since his connection with spiritualistic teachings and phenomena, would of themselves fill a volume, and are by no means admissible in this exceedingly brief sketch of an eventful career, but we note as prominent among them, that he was for a long time a public speaker, and spoke in a trance or unconscious condition, to the great dismay and astonishment of those who opposed, and the satisfaction and encouragement of those who coincided to some extent with his teachings. But in process of time he seemed to become so extremely radical, and announced in public, ideas so much in advance of his time, and he was withal constitutionally so firm, and somewhat harsh and severe in his language, that, as he says, his speech was confounded, or he was unable to give utterance to his thoughts in public, and of course he ceased lecturing. But there seemed to be another field opened before him, and like Paul and Swedenborg and many other seers, he was called upon to make his personal survey of some portion of the spirit realms, and at several different times, has been thrown into a semi-trance condition becoming partially unconscious of his earthly surroundings, and permitted to pass through the most vivid experiences that he was capable of appreciating in the spiritual spheres. These different seasons of trance, in which he partook of no earthly food or drink except a little vinegar, were from three to twelve days each, making over forty days in all, and for four days of this time he was to all appearance dead, so much so that a prominent physician of the town pronounced him dead to all intents, with the remark that they might use his head for a foot-ball if he ever breathed again upon the earth, and it required the utmost exertion of the friend at whose house he lay, who was a man of some influence, to keep the authorities from consigning him to a premature grave, thus adding another to the numerous human sacrifices that have been made in this manner by people ignorant of some of nature's laws.

Yet, notwithstanding all the learned Doctor's opinions and assertions, he did breathe again, and after lying twelve days in this comatose, apparently lifeless condition, without food of any kind, his spirit came back from its wanderings once more, took possession of the earthly tabernacle, and he lived to write a brief account of what he saw during his several trance conditions, and published to the world a small work of thirty-eight pages, entitled "My Experiences in Spiritual Phenomena," and to all appearance he seems likely to live for many years to come.

This work, in consequence of its strange and radical ideas, was not well received, even by those minds who supposed they had laid off the trammels of old orthodoxy, but most likely the day is not distant when this little book will be re-published, and properly appreciated by those who are attaining to a clearer perception of spiritual truths and philosophy, than was enjoyed twenty years since by the most enlightened persons.

Up to the 1st of January, 1870, I think we had obtained no clue whatever, to the meaning of the language made use of when he first entered my office, and introduced himself. About that time, however, we discovered the fact that he seeemed to go under an influence when I came into his presence, and he and Mrs. Sherman who is remarkably mediumistic, began to see clairvoyantly many curious visions or symbols that were to us quite dark and mysterious, among which was one of a book, seen by him, sealed with five seals, three in front and one at each end. It appeared to be a large, finely bound volume, and it was presented me with instructions that I was to take the book, and unloose the seals thereof, all of which was Greek to us at the time. At other times large quantities of paper and pens with beautiful inkstands, and writing materials generally were brought and presented to me; and among many other things it was finally told us, that through the Doctor's mediumship we were to obtain the general ideas, and that I, in my room, by the aid of my own impressional powers was to mold and fashion and weave them into a book, to be entitled the *World's Agitator and Reconciler*, and in due time they began through the Doctor's organism to teach concerning the nature of the book and its contents. However, the teachings were of such a character that we were very slow to receive them, and, in fact, it was a very tedious process upon their part to make us understand and comprehend their ideas. They came to us in such broken fragments, and apparently dark and mystified manner, but they urged me to commence writing, for it was no matter where and how I commenced, they would find a place in the book for my productions, and so I began about the middle of March, and was urged as nearly as may be, to finish the book by the first of November.

The whole affair has been extremely novel to us all, and I doubt not these pages may appear somewhat novel to the reader, and if he will go through them with some little attention, he may arise from their perusal quite well convinced, at least, that old things are passing away, and that many things are becoming new. I have written these pages in an entirely normal condition, and perfectly unconscious of any influence, only there were times when I could not write a sentence, and felt very much averse to doing anything in connection with the book, and would get up and leave the room, almost involuntarily. At other times I would write with ease, quite generally commencing a sentence without knowing how it was to terminate. I have copied and to a certain extent, modified about half of the manuscript that was first written; the remainder is just about as it was presented. The different chapters or subjects, are by no means arranged as they were written, as some were partly finished, and laid aside, as there were times when I could write upon one subject and not upon another.

They informed us at the commencement that the teachings would come through the Doctor's organism in an indirect manner, or in chips as they termed them, but they would be enabled by that mode of procedure to transfer the ideas to my organism, and thus enable me in my own study, to weave them into the web which they wished to produce to the world, at this period in its history. They remarked, the time had arrived to make these revealments, and they, (as they termed themselves the delegation) had searched the nations for the Key or Keys that would unlock to the world,the profound secrets contained in this book, and they had found the Keys hidden away in our organisms, and had watched our outgoings, and incomings, and made use of the means that would bring us together at the fixed time for the accomplishment of this purpose. I do not claim any large amount of credit for the authorship of this work, though much of the time it has been quite a severe tax upon all the mental energies that I possessed, and although the prominent ideas were given to us, yet they seem to have passed through my organism in such a manner that it is quite difficult for me to determine from whence they came, and how I have been able to present them in this form

We learned in process of time that the five seals of the book presented in the early stage of these proceedings, had allusion to prominent ideas, or facts concerning the physical globe upon which we dwell, and its various appertainings.

The first seal is supposed to allude to the great fact that this globe is a hollow or spherical shell with an interior as well as an exterior surface, and that it contains an inner concave as well as outer convex world, and that the inner is accessible by an extensive spirally formed aperture, provided with a deep and commodious channel suited to the purposes of navigation for the largest vessels that float, and that this aperture may be found in the unexplored open Polar Sea.

The opening of the second seal, is supposed to reveal the fact that this globe is a mechanical structure, in which is introduced the highest principles of the art, and that it is consequently, built by mechanics who are well versed in all the acquirements necessary to produce such a structure, and that to be built in accordance with correct principles, it must be formed from the least amount of material compatible with the needed strength, and hence it must be in the form of a shell, with an outer and an inner surface.

The third seal seems to open to our view, the fact that the mechanics who are competent to build a world, must have acquired their knowledge like all other intelligent beings, by experience and observation, and hence they must have necessarily passed through all possible conditions below them, in order to have attained the needed acquirements, or the wisdom and power that would be absolutely essential in the construction of a world;

and further, that worlds are not created from nothing, by a self constituted infinite being who has never passed through all this entire routine of experience, but sprang into existence without law or cause, with wisdom and power sufficient to produce all things from nothing by his own fiat, as the human mind is entirely incapable of conceiving the existence of any such being, within the boundaries of universal nature.

The fourth seal would seem to disclose to our view, a number of facts concerning the inherent powers contained in our globe, by which it performs its axial and orbital movements, and manufactures its interior light and warmth, and is destined to unfold to that higher and more independent and matured condition, that will ultimately enable it to take its proper place as a *sun* in the vast firmament.

And the fifth seal has allusion to human vision, and will be fully explained by a perusal of the chapter upon that subject.

When I rather reluctantly consented to commence the ostensible authorship of this book, I had determined that nothing should be introduced into its pages that would conflict in any manner with well settled scientific opinions, and I supposed I should spend a large portion of the summer, in the study of scientific works; but we were constantly admonished, that with regard to most of the subjects upon which I was to write, science was entirely at fault, and her votaries were wandering in a maze of darkness, and that all I needed was a general idea of their opinions upon matters that would be brought to light, so we could demolish them more effectually. That if scientific men had already arrived at truth concerning all these matters, it would be quite unnecessary to say more, as no one could be benefited by a vain repetition of what was already written, and well understood; and instead of being particularly enlightened by scientific theories already established, I have been compelled to adopt many directly in conflict with those entertained by the most eminent men of the present day. I have been also impelled to introduce an array of argument in support of the new ideas and theories, entirely novel to myself, but yet, arguments that in most cases seem to be astonishingly conclusive, and that will no doubt, stand the test of the most critical examination; and we have every reason to believe viewing the matter from our standpoint, that these pages will prove of no little interest to the public generally.

It will not be very surprising, if in treating upon subjects of such vast magnitude as those introduced into this work, that an author so unprepared as myself, by an intimate acquaintance with the scientific works designed to throw light upon these matters, should frequently meet with almost insurmountable obstacles and impediments, that would seem to tower mountain high before him, and thus not only obscure his vision, but obstruct his pathway; but strange to say in every instance of this character, which have not been infrequent during the progress of this work, all the obstructions and difficulties have not only been removed, but they have invariably strengthened our arguments, and been but stepping stones upon which we could stand, and if possible take a broader and more extensive survey of the realms of nature, beholding more clearly and vividly, those harmonies and beauties that present themselves everywhere in the universe.

The book itself presents upon its face but few characteristics that came within the reach of my interior vision, when I consented to commence its authorship. In fact, I had but little idea concerning the matter, and it has been unfolded to my view during its progress, partly by the teachings given through the Doctor, and partly by the vivid impressions that seemed to be made upon my own organism, and I cannot exactly determine how far the work had progressed, when I became fully convinced that the views promulgated were substantial facts, and fully in accordance with the established principles existing in the universal realms, but I at length succumbed to what appeared to be my own reasoning, as the arguments introdnced were beyond my reach, and demolished my preconceived theories, and I trust many individuals who carefully peruse this volume, will pass through a similar experience.

I seem to be deeply impressed with the idea that many of the thoughts that are briefly presented in this work, will be seized upon in the future by other minds and elaborated, so as to become of great utility to the human race, and I must be permitted to entertain the thought that the elucidation contained therein, concerning the great positive and negative forces existing in nature, will ultimate in their final introduction, and general application to mechanical purposes.

WM. F. LYON.

Sacramento, Nov. 1, 1870.

THE WORLD'S AGITATOR
AND
RECONCILER.

CHAPTER I.

SOME SCRAPS OF HISTORY.

If with an intelligent eye, we glance back through the pages of recorded history, we shall find, we trust, that every event noted has occurred in its exact order, and at its proper time and place, so that the known record of human transactions, is somewhat prophetic, beautifully progressive, and singularly symmetrical, in all its proportions. Each event has transpired at its fixed time, in its regular succession, it could not have possibly occurred sooner, neither could it have been longer delayed, *as*, in the advancement of human intelligence, and in the accumulations of human experience, events must necessarily take place in accordance with man's condition at the period of their occurrence, and we see it could not be otherwise; for it would be impossible for human society to enact, in an ignorant and semi-barbarous condition, what would be very natural in a more advanced and civilized period of its history.

And thus we find the earlier history of the human

race is in perfect accordance with the more undeveloped conditions that existed at the period when the event occurred, and the records of all succeeding ages have kept even pace with the onward march of human advancement. The people who lived even a hundred years since, could not by any possibility, have enacted the most commonplace events that are occurring every where in civilized society, at the present, simply because they had not the means, and the appliances that would produce any of the ordinary occurrences of to-day, that we witness with no apparent or appreciative interest, because of our familiarity with them as every day transactions.

We now upon the Pacific coast, scarcely walk a block to witness the advent of a large party of distinguished gentlemen, who left their homes in Boston, over three thousand miles away, a week since, and have traveled across the entire continent, at that rapid rate, faring sumptuously the whole distance, being boarded and bedded and dined and wined, in flying palaces that are fitted up and most elaborately adorned, with a luxurious magnificence unknown to our wealthiest ancestors in their private residences, a century since; while only a few short years in the past, the residents here would have been deeply interested in the approach of an ox wagon, and a small party of emigrants. And thus we find to-day, the schoolboy familiar with facts, principles and phenomena, unknown to the college professor of a hundred years ago. Formerly, history lagged and traveled sluggishly in lumbering vehicles, upon the common highway, or it waited for the winds to fill the sails of its diminutive, ill shapen crafts, before it could move onward in its journey. *Now* it rushes forward with all the accelerated speed of the locomotive, and with the still increased celerity of the electric telegraph, making half the circuit of the globe while the sun is washing his face, preparatory to his day's journey, or without waiting for winds or tides, it moves on in the accomplishment of its high destinies, with certainty in the measured tread of the ocean steamer.

Formerly, history seemed to be working out all its problems with great moderation, by the unaided hands of men and women; it brought into requisition the simplest instruments to aid in its handicraft, and performed comparatively little, but now it calls to its assistance, the most wonderfully complicated machinery, set in motion by powers unknown as such to our ancestors, and by the aid of steam and electricity, it may now rattle off a volume in the same time that in ages past, by their simple appliances, it could scarce produce a single page.

As we have said, the history of each succeeding age, must have had a perfect correspondence with the condition of the age to which it belonged, and must comport exactly with the experience and advancement of the people of that particular era, in the varied branches of human knowledge; for instance, the written particulars of a battle, occurring previous to the knowledge and use of gunpowder, must have been a very different affair, in all its details, to a similar combat at the *present* time, when columbiads and Henry rifles, and all the numerous improved destructive weapons are brought to bear by the belligerents, in their efforts to destroy each other.

If old Homer could have provided his heroes with

some of our modern implements of warfare, they might have planted their mortars and Parrot guns, and bombarded, and battered down the walls of ancient Troy in a single week, taken the fair Helen, and returned to Greece, with victory perched upon their banners, by the next steamer, instead of remaining there for ten long years, and wasting so much time in hand to hand encounters, and the whole history could have been given in the daily papers the next morning after the steamer arrived. But then a great amount of fine poetry, would have subsided into a small matter of fact, so we see the whole history was admirably adapted to the age that gave it birth, and the minds of our youth are charmed and developed to a certain extent, by a perusal of the exhilerating poetic lines of the famous Grecian bard, all about a contest that would have been decided at the present period, in a few days or weeks at most.

And we find that the religious history of the different ages is marked with the same great disparity, for certainly no one can deny, but it gradually changed its forms, among the different people of the earth, as they have advanced in experience and knowledge, till at the present day, we may behold numerous religious organizations so widely different from each other, and so extremely at variance with those of a past age, that we can scarcely recognize the fact that their views and devotional exercises, are prompted by the same elements as those which existed in the natural and spiritual organisms of their ancestors. Nevertheless, we are compelled to acknowledge that such is the case, and we must admit that the same peculiar powers and faculties of mind that were found in the Egyptian, which prompted him under his conditions, to establish a priesthood whose duties were, to offer certain sacrifices to those beings who were the representatives of their highest conceptions of God, or supreme power and wisdom, are the same precisely, that are found in a more advanced condition, in the people of New England who adopt such different modes of worship, and are supposed upon their set days, to listen to the most advanced spiritual thoughts of that highly cultivated class of divines, who officiate as priests, in accordance with the most approved forms and ceremonies of this enlightened age. And no doubt, the Egyptian was as sincere, devout, earnest, and worshipful, as is the more cultivated and refined citizen of New England, who is a constant and devout attendant upon one of the popular churches of the present day; and though his form of religious worship would be illy adapted to us in our condition, yet it served him in his condition, far better, and doubtless was quite as acceptable to the powers to whom it was addressed.

The same disparity must obtain in the history of the different ages of men, in reference to their scientific, mechanical and agricultural attainments. One discovery in any one of these departments, must have preceded another, in regular order, as it was necessary that men should be familiarized with the more simple, before they could comprehend the more complex, and the one only made way for the other, and was absolutely prophetic of what would follow. So we perceive that one page of history has prepared the way, and made it possible for the next page to occur; for had there been no infancy, there could have been no growth and consequent maturity, so that history has passed througn all these various changes ; one event depending entirely for its occurrence, upon the one that preceded, and thus on down through all its recorded pages, each occurring in its own appointed time, in accordance with fixed, unchangeable laws. We must conclude that all has been foreseen by some exalted minds, and that no written page has occurred in a hap-hazard manner, but all was and is, in accordance with the best designs of that power and wisdom that guides and directs all, for the highest purposes and best good of all the parties concerned. This may be called *fatality* or predestination, or special or general Providence, or what you will, but we consider it simply an acknowledgment, that there was power and wisdom in existence before the foundations of the world were established, entirely adequate to comprehend all that was in any way connected with the grand undertaking, from its inception to its ultimate completion, and that in all its minutiæ, it was designed to work out the highest possible purposes, and that consequently all of human history, must have been taken into account, and that these events have been, and are transpiring in accordance with the direction of the powers that are delegated to watch over and direct the affairs and destinies of humanity.

Mankind have been placed here under certain conditions,and endowed with certain faculties,and peculiar organized mentalities,and this fact has been followed by the events of history. They have been ushered into life, and upon the stage of action, and rushed off upon the other side, without even being consulted in regard to the conditions and surroundings in which they were to be placed, the peculiar faculties and organisms they were to inherit, or influences that should be brought to bear upon them; and under these peculiar circumstances, can it be supposed that individuals have exerted a great amount of uncontrolled power, in producing the history of the world? It must be conceded, that we *as* individuals can do little else, than to watch the progress of events, as humanity passes on from its lower to its higher and more advanced conditions, impelled forward by the varied influences by which we are surrounded, and which exist in our interior natures.

Men may conceive that they occupy a high position in the world, and that they individually are wielding a powerful influence in their spheres, but if our eye could be opened to a discernment of that invisible power that dominates behind the scenes, we should discover that they are only agents, instead of principals in the great work they appear to accomplish.

There can be no doubt, but the same general elements existed in the organizations of our ancestors, as are found in our own, yet with what very different reresults, simply because they had not enjoyed the same length of time for experience and development. Our ancestors had not passed through all these multitudinous changes—hence their hopes, aspirations and yearnings, their joys and their sorrows, were all of a different character. People doubtless in all ages have had, as they do now, hopes and aspirations that reached out somewhat beyond their possible attainments, so that those of one age have overleaped the bounds of their own day and generation, and only become the realizations of their successors :—thus coming events cast their shadows before, from age to age; and the ideal yearnings of the one reaches over into the actual experience of the succeeding,—and doubtless the same order and harmony will continue in the experiences of humanity during all the ages to come.

Thus the laws of progressive development are carried forward, the thinking men of one age, evolve reforms, or devise schemes, for the general improvement of humanity, and cherish some ideal that can only be realized by a later generation, and thus it has been said, and doubtless very truly, that the strong desire upon the part of a people, or perhaps an individual, for the attainment of a certain object, proves most conclusively, that the object is attainable, or it may be prophetic, and a sure precursor of its realization. For instance, when the slave population of the South sent up their united cry for freedom, and were joined by the fervent petitions of all liberty loving souls, everywhere, it was prophetic and substantial evidence, that their cry would be heard, and that means would be instituted, by which their freedom would be obtained, not that some great infinite power, who had carelessly left them in bondage for so long a time, would have his attention called to the subject by their importunities, and be moved to pity and extend his clemency toward them, in procuring their release; but that in the order of events the time had arrived. That the spontaneous yearnings engendered in their souls, was a premonition, and silently conveyed the information, that their release from bondage must follow as a natural result, not because of their strong anxiety and yearnings, but because the time for that event had transpired, and all nature that had been groaning and travailing in pain until then, demanded its just fulfillment; and the great movement in the North, and the excessive cries and groans of the slave, were only prophetic of such a consummation, thus the multifarious events connected with this great revolution, transpired in their regular order, and no amount of petitions could have hastened them a single day.

If we turn our attention back to the history connected with the discovery, settlement, and advancing progress of our own country, we shall ascertain that events have been singularly prophetic of their successors, in all their recorded pages, and that they have shaped themselves in accordance with the absolute necessities of an advancing civilization, very naturally, to meet the demands of the age, and we shall also discover evidence of an undoubted character, proving conclusively, that somewhere, very high intelligence was brought to bear, and stood at the helm, guiding the ship, molding and fashioning this wondrous succession of important events, that have ultimated in the building up of a great and powerful nation; with the freest and most liberalized government known upon earth.

It will be remembered that when Catholic supremacy and intolerance, over-ran all Western Europe, that an obscure young sailor was deeply impressed with an idea that finally resulted in the discovery of what they termed a new world, because they supposed then as now, their previous knowledge embraced all of the world, that could possibly exist. The idea to them that there was any more, beyond the bounds of their research, was quite as ridiculous, as it is to-day, to suppose that there is a vast interior world, already developed, and elaborately and beautifully fitted up, in all its appointments, and only waiting to be discovered, and occupied, the same as this new world waited till the set time had fully come, and the individual appeared, who had within his organism, the key that should unlock the mystery, and make known the astounding fact that a grand continent was theirs, to bequeath to their posterity, as an inheritance forever. As Columbus announced to the people, and authorities of old Spain, that across the seas to the west, was something of vast importance to them, and worthy of being searched out by a national expedition, so we announce to-day, to the people of the self-same country he discovered, nearly four hundred years later, that to the North-West of here, within the unexplored Polar circle, may be found a gateway that will lead the astonished navigator to a world far more magnificent, and of more value to the generations to come, than Columbus ever realized, or of which he ever dreamed in his most enthusiastic contemplations and visionary moments, and we feel some confidence, if the reader will follow us through these pages, with patience, we will convince him that such not only may be *possible*, but that it is, and must necessarily be a *living fact*, that will be demonstrated with far more ease, than the American continent was discovered by the famed navigator of the fifteenth century.

We shall not probably be exposed to any more ridicule than was Columbus, and many other individuals who have had the daring to present a comparatively new idea to the world, and to labor assiduously in its vindication and support, and as our great prototype did not succumb to ridicule, nor yield to the difficulties and various impediments that were thrown in his pathway, quite likely *we* may be encouraged to follow his example, for in the present more advanced state of scientific research, it is no greater stretch of the imagination to suppose there may be an interior surface to the shell that is quite generally admitted to exist, as the exterior portion of the globe, than it then was, to suppose there was a vast continent to be found away in the unexplored regions of the western waters, for it was universally considered that the pillars of Hercules were the *ultima thule*, and that there was nothing of great importance to be found beyond.

But not so thought Columbus, and he most obstinately persisted in presenting his ideas, first to his own circle of friends, and then to the public; and to different courts, year after year, for what appeared to him, doubtless an interminable length of time, before he could obtain the amount necessary to fit out the feeble expedition, that would at this day be considered entirely inadequate to cross the ocean.

And let us contemplate for a moment, the doubts and wavering uncertainties, and then the unexpected streams of light that penetrated the mass of darkness that clouded the whole subject, as viewed from his own standpoint, the brilliant hopes that led him onwards, and then those dismal fears that it might be all a misconception, some visionary hallucination of the brain, and then the discouragements of friends who expressed a warm interest in his welfare. What vivid, strange and complicated experiences must this energetic, persevering young man have passed through, while pursuing his profitless journies from city to city, and from court to court, presenting his grand idea to unappreciative listeners, or perhaps to those sympathizing friends who were entirely unable to aid in a practical demonstration of his great theory?

It is very doubtful whether Columbus could, during this entire period of struggle, absolutely define his own position in relation to the great project he had in view; and it is probable that from the time the first germs of thought were projected upon his mentality, up to the hour of the discovery of San Salvador, he could not have said he possessed entire, absolute, unwavering confidence in the undertaking; and thus it is, that men who are capable of the conception of a great thought, or rather whose organisms are susceptible to the impression of expanded ideas, are necessarily perplexed with shadows and uncertainties, and sometimes darkness; until by almost superhuman energies, they are enabled to materialize, and demonstrate their highest thought, thus the great discoverer, though he could not absolutely say his impressions were true, yet his convictions were of that permanent character, that impelled him to devote the best energies of his enlarged soul, for so many years in promoting the one great object of his life.

Convictions less firm would not have enabled him to consecrate all his powers of mind, and press them into the work, and urged him onward until he overcame all the impediments, and obstacles that beset his pathway, and impeded his progress. The unwavering convictions he experieneed, doubtless were the prophecy that a great event was about to transpire, that would be of vast importance to the human *race*, and the set time had arrived in human history, for that grandly illuminated page to be recorded; and that the individual had been found with the ability and daring requisite to make the sublime record.

And if we take the time to study the condition of Western Europe at that period, we may readily discover that the necessities of the then civilized world, demanded that the existence of the American continent, with its varied resources, and capabilities, should be made known to humanity, at the time of its discovery, and thus we see that an obscure young man, an individual from the ranks of comparative poverty, but endowed by the peculiarly requisite qualities of mind, was raised up, impelled to go forward, and prosecute the enterprise, until his assiduous labors were crowned with such distinguished success. It will be remembered that in the year 1492, Martin Luther, he who was destined to occupy such a conspicuous position in revolutionizing the religious world, in unsettling old established opinions, and consequently introducing discord and inharmonious elements that must in the future, result in violent persecutions, was a boy nine years of age, and that Ulrich Zwingle, the shepherd boy of the Alps, but subsequently the distinguished Swiss reformer, was eight years of age, so that the great reformation of the sixteenth century, was already in embryo, that finally resulted in such unhappy consequences to untold thousands of individual dissenters, and protesters against the dogmas of the established church; and how absolutely necessary that an asylum should be found, where the victims of this terrible intolerance and persecution, could find a refuge from their enemies, with the needed peace and security, and where they might be permitted to worship in their own manner, and under their own vines, and in accordance with their own conscientious opinions, and beliefs. And how readily large numbers of these sufferers, availed themselves of this privilege, and left the homes of their childhood, their altar-fires, and all their cherished attachments, and came to this new world, to swell that patriot band that were laying there, the foundations of what should some day, become a great and powerful nationality, that would be composed of the peculiar elements best calculated to promote the growth of a more liberalized government, as well as more exalted opinions, concerning man's inherent rights to think and act for himself. And in order to establish new institutions, then, as well as now, it was absolutely necessary, that new territory should be found, upon which they might be established, that new societies might be reared out of a combination of elements, that would naturally gravitate to the new and unsettled terrritory. And strange to say the condition of the European states, has from that period been such, that very large numbers were induced to flee, and seek this asylum where they could enjoy that liberty they so much craved, but could not find at home.

It was certainly much easier to build up and establish new forms of thought, and carry out more advanced ideas, where all was new and unformed, than in the old world, where all their ideas and opinions were running in deep grooves, worn down by time, customs and usage, and where aristocratic and pecuniary interests were mingled with the civil and religious institutions of their fathers. And the long succession of events that culminated in the emancipation of the people from the injustice and oppression of British domination, is no less singularly prophetic, all tending towards a great consummation of immense import to the whole civilized race. And now it became a necessity, that the enfranchised minds of the liberty-loving subjects of the different nations of Europe, after they had found this asylum, should also establish a government of their own, based upon individual rights, under which they might enjoy all those privileges, both civil and religious, they had so clearly inherited from the great supreme power that sways the destinies of this universe, and that they and their posterity should assist in building up and giving permanence to those free institutions, that might eventually and for all time to come, exert a wide spread, libèralizing influence over all the nations of the earth.

It would give us great pleasure if we could pause here, and pay some slight tribute of respect to the long catalogue of names that appeared conspicuously at this stage of American history, who were ready to gird on their swords, and go out to battle valiantly for the liberties of their chosen country, in its hour of deepest trial; but perhaps the halo of glory that does, and will surround until the latest generations, the memories of such men as Washington, Jefferson, and the much abused and vilified Thomas Paine, and a host of others that figured in those perilous times, might receive no additional lustre from the pens of obscure individuals, but such as we have, we offer, and only wish the incense proceeding from hearts th at are grateful for the civil and religious rights of this great people, may be wafted to the spirit abodes of every individual, high and low, who took part in the great struggle that purchased the liberties *we now* so abundantly enjoy.

And, now, we need notice but few of the many remarkable occurrences in American history, to show most conclusively, that they are all tending towards, and are singularly prophetic of a final culmination *still more* marvelous than the discovery and settlement of this continent, and its subsequent startling historic events, that have really been productive of a progressive influence in the European States, and have caused many monarchs to tremble upon their thrones.

The American people, being direct descendants from the different states of Western Europe, whose fathers fled from religious intolerance and political oppression, the natural result of long established institutions upon the continent, marrying and inter-marrying with each other, must, of course, possess peculiar elements and national characteristics entirely distinct from their brethren at home; in fact, they became a people, *sui generis*, with elemental qualities that no nation upon the face of the earth had ever before exhibited; an outgrowth of that conglomeration produced by the mingling of so many European nationalities, under such peculiar circumstances. Inheriting from their ancestry that energy and freedom of thought, that impelled them to leave their paternal home, and seek a refuge in a new country and many times in an uncultivated wilderness, they have exhibited those remarkable energies from the earlier settlement to the present, in subduing the wilderness, and making almost the entire country subservient in supplying the necessities of an advanced civilization. We remark with what rapidity the population of the Old

Thirteen overleaped their limited boundaries, and surged onward until it spread over the larger portion of the valley of the Mississippi. And subsequent events have taught us, that it was of the utmost importance, that our people should occupy and cultivate, as early as possible, this extensive granary of the American continent in order to be prepared for circumstances that must occur in our progressive course. For although our people had experienced unexampled prosperity, with trifling exceptions, since the achievment of their independence; yet they had fostered an unfortunate relic of a most barbarous age, in their own body politic, that was sure to ultimate in a fierce conflict, as it had been a bone of contention for many years, and each year the strife waxed hotter and hotter. And we are compelled to notice here as briefly as possible, this darkest feature in American history, that has been for so many long years, a plague spot and malignant curse upon this goverment, and that finally culminated in the shedding of such vast torrents of blood.

Less than forty years since, the idea was seized upon by certain persons, as having been announced in our Declaration of rights, that all "Men were born free and equal, and possessed certain inalienable rights," and they conceived this idea *meant* something; and that it ought to be enjoyed by *all* without regard to *race*, color, or condition; they made bold to express this idea, both *in* season and *out* of season, and became what was then termed abolitionists, for it must be remembered, that there were then nearly 3,000,000 of colored people in the Southern States, enduring the most abject bondage. Their masters of course, took the alarm, and hence the doctrine of State's' rights was promulgated, as far as slavery extended, most industriously, from the press, the rostrum, and the pulpit, and became the central idea in the political, if not the religious creed of the entire Southern people. These two opposing elements, at first no larger than a man's hand, above the horizon, gave no great alarm to any party; but after no inconsiderable wrangling upon the part of private and public men, the set time seemed to arrive when this contest should assume larger and still larger proportions, and finally permeate and interweave itself into the entire political fabric of the Government; so that it became intimately connected with almost every important measure that agitated the public mind, and received the attention of our National Legislature. Not a State could be admitted into the sisterhood, but these opposing partizans were terribly excited, until it was temporarily supposed that the increasing fires of this volcano, were quenched by the waters of the various Compromises. But in process of time, and during this controversy, the entire country was startled by the announcement that there was a war in progress between the United States and Mexico,—and although it was very difficult, at the time, to ascertain by what authority, we were involved in a war with a neighboring nation, nevertheless it proved to be a very serious fact, and the whole people were suddenly awakened to the knowledge that General Taylor had absolutely opened his batteries, beseiged and taken Matamoras, and that the war was in actual progress, whether justly or unjustly, was the great question now to be debated, and if possible determined. And that question was agitated and discussed in the halls of Congress, in the Legislatures of the different States, and extensively among the masses of the people, in their town halls, in their debating clubs, in their places of business, and upon the streets, with great zeal, and many times violent acrimony. Parties arraying themselves generally in accordance with their political proclivities, the Democratic party in consequence of their more intimate relationship with the political influence of the South, and having in their possession the administration at the time, favored the war, while the Whigs generally united with the Anti-Slavery party, in very strong opposition, as they conceived they discovered a great amount of injustice mingled in the transaction, and were fully impressed that the grand central idea of the instigators and promoters of this war, was an intention to extend the area of African slavery.

This fierce contest continued with unabated warmth, until our so-called Mexican invasion, like all other wars, came to its end, and terminated in the triumph of the arms of our Government; and those inferior races were compelled to acknowledge themselves conquered by a superior people, and doubtless were happy to enter into very favorable treaty stipulations with their conquerors.

Our Government with great magnanimity, agreed to defray their own war expenses, granting entire immunity for damages sustained, relinquish a large debt which was held against them, and then pay them $15,000,000 besides, and only receive in exchange for all these gratuities, a simple quit-claim for the disputed part of Texas which we already held, the territory of New Mexico, and California, all of which was at that time supposed by the masses, to be about worthless; and more particularly, by those who opposed the war, and that party fairly howled over such a reckles and extravagant waste of the toil-earned money of the people, that had been gathered into the coffers of the Government.

But lo! about this time a change came over the spirit of the dream,—and very rich mines of gold were discovered in California, upon the newly acquired territory, and busy rumor heralded this exciting news back to the Atlantic States, and the restless, uneasy element that has ever existed in the descendants of the Anglo-Saxon race, began to be aroused, and very soon exhibited itself with redoubled energy. The great thoroughfares both by sea and land, were in a short period, crowded by adventurous spirits who were bound to this new found land of golden promise, but in very many instances, disappointed hopes, and from that day to the present, we have never heard an American citizen, of any party, breathe forth a single lisp, in relation to the horrible injustice of the Mexican war, or hint that our people made an unprofitable bargain, when we acquired the purchased possession of the great territory, reaching from the Gulf of Mexico to this Pacific coast, and containing within its borders, mineral and agricultural resources, scarcely equalled upon the face of the globe.

However much any of us might have been opposed to those passages, in our history when they occurred, we are compelled to admit they grew out of the necessities of the case, and evidently carry upon their face, the deep marks of design, and that the parties that were invested with power at the time, were only agents in the performance of their parts in those several transactions, and every intelligent man is also driven to the admission, that the exigencies of the case, and the peculiar condition of our people at that period, and since that day, absolutely demanded that the key should be found at that fixed time, which would unlock this vast treasure house of mineral wealth for the benefit of the American people, in order to aid our Government to march on, in the fulfillment of her great destinies.

Who, now, that looks backward upon the line of this strange concatenation of human events, and examines the prominent occurrences that have culminated in the possession and development of the untold resources of the Pacific slope, but must acknowledge that each successive link in this connected chain of history, was but a prophecy of the one that would follow, and that all are tending toward some other grand consummation in the future.

But while this part of the historical problem was working out, and arriving at a partial solution that has thus far resulted in placing a million of enterprising and energetic inhabitants west of the Rocky Mountains, and in part developing the immense resources of this golden country, time was effecting its wonderful changes upon our Atlantic borders, and in the older States, for, notwithstanding all the agreements and compromises that had been entered into by our statesmen, and all the efforts that had been made by our patriotic citizens, to stay or avert any serious difficulty that might arise from this slavery question, yet the contest waxed warmer and still warmer; although the party of the North had consented to let it remain intact where it was already established, they strenuously opposed its extension into new territory. It was also discovered that North of Mason and Dixon's line, the free institutions that prevailed were more congenial with the masses of emigrants that were continuously arriving from Europe, and that the large portion of the accessions to our population, were attracted thither; and, again, it was ascertained, that freedom was more conducive to growth and expansion, because it called into active exercise, the energies and enterprise of the great mass of the population, placing each man upon an equality. Every individual had a personal interest in the well-being and advancement of the whole, and hence, it was found, that the Northern States were rapidly outstripping, and gaining upon the Southern, both in wealth and population. This fact was of course, a great cause of distrust, and fear upon the part of the people of the South, for they discovered very readily, if that state of things should continue any great length of time, their cherished institution would only occupy a corner of the territory, and ultimately be swept out of existence, by the overwhelming numbers and power of its opponents.

Hence, it became a necessity, if they wished to preserve slavery as an inheritance for their children, and to perpetuate the institution for the benefit of succeeding generations, that they should separate themselves from the free states, and establish a government of their own, with slavery as its chief corner stone. The prominent statesmen of the South only waited an opportune moment, to carry into execution, this darling project, and place themselves beyond the dictation, or interference of those they considered their most bitter enemies, and whom they viewed with such utter contempt.

Thus far, they had by some means, been enabled to

exert a preponderating influence in the National Legislature, and in the election of the Executive Officers, and the appointment of men, to fill prominent stations under the Government, and they boldly declared that when their influence should wane, and their power declined, and a President should be elected, who represented the Northern idea, or possessed abolition proclivities, they would secede from the Union, as they averred was their right, in accordance with the national Constitution, and establish a confederacy of their own, embodying their peculiar views and principles in its fundamental laws.

It was impossible in that political condition of our country, that a crisis should not arrive when these men would seek to put their bold threats into execution, and when Abraham Lincoln, in every sense a man of the people, and a moderate representative of the ideas then prevalent in the Northern States, was elected to fill the office of Chief Magistrate, and some time before he had taken his seat in the presidential chair, many Senators and Representatives had left their places in Congress, and the doctrine of States' Rights had culminated in the secession of a number of the Southern States, and finally a rebellion was inaugurated of vaster proportions, and more terrible in its consequences, than any that ever occurred since history has recorded the annals of national events.

Slavery had made its mark so deeply upon our body politic, had become so intimately interwoven into our governmental institutions, that nothing less than a bloody and desolating war could wash out its stains, and cleanse and purify our national escutcheon from the dark spots and murky clouds that could not be covered up, and hidden from view by all the glory of the free and liberal principles adopted by our Government, and taught by our citizens. Such a war have we passed through, that for bitterness and hatred upon the part of the belligerents, has perhaps never had its equal, and it is devoutly hoped our country may never experience its like again.

This terrible conflict, too, has doubtless had much to do in working out the destinies, not only of this nation, but perhaps the entire civilized race. But for the war, there would not have been a Pacific Railroad; no such easy and speedy means of communication would have existed between the East and the West; no opening up of the great territory lying upon both slopes of the Rocky Mountains, bringing all those vast regions comparatively within the neighborhood of the older settled States, enabling their great commercial marts to extend a friendly hand in developing their latent resources, and thus helping them to lay the foundations of their future greatness. It is said "The mills of the gods grind slowly,"—but it would seem, since the days of railroads and electric telegraphs, that these mills have been grinding with accelerated speed, and events succeed each other with such rapidity, and seem to follow upon the heels of their predecessors so suddenly, that we are almost overcome, and bewildered in their contemplation.

It would almost seem that the power that holds in its hands the destiny of nations, was hurrying up matters, and propelling the machine with increased motion, and working out the details of history, with railroad or telegraphic speed, so that the great denouement may be sooner witnessed by the astonished multitude. That some power does preside and direct in working out these great national problems, no one can doubt, who has ever given the most careless glance at the continuous history of past events.

There must be some presiding intelligence somewhere, possessed of power and wisdom adequate to the great duties performed, and the influence exerted over men, causing them to act in accordance with a certain programme, well understanding, that those acts, although unseen by the individuals, will tend directly toward the accomplishment of a fixed purpose. When Jefferson Davis left the United States Senate, over ten years ago, how little did he know what would be the result of that movement he was so desirous to inaugurate. It was absolutely necessary he should pursue the course he did, in order to aid in the accomplishment of the great result that followed. Thus, somehow, he was made an instrument in working out the very object that he was taking measures to prevent, and had he and his coadjutors remained quiet, might have been prevented for many years to come. How exceeding strange, that after ten years' struggle through so many unhappy vicissitudes of fortune, he should find himself occupying an obscure position in an insurance office, that any person of ordinary ability might fill with honor, while the seat he deserted in the Senate Chamber, is to-day filled by a black man as his direct successor. He left his place in the Senate with the full determination to aid and assist, to the utmost of his ability, in forging and riveting chains upon this honorable Senator and his posterity forever, so that neither he, nor any of his generation, might hope to enjoy the glorious boon of freedom in all the ages to come. He left for the base purpose of aiding in the establishment of a government that would entail bondage upon every man, woman and child, in whose veins coursed a single drop of African blood; but he, against his own will, was made instrumental in working out the great problem of universal *Freedom*, for black as well as white; in unloosing the bonds, taking off the shackles, and bestowing that liberty upon the oppressed, for which they had so long sighed, but sighed in vain.

Not only that, but what the most ardent advocate of universal freedom had scarcely dreamed of, raising them to citizenship, and bestowing upon them the right of suffrage, and eligibility to official position, thus making men of them, in the broadest political sense of that term, and placing them upon the high road to intellectual growth and advancement. Now, we are fairly rid of the blighting influences of African Slavery, that has so long hung around us as a black pall, darkening and obscuring our national greatness, and increasing glory.

We have one railroad completed across the continent, and a number more in progress, and in contemplation; we have a million of enterprising people upon the Pacific slope; and the intermediate States and Territories are rapidly opening to settlement, and being occupied by the abodes of industry and civilization, and the very natural inquiry is now—what next? Perhaps the most momentous question of the present century, that can be propounded by an intelligent mind, after all that has transpired, is—what next will be the great prominent event that shall startle the world, with its magnitude and vast importance to humanity. We have seen that "Westward the star of Empire has taken its way," thus far; steadily the ever surging tide of emigration has rolled in its onward course, from Central Asia through the continent of Europe, and then across the Atlantic to the Eastern shores of America; and barely resting, as if to take breath, it has urged its way through the wilderness, and across the desert plains, and precipitous mountain ranges; until it has finally found this lengthened line of Pacific coast, and here it looks out upon one wide waste of waters, seven thousand miles in extent, that speaks a language to the restless, uneasy, ever moving mass of rolling emigration, too plain to be misundertood, and says, "Thus far shalt thou go, and here let thy proud waves be stayed." The tides of the Pacific oppose themselves in stout defiance to the tides of emigration, and there can be no question concerning which will prove the conqueror.

Thus it commenced and has gone forward in its ceaseless march, made, as far as possible, the circuit of the globe, and must now find some other territory upon which it can continue its onward course, or else coil itself up in its own body and die for want of those activities that living principles always exercise; hence we conclude that some new field still broader, shall be opened up, as living elements in our nature cannot die. There are certain powers in man's interior organism, that produce all his varied activities, and give rise to those proclivities that are found within them, and if an individual or a class, manifest a disposition to wander from home, and seek new places of abode, it becomes evident there is something about their mental organisms, some peculiar constitutional element in their interiors, that necessarily leads to such a result.

This has all been ordered for the wisest purposes, for suppose every one was possessed of large inhabitiveness, and a general distaste for leaving the parental rooftree, forming such lasting attachments to the scenes of childhood, that they could not sunder the ties that bind them to the homes of their ancestors, and the faces of their early friends. We perceive that humanity, and especially the civilized part, would have confined itself to the narrowest possible limits, and the larger portion of God's green earth, would have remained an uncultivated wilderness, unadorned by the labor and improvements of an advancing civilization; that society would have crowded itself into compact cities, and overflowing neighborhoods, and endured a thousand inconveniences that would have been entailed upon them for the want of sufficient room. So far from this being the case, the very opposite has seemed to prevail, and a large portion of the human race, have actually possessed very small inhabitiveness, and have manifested a remarkable disposition to wander from home, and penetrate into unexplored and uninhabited countries.

Such has been the case to a wonderful extent in the settling and peopling of the American continent, where, as yet, there has been such a large area of country, in proportion to the number of its inhabitants.

It will be perceived, that our ancestors must have been largely permeated by this element, or the new world would not have received this continuous influx of population from the old, and in this respect it cannot be denied, that the children have done full credit to the fathers, for not a few have adopted almost nomadic habits, wandering from place to place, with scarcely a fixed habitation, and very large numbers have preferred a frontier life, moving on still further when the population became too numerous to suit their tastes.

Thus they have continued to spread out, and extend their borders, impelled forward, and gradually surging onward, scarcely heeding, much less comprehending the great problem, they were assisting to work out, until they have reached, and are now standing upon this extended line of Pacific waters, and the important query that we have propounded—what is to be the next move? demands a reply.

Emigration, like revolutions,never moves backward, it has manifested thus far, no inclination to return, and recoil upon itself, but onward has been its watchword heretofore. We doubt not, such must of necessity, continue to be the case, or we might conclude that this tide would roll back, and fill up all the unoccupied territory, lying between this and the older settled portions of our country. But, such is not in the order of things. Men may stand upon the shores of the Pacific, destitute of employment and means, and there sigh and wait, and sigh again, for some other inviting land that holds out glittering promises, but they cannot, they will not go back,it is not in their natures. There is as a general rule, some principle in their mental organizations, that forbids any return; a something within them that speaks in language too plain to be misinterpreted, and says *go forward*; and they must obey those imperative commands, or remain at this their journey's end.

The great portion of our present population, came to this coast, with the full purpose of acquiring a competency, and returning to enjoy their gains among those scenes with which they had been familiar in their earlier years, but how very few comparatively have carried out these designs. The larger number did not acquire the competency—and those that did, found fortune tardy in answering to their earnest appeals, and proved it a work of years instead of months, to obtain what they considered sufficient to supply their wants in the future, and when that period arrived, they found themselves surrounded by circumstances that rendered it extremely inconvenient to leave, and they have discovered so many attractions here, in fact, they have had no desire to return, and many of those that really did go back to their old homes, for the purpose of spending their days there, in ease and plenty, have become dissatisfied, and found their way back again to these shores, as more congenial to their newly acquired tastes and habits. Arrange the matter as you choose, there can be no retrogression, and the material to fill up the intervening space beyond the Missisippi, must come from the Eastward. There is a great surplus of population still in Europe, and it is accumulating every year, and only waiting for time and transportation to come and take possession of the vast unoccupied territory of these States, and when the waste places are built up, and filled to overflowing, as they will be in a few years, then emigration must roll onward from there; and the query still urges itself upon our attention, where will it go? It may appear to many this question is not one that necessarily demands our consideration to-day, as, there is ample room for all that may come to our shores. But it may be well to inquire how the matter may stand when a century or two have rolled away, and have added their prolific pages to the history of this continent, and of this Government.

Another remarkable event in this continuous chain of history, that all seems looking in one direction, is the purchase of the Russian Possessions in North America, by our Government. What strange prescience could have taken possession of the far-seeing mind of the Secretary of State, Wm. H. Seward, that prompted him, to use every exertion in promoting the purchase of this cold, forbidding, and comparatively worthless territory, that would seem to contain so little worthy the attention of our citizens? Perhaps no purchase could be made, within the boundaries of the North American Continent, of any portion of its lands, that would appear less desirable as an acquisition, or that would meet with greater opposition from the people; notwithstanding this, the purchase has been ratified, and the transfer accomplished, and our Government is in full possession of this great tract of barren mountains, with all the appurtenances of Indians, bears, foxes, and dwarfed growth of timber, and whatever else, this extensive, far-off region may contain of value. Doubtless it never entered the mind of the shrewd Statesman that this same Alaska was purchased preparatory to the grandest event that has ever embellished the pages of history, and that it was absolutely necessary that our people should own this half way house, or resting place between San Francisco and the new world, that the extensive steamship lines which must be established at no remote period, would require supplies of coal, and numerous articles that might be found upon this territory, and that it was absolutely of the greatest possible importance to our country, that the purchase should be consummated when it was; thus giving into our possession the key that will perhaps unlock the vast treasure house of a new world.

If we go ahead for one hundred years at this rapid pace, the question referred to will be of great import. Our population since 1790 has increased thirty-three and one-third per cent. each decade, and if we may suppose it will continue to increase for the next thirty years upon a similar ratio, our numbers will swell to nearly 100,000,000, and if we then suppose it may increase 25 per cent. each succeeding decade until 1970, we shall have a population of nearly 400,000,000. And in view of all the circumstances connected with the case, there can be no doubt, but our numbers will continue to increase for centuries to come, until every acre or rood of land within our borders is occupied.

In the meantime we inquire—what is to be done with that restless, uneasy mass that have always been going ahead, seeking out new territory, and preparing the way for the more quiet, stay-at-home class who only follow in the wake of the Pioneers.

We think the reader will be driven to the conclusion that one of two facts must occur, either new territory must be found upon which this roving element may exercise its powers, or this element existing so prominently in a portion of our race, must die for want of the needed activity, and human organisms must change to meet that condition, when emigration is impossible for the want of new territory to be occupied. Then it will be found that Divine wisdom has essentially failed in arranging mental organisms, for, we find within them permanently placed, that which could only have been required for temporary purposes, as such a change of condition would necessarily render nugatory, all those restless, migratory proclivities found so extensively in the American or Anglo-Saxon race.

As we cannot suppose Divine wisdom can make any such error, man of course cannot possess organs that will not be adapted to his condition during the entire existence of the race; and all the elements in his nature must, at all times, have their appropriate uses, and fields must be provided wherein they may exercise their activities. Hence the required territory must be found of necessity, and for this reason we are deeply impressed at this particular juncture, to call the public attention to its probable discovery at no distant period, and to announce the fact that within a few short years, in our explorations in the open Polar Sea, a passage to which may be easily found, by following the warm Oceanic current through Behring's Straits; an accessible gateway will be discovered that will lead the navigator to all the territory we can occupy for many thousand years.

We think the reader must perceive by a cursory glance at past historic events, a few of which we have faintly delineated, that the fixed time has nearly arrived for this grand culmination, and that the day is not far distant when this Polar Sea must be explored, and when the new territory must be found where this most active element existing in our race, may find ample scope for its exercise and development; and we dare predict that within the next five years this grand discovery will be made and published to the world.

CHAP. II.

THE OPEN POLAR SEA.

This sea is a circle surrounding the North Pole, of some ten or twelve hundred miles in diameter, enjoying a temperate clime, and thus far in our history, almost shut out from human observation, by a formidable barrier of cold, where may be found a belt, or zone of about ten degrees in width, rendered nearly impassible, by a climate so rigorous, that none but the most adventurous and daring will attempt its exploration. Within this frigid belt, seems to be a charmed circle that possesses a sort of fascinating interest, as well for the scientific explorer as the enterprising navigator. It is doubtless the great geographical enigma of the present age, but we trust at no distant period, it will be entered upon the catalogue of those problems that have been solved by long and unwearied exertion, and the enlightened researches of a steadily advancing civilization.

Doubtless the contributions of Prof. T. B. Maury to Putnam's Magazine of November and December, 1869, give the ablest exposition of the whole subject, as yet produced by any author, presenting the theory of Capt. Bent, and a great array of valuable ideas of his own, that are quite new and worthy the highest consideration; however, we may be compelled to differ with him in some of his conclusions. He complains also that scientific men have been guilty of very serious blunders, and do not always make the proper deductions from the facts presented, because in many instances, other facts may be connected with a subject, that are obscure and hidden from view. Very possibly, this may be the case in relation to the great unsolved problem in question; for surely there must be room for many unknown facts, within an area of a million square miles of unexplored territory. There may exist causes within the borders of that charmed circle, for external phenomena, little dreamed of by those who have not been introduced to the scenes that lie hidden within its recesses; hence the great difficulty in arriving at proper conclusions, and those that may not be overthrown by subsequent research.

However, it is quite apparent, notwithstanding all the errors and miscalculations that have been made in relation to this matter, for the last three hundred years, that the deep interest which has existed all this long time, in the minds of so many individuals of different countries, is by no means abated, and that the zeal for new discoveries in that direction, is no less untiring than it has been in the past; while so many expeditions have been sent out by the different maritime nations, at such great sacrifice of money and human life; and that inquiring minds will not be satisfied nntil the problem is solved, and will not cease their efforts, until the mystery is entirely explained.

Captain Bent, under the instruction of Commodore Perry of the United States' navy, while stationed in Japanese and Chinese waters; by a long series of experiments and observations made since 1853, ascertained that there exists a very extensive Oceanic current of warm water flowing from the tropical regions of the Pacific ocean, as well as the Atlantic; that it is probably more than equal in volume and influences to the Gulf Stream, and appears to subserve similar purposes; that in its northern course it passes to the eastward of the Chinese and Japanese coasts, and thus on to Behring's Straits. From thence, he supposes it makes a direct course northward, through the great icy belt that surrounds the Polar Sea. He thinks a passage or gateway may be very easily found through this frozen zone, by keeping the track of this warm current, which may be done by continuous thermometrical observations. He also supposes that a similar passage way may be found by following the Gulf Stream by way of Nova Zembla, and that both these currents meet at one common center near the pole, and thus a great maritime highway may be opened through the Arctic Ocean, that will wonderfully shorten distances, and prove an incomparable benefit to the commercial intercourse of the entire world.

There is no doubt that the Arctic seas will at some time become accessible, and easily navigated, because, as we are fully satisfied, this open Polar Sea and warm circle of the North will make encroachments upon the frozen belt by which it is at present surrounded, and be very much enlarged. In fact, we are driven to the conclusion that long before this globe of ours is finished, the whole icy belt must melt away, and that our temperate zone will ultimately reach the Polar Sea, and then, when the great glacial period has passed away, in the far North, as it did at some time from the more southern latitudes, all those waters will be easily navigated; and doubtless long before that period, they may be traversed, by passing through the warmer currents, that extend into their borders. We conclude at the present time, if that goal is reached by vessels of any considerable magnitude, the navigator must follow one or the other of the Oceanic currents, alluded to by Capt. Bent.

Furthermore, we think the attempt to reach the open sea, regardless of these natural gateways, will as heretofore, prove abortive, and viewing the matter from our standpoint upon this Pacific coast, and from the evidences presented to our minds, we are fully of the opinion, that the successful expedition is bound to pass through Behring's Straits, upon the Kuro Siwo, or the Black Stream of Japan. We are convinced that such a passage is now open, and may be navigated, whenever a party with a suitable craft may make the attempt, and indeed, before we heard of Capt. Bent and his theory, or the contributions of Prof. Maury to Putnam's Magazine, we received information upon this subject, and had arrived at the same conclusions, and announced them to a public audience in Sacramento.

The frozen regions of the North are mostly contained within a zone, or belt of some ten degrees latitude; generally ranging from seventy to eighty degrees, and most probably, this belt is very much narrower in many places, and particularly in the vicinity of the warm Oceanic currents. Within, or north of this icy belt, the climate is comparatively temperate, the sea open, with no continuous accumulation of ice; either in winter or summer, and it cannot be dependent for its climatic temperature, to any considerable extent, upon those causes that regulate the changes of the seasons, south of the glacial belt, by which it is surrounded.

For it will readily be discovered if this polar region is dependent upon such causes, it would forever remain locked in the frozen embrace of the vast fields of ice that would accumulate from year to year and from age to age. Those great formations would have naturally encroached upon the temperate latitudes, thus extending their area and depth, until all the waters upon the face of the earth would have been attracted thither to swell the increasing glaciers of the Arctic regions; and all the solar and other influences operating in the temperate zones, could not have prevented the catastrophe.

For if, between the seventieth and eightieth parallels of latitude, spite of these influences, there exists continuously increasing bodies of ice, four to five thousand feet in thickness, and which in accordance with a certain well-known law, are urging their way forward to the sea, slowly and surely, and ultimately breaking off in the immense icebergs, that come floating to the south; what would naturally be the condition in a latitude still farther to the north, or at the pole, if no other causes were brought to bear, to regulate the climate, and prevent such a state of things?

We plainly discover that these mountainous accumulations, must have increased until they would have towered to the skies, had not the great presiding mind ordered it differently, and arranged this globe in such a manner, that a temperate clime might also exist at this polar extreme, as well as at the other apparently more favored latitudes. And we clearly see, without going into an accurate computation concerning the annual amount of absorption, that if a portion of the water was locked up each year in the glacial formations of the polar regions, then at some time the waters of the ocean would all be drawn thither. But as there is no perceptible diminution of the waters upon the globe, we may conclude that a large portion of the Arctic regions are free from such vast bodies of ice, and hence it would seem to be established if there was no other evidence, that there must be a temperate clime, and an open polar sea.

This subject has been of great interest to navigators and men of science, for a very long period, and they have given the matter great attention, and numerous expeditions have been fitted out, with a view of exploring all those regions; not only to bring to light the mysteries that might lie hidden in this *terra incognita*, but also to aid commerce, by discovering the long talked of northwest passage from Europe to India; and navigators from time to time, with one or the other of these purposes in view, have penetrated into very high latitudes. They have made what discoveries they could, but evidently the time had not yet arrived in the history of human affairs, when all the secrets of that mysterious circle should be made known to the world. There seems thus far to have been a barrier that has kept navigators ftom penetrating into the extreme northern regions, and yet some of them declare there was nothing in view to hinder, for they could look to the north as far as the eye, or their glasses could penetrate, and all was open; no impediments in the way; but they did not go on. Some inexplicable reason prevented those parties from pursuing where the road lay open before them, and has prevented their successors from finding any open pathway until the present time, and we are still in the same condition of ignorance concerning the mystery; the great geographical enigma of our globe still remains unsolved, and our ideas of the extreme North are but little clearer than in the days of Columbus.

It is known that captains of whalers have penetrated far to the north of Behring's Straits, without seeing any traces of ice; aud whalemen who have visited the harbor of San Francisco, state from personal knowledge, that it is much easier when as high as latitude seventy-two degrees, a little north of the Straits, to find moderate weather in which to winter, by going northward, than by going southward. Capt. Parry in 1810, saw no visible signs of ice in the very highest latitude he reached. Wrangle in 1820, far to the north and east of Behring's Straits, saw no appearance of ice; but for some strange reason, when these navigators were in those waters, and had such precious opportunities, they did not prosecute their explorations, and those rare chances for more extended research, seem to be lost forever to the world, while the great problem is still presented for solution.

Without doubt the best authenticated evidence in relation to the whole subject may be found in Dr. Kane's journal of the second Grinnell expedition, and perhaps Dr. I. I. Hayes in his Open Polar Sea, may throw some further light upon the matter, though we fail to see that he added much to the stock of information given by Morton, the steward of Kane's second expedition, who has never received the credit justly due for the great discovery he personally made in relation to the Polar Sea.

Capt. Bent feels quite confident that some Dutch whalers in 1655, sailed to the vicinity of the pole, from the eastward, or from their whaling ground near Nova Zembla; and quotes from the archives of the Royal Society of London, in support of the idea; but there are some doubts whether the authority of whale captains in that age, would be quite reliable, science having made some revealments since that day, of which they were entirely ignorant. Navigators of a far later period, have been much puzzled to find their whereabouts in the northern seas, in consequence of the unknown position of the magnetic pole, discovered by Capt. Ross in 1832, and if in a more advanced condition of science, they have been at a loss to find their latitude and longitude, how can we place implicit confidence in the unlearned whalemen of 1650. We are also persuaded that very dangerous phenomena exist in that vicinity, where the Electro-Magnetic currents converge to a common center, phenomena that have not yet been revealed to mortal eyes, and of which we may hereafter speak at greater length.

It does not seem to occur to northern navigators, that the immense glacial formation, upon the land in those frozen latitudes, have produced increased chilling influences upon the water; and that of course by the processess that are continuously going forward, the comparatively narrow channels must necessarily be filled with icebergs, thus rendering the waters of those channels and bays still colder. In all those explorations, they have seemed very desirous to keep near shore;

which may be very proper in some cases, but we conclude this course has been fatal heretofore to the success of the arctic discoverer; for there can be no doubt, it would be wisdom to get as far as possible, from the cold influences of the vast glacial formations upon these northern continents and islands, and doubtless when the gateways are discovered, they will be found as far as possible from the land.

The German Arctic expedition that was heard from some time since upon the eastern coast of Greenland, and almost upon the track of Henry Hudson, are experiencing the same difficulties, a great deal of mist and more cold than in 1868, with adverse winds; because they have placed themselves directly under the influence of the vast glaciers of the coast of Greenland, and of necessity they must experience the result—adverse winds, fogs, mists and severe cold. That expedition is fated like its predecessors to return, (if it does return,) unsuccessful.

We have perhaps said already, what is necessary upon the phenomena of the polar climate, the fact of an open sea, and a territory of great interest to humanity, at the far North; if not, the reader can find a great fund of information in the various books published that we need not repeat here, and now we may examine a little into the causes for these phenomena, that have been presented by navigators and scientific men.

Capt. Bent says, "And I, therefore reiterate the conviction expressed in my communication to the President of the Geographical Society of New York, that the Gulf Stream, and the Kuro Siwo, are the prime and only cause of the open sea about the pole, with its temperature so much above that due to its latitude."

Prof. Maury fully endorses this opinion, and claims that the "warm oceanic currents carry an amount of water to the polar regions, of about forty-eight to fifty degrees, and more probably sixty degrees temperature, entirely sufficient to displace all the cold water that can accumulate there, or that can become chilled after its arrival, which rushes off in under currents to the south." Secondly, "An untold amount of aqueous vapors arising from the waters of the warmer latitudes, and forced by the prevailing winds to the northern polar circle, spreading out accumulates, as a vast blanket of non-conducting material which prevents the latent heat carried forward by the warm currents, from radiating and passing off into space." Thirdly, "The all-potent influences of the solar rays that are permitted to penetrate the atmosphere of that region during the six months of the year," also "Heat radiates upon the earth from every quarter of the starry heavens, which has been ascertained by scientific experiments, to equal five-sixths of the solar heat.

Fourthly, "The agitation of the waters by these two counter currents, as they come in contact at the pole, and form a sort of commingling eddy, the friction attending this violent clashing of currents would necessarily produce great and extended heat.

Fifthly and lastly, "The internal heat of the earth, which Fourier has proved to be equal to incandescence, and as miners, when they penetrate beneath the earth's surface, find a constantly increasing temperature of one degree Fahrenheit in about fifty feet,it would be easy to prove that at the distance of twenty-five miles, every thing, even the most refractory rocks are in a molten condition, and brought to a white heat, and that in consequence of the depression or flattening at the pole, the crust would be thinner, bringing this region nearer to the vast Cyclopean furnace, by about thirteen miles, than any other portion of the globe," and thus the Professor makes his case. It cannot be doubted, the most sceptical mind will be compelled to admit, that the array of causes are truly formidable, and ought to be entirely satisfactory, if they can be brought to bear by any of the laws and processes that are used in accomplishing the great purposes of nature, upon this particular portion of the globe. He has elaborated the subject to an extent that would seem final and conclusive, and no doubt the Professor has presented the most advanced scientific thoughts of the present age, but the careful reader will discover that any one of the causes he has introduced, would be quite sufficient of itself to produce the desired result, if there were no impediments in the way, and nothing to prevent their direct action.

If these warm oceanic currents go up there in such great volume, sufficient to displace all the cold water and they are at a temperature of fifty degrees, nothing more is needed to produce an open sea, than to fill it up with warm water and keep a constant supply running in as fast as it cools, and passes out. It requires no great stretch of the intellect to discover that fact, and we cannot help thinking, the gentleman has thrown distrust and uncertainty around his own theories, by entering the fields of scientific research, and bringing meteorological and internal geological influences to bear, in assisting a cause, which he makes entirely adequate to produce all the results that have been made known in the polar regions.

It is quite as damaging to any hypothesis, to prove too much, and weakens our cause as effectually as if the evidence presented in its support, lacked sufficient force and authority. If we simply wish to show that within the ice-bound regions of the North, there is an open, unfrozen sea of a certain diameter, with a climate that is temperate, there can be no propriety in traveling out into the regions of ideality, and producing in support of such theory, causes sufficient to bring all the waters upon the entire globe, to the boiling point. We only need to show that causes exist commensurate with the effects produced.

The fact that two immense warm oceanic currents are now running from the tropical regions, carrying up large quantities of vegetable food for the Arctic whales and influencing the climate of the extreme North to a certain extent will not be disputed, but that the effects of these currents are sufficient to warm all the waters of the polar sea, is extremely doubtful. We doubt also that those waters are warmed by any terrible Cyclopean furnace of such awful magnitude and intense heat as the one spoken of, which our friend thinks must be more contiguous in consequence of the spheroidicity of the earth.

If these currents are so potent in their influences in this unexplored Polar Sea, where navigators have never penetrated to mark their effects, we can but wonder why they have not operated upon a grander scale farther to the South, where very many travelers have been, for several hundred years, searching for a pathway. It certainly seems that they would exert an influence upon the icy belt, quite as powerful as they do further to the north, and that a passage way as wide as one of these warm oceanic currents, would have been discovered long since. These currents, it is said, rest upon a cushion of cold water, during their entire passage, and radiate a very large quantity of heat, so much so, that the temperature is materially affected both by land and sea, all along their entire course, and we must suppose the heat that is radiated and passes off during the journey, is not carried to the North Pole. Again, the line which marks the waters of the Gulf Stream, is very sharply drawn, so that a vessel may have one-half in the warm current, and the other half in the colder waters of the ocean.

"As cold water is a bad conductor of caloric, it is not affected to any considerable extent, and this is a wise provision of nature, lest the stream should come in contact with the bottom, or with the shore, the earth being a better conductor, allowing the heat to radiate and pass off, and in no place during this long journey, does this stream approximate very nearly to the shore, or to the ocean bottom, but rests during the entire circuitous route from the Gulf of Mexico to the Pole upon this cushion of cold water."

We may now learn some of the wonders of this marvelous Gulf Stream during its journey northward, as represented by scientific men. It radiates caloric sufficient to produce a stream of molten lava as large or larger than the Mississippi at its mouth. It renders the climate that would otherwise be cold and cheerless, balmy and genial almost its entire distance, and yet arrives after a lengthy journey of 4,500 miles, through all the rigors of the northern latitudes, so little changed in temperature that it is capable of warming one-half the Polar Sea. This is what it does above the ocean's surface; mark what it does beneath. Although it never approaches the shore, but rests and travels upon its cold cushion, at a respectful distance, yet they say its influence is such that it produees beautiful coral formations in the chasms of the rocks near the coasts of Norway and Lapland; and what it may do when it gets to its destination, perhaps will only be known, when men get there to see.

It is unnecessary for our purpose to inquire into the exact amount of iron that might be fused by the caloric radiated from the Gulf Stream, but we consider there are some doubts concerning the isothermal influence produced upon the western coast of Europe, as the climatic temperature does not materially differ from the same latitudes upon the western shores of this continent, where the prevailing oceanic currents are from the opposite direction, and we must conclude the causes co-incident, that produce similar results upon either continent.

The coral specimens found by the fishermen of Norway and Lapland, require more than a passing notice, so we give the author's own words: "A beautiful coral forming long rose colored branches, was found in the rocky chasms of the sea, on the north-western shore of Norway, in latitude sixty-seven, or about twenty-three degrees from the Pole, and pieces of this coral have been obtained, where the Laplanders fishing for cod, have brought it up from the sea with their lines." These silent monitors that are fished up from the depths of the sea, and are found in the depths of this earth, ever speak a dumb language of their own, though that language may at times, be misinterpreted by men of scientific attainments. Our author says: "It is a startling commentary upon the power of the Gulf Stream to transfer climatic submarine temperatures," and still further, "As a rule the hottest water of the Gulf Stream is at or near the surface, and there is reason to believe, that its waters are nowhere permitted in the oceanic economy, to touch the bottom of the sea. There is every where a cushion of cold water between them and the solid parts of the earth's crust.

Where was the beautiful branching rose colored coral found? In the warm, genial currents of the Gulf Stream, where a sub-marine temperature might have been brought from tropical climes, suited to that kind of productions? By no means. It was fished up from the rocky chasms at the bottom of the sea, and nearer the shore, and upon the solid parts of the earth's crust, cosily nestled in this cushion of cold water, where, in the oceanic economy, the Gulf Stream never approaches and where the temperature could have been, in accordance with this theory, and doubtless in fact, no way influenced by the Gulf Stream or its proximity, any more than if it had been a thousand miles distant. We discover very clearly if corals exist off the coast of Norway and Lapland, produced by the Gulf Stream, they would more likely exist far to the south, where the stream must be warmer, and approaches quite as near the land as is the case at the Shetland, the Hebrides and Faroe Isles, and off the coast of Ireland, where this cause must exert a far stronger influence. All these places being destitute of such phenomena, we are compelled to conclude when they occur so far to the north, some other cause has been brought into activity, in their production.

We cannot think the Gulf Stream, wonderful and sublime as it may be in its operations, as it pursues its majestic pathway to the North, and presses onward through the icy belt that guards the Polar Sea, performs all the submarine marvels that may be found to exist in the depths of the ocean. We do not think it can possibly warm the harbor of Hamerfest, that is land-locked and almost upon the northern verge of the coast of Norway, and is a favorite resort of navigators in the winter season, because it remains nearly free from ice, or that it can produce coral upon the shores of Lapland; for both these points are certainly quite remote from its influences. Prof. F. M. Maury, in his charts, represents the currents as coming from the North, the entire length of the coasts of Norway, placing the Gulf Stream considerably to the west; and we suppose, his charts must be received as authority, until they are superseded by something more accurate.

So we think we shall be compelled to turn our attention in some other direction, in order to find a cause that will explain the phenomenon of the corals, and it is barely possible, that these tropical submarine productions existing so far from their native climes within the tropics, may throw some light upon another subject that now lies involved in mystery. It is a remarkable fact, that these corals were found in the immediate vicinity, the one, of the famous Maelstrom, off the coast of Norway, and the other, near a similar whirlpool of nearly the same magnitude, that lies still to the north, and in the vicinity of the Lapland fisheries. There is something extremely marvelous that such productions should be found in close proximity to these whirlpools, and to say the least it is a remarkable co-incidence, and would lead us to suppose they might have some connnection with those unexplained phenomena, and that possibly, there was a more intimate relationship existing between them than has been supposed. In the absence of thermometrical observations, we must make the best use we can of the rays of light that are dawning upon our minds in regard to these marine vortices that occur in the higher latitudes, and there can be no doubt, they are numerous in those untraversed seas, both in the Northern and Southern Hemispheres.

The Electro-Magnetic currents are known to exist upon every quarter of the globe, running from north to south, or in a longitudinal direction. They permeate the whole atmosphere, and in all places where no local impediments are found, guide the magnetic needle. Being longitudinal they must as they approximate either pole, converge towards a common focus; thus impinging upon each other, they might be attended with a friction productive of dangerous results, if all these currents continued to the pole. To avoid this danger, certain of these currents must drop out from the great body as they approach the common polar center. It will be noticed that the currents spoken of must be continuous and form a complete circuit, as any break or disruptions would permit the Electro-Magnetic fluids to accumulate and cause serious disturbances. Now, we perceive if these currents are continuous, they must pass from the exterior atmosphere, and then on to the south, near the concave surface of the shell, passing to the exterior again at the southern pole, thus continuing the circuit, and they form the warp of numerous webs that seem to enwrap the physical parts of the earth upon every side, both without and within. There is little doubt but the larger portion of these Electro-Magnetic currents, passes through the shell at different points within the unknown polar circle; but, as they converge together from some unknown cause of attraction, as we have said, some of them drop out and pass through in lower latitudes, and we discover disturbances would necessarily be produced, wherever such is the case to any great extent.

There is but little doubt further investigation will prove conclusively that Electro-Magnetic action is the cause of the disturbance in the waters of the Maelstrom, and also at the whirlpool still to the north, and the consequent friction is productive of a tropical submarine temperature, congenial to the coral insect, or marine vegetation, belonging to the warmer latitudes; we are quite sure if you leave the vicinity of those vortices, you will find no coral. We presume scientific men of the present day will not endorse this hypothesis, but leave it for their children. However, we may safely challenge them to look out into the realm of causes, and find any other reasonable view of the subject that can be supported by a shadow of evidence. It will be observed that these whirlpools are always more agitated, and more dangerous at times when there is any considerable electric activity.

We are not writing this work for the purpose of combatting any person's theories or opinions, and do not wish to do so, only so far as they are in direct conflict with those we are endeavoring to support, and hence, in our opinion, untenable. So we are perfectly willing that the prevailing winds should carry all the aqueous vapor to the polar regions, any one wishes to send, however difficult it might seem, from the point we occupy, to get it across the icy belt, during the cold part of the year, when it is most needed. We had conceived that a temperature usually sixty degrees below zero, was quite unfavorable for such purposes of transportation, but if it will go, under those circumstances, we make no objections. Again, if the solar influences have manifested any disposition to go straight ahead to the polar sea, and concentrate all their power there, without regard to that portion of the globe lying between seventy and eighty degrees, or the icy belt, we shall be compelled to accede to that state of things, still we cannot discover how it is they can give that frozen zone the go by, and not let their rays fall with equal potency upon the vast glaciers of Northern Greenland, that are accumulating from year to year. We had supposed the god of day impartial in bestowing his blessings upon our world, and that he would, as far as circumstances permitted, treat all portions of the globe alike, and certainly he has a better opportunity to let his warming influences fall upon the icy belt than upon the polar sea, and yet those frozen regions remain from age to age, locked in the cold embrace of the frost king, spite of the sun's fiercest rays. And if the "sun-studded heavens" choose to radiate all their virtues and influences upon those regions, we submit; though we are quite unable to discover why the effects of any warmth from that source, would not be general, and expended upon all parts of the globe alike. We are at a loss to know why such causes should be introduced by scientific men who seem to have others in their possession so all-potent and overwhelming, and why they should go out into the interminable regions of space, to bring down a trifle of stellar heat to assist in keeping the polar sea from freezing, when they had already succeeded in placing, by accurate mathematical computation, a vast globe of incandescent molten material, only twelve miles distant from the waters they wish to keep warm.

We think if this vast body of incandescent heat really exists where the figures have placed it, there will be no difficulty in keeping the polar circle from freezing; but there may be very serious doubts whether we can keep it from boiling; and perhaps if we canvass the matter a little, we may find other difficulties that have not been contemplated. It becomes necessary to take a more extended consideration of such an all-powerful cause of polar warmth, as this fire theory is very much in the way of our grand central idea, and of course would totally annihilate the position we have assumed, and the theory we are endeavoring to substantiate, and in self-defense, although we have devoted a chapter to this subject, we shall be compelled to allude to the matter in this connection. If the diameter of the globe is eight thousand miles, and it has a solidified crust twenty-five miles in thickness, and the balance is molten lava, then there must be an orb of that material within this crust, 7,950 miles in diameter, containing fifty-four fifty-fifths of the solid contents of the whole superstructure, leaving one fifty-fifth of all this vast body of material, in a partially elaborated condition, that is, so much has passed out of this fiery, unevolved, primal condition, or cooled and assumed the form of granite, then disintegrated and formed sedimentary deposits, and so on, until it is covered with sufficient alluvial soil to produce the vegetable, and sustain all this scene of animal life, and activity. We hesitate not to pronounce this theory one of those learned humbugs that will give place at the proper time to more intelligent and enlightened views, which are harmonious with all known facts and phenomena that exist.

They claim that this immense mass of molten lava is sufficiently heated to melt the most refractory rocks, and if so, we can but wonder the refractory rocks are not melted, as in accordance with Fourier's computation there is fifty-five times the amount of molten lava that there is of rock, or crust of any description, and if this lava is capable of melting the most refractory rocks, how did these rocks happen to cool when they were originally right in the midst, and a part and parcel of this huge, super-heated mass. We do not like to be inquisitive, but would simply inquire where the fuel is obtained that keeps up this vast amount of glowing heat throughout the eternal ages, for no philosopher has ever yet devised a means that would be effectual in producing a great or small mass of molten lava, or in reducing mineral substances to a state of fusion, and holding them in that condition for any length of time, without using combustible material to generate the requisite amount of heat, and as heat being a positive element, is exhaustive of its own forces, a continuous supply of fuel must be provided, else the fire will go out, and the heat discontinue, whether under or above the earth. If philosophers can keep up such a terrible fire in the bowels of the earth without fuel, why do they not do the same upon the earth's surface? they could soon make their fortunes. But we refer the reader to the chapter upon this subject, where he will find it considered in many of its deformities and ugly details.

It cannot be doubted but there are causes sufficient in the realms of the natural universe, to produce all the effects that will ever come to the knowledge of men, but causes must always when found, be commensurate with the effects produced, and the intimate relationship betweeen the one and the other, will be apparent. If we should discover an elephant in labor, we should not expect the result would be a mouse, but that it would correspond with the magnitude of the producing cause. If we should ascertain that at a fixed locality upon the surface of this globe, certain phenomena existed, that could be found nowhere else, we should conclude the causes that produced such local phenomena, could not exert general influences upon all parts of the globe alike, and hence they must be confined to that locality. When we find a temperate polar circle of a million or so square miles, surrounded and enclosed upon all sides by a broad extent of territory extremely cold and frozen, we must conclude, that some causes are operating within the warmer circle, that do not expend their forces upon the surrounding frigid zone; for most assuredly, any cause that would keep that circle free from ice, and render its climate warm and genial, would produce the same result, if brought to bear uoon any other portion of the globe. We must look for causes entirely local, that exist within the circle, and do not extend their influences beyond its borders, or that are universal in their character, and originate away out in the "sun studded heavens," or in the rays of the sun for one-half the year. For it is quite clear that all these influences would be as effectual in dissolving the vast glaciers of the frozen belt southward of the warm circle, and would render the entire arctic regions as mild and temperate as the open polar sea.

We have already spoken of the longitudinal, Electro-Magnetic currents, that they must converge to a common focus at or near the pole, and pass through the spherical shell, continuing southward upon the interior concave surface, thus making a complete circuit, and that where these currents pass through the water, they will necessarily produce friction, creating disturbances and agitation, thus imparting great heat to the surrounding waters, as is evidently the case at the Maelstrom off Norway, and other whirlpools in the Northern Seas, near which the corals and other tropical marine productions are found. These attenuated fluid elements may pass with the utmost facility the most solid material substances, but in their pathway they always produce certain results, and quite generally heat ensues where there are any considerable Electro-Magnetic activities, and we readily discover, if all or most of these currents or threads that exist in every portion of the atmosphere converge at or near this point, or within the polar circle, and there pass through the water or more solid earth to the interior surface; then very great disturbances must exist, and very considerable heat must be produced; doubtless quite sufficient to prevent the freezing of the waters of the entire polar circle.

If the reader would dare admit that there might be an extensive spiral gateway within this circle, leading to the interior surface, and to a beautiful, more highly developed world than can be found upon the exterior, where every thing is warm and cheerful, and which receives its light and heat from the aural instead of the magnetic element; then he might find a prolific source for those influences that not only aid in rendering the open polar sea genial and temperate in its climate, but also assist in presenting to the human vision, those grand auroral displays that strike the mind with such profound astonishment, and which are so little understood by the philosophers of the present age.

I think we shall readily discover that these two local causes will prove entirely sufficient to produce all the climatic influences that can be experienced in the northern polar circle, without importing any from the far-off heavens, or sending them up from the tropical regions. If it can be supposed that "the clashing of the waters," in that region, caused by the convergence and commingling of the two great oceanic currents," can produce sensible heat sufficient to change the temperature of the Polar Sea; then we may well conclude that the disturbances and agitations produced by a continuous passage of the Electro-Magnetic fluids, would be most potent in their character, and productive of very extended climatic influences. It will be noticed that the fluid particles of Electro-Magnetism pass through the denser portions of the earth in a spiral form as the particles of water escape through an aperture, or as the atmosphere rushes through a seeming vacuum; thus increasing the agitation and consequent friction, and when we consider that the great majority of the Electro-Magnetic currents that surround the globe, have converged to this central focus within the polar circle, we may well suppose that the effects produced are very terrible, and the frictionizing and heating processes quite sufficient to change and materially modify the temperature of the entire Polar Sea.

We present these two *causes*, entirely local in their character, as explanatory of the great secret of a warmer clime in the extreme North, which must exist independent of those general laws that seem to produce changes and conditions of temperature between the icy belts that have thus far guarded the polar circles, and kept the most enterprising navigators at a distance that has precluded any very minute observations. We notice here the obvious fact, that this earth is a huge mechanical, self-moving machine, and like all other machines, it requires *motive-power*, which philosophers in all their researches into its physical structure have never been able to supply. No scientific mind has been qualified to inform us where the power originated, that rolls this earth upon its axis once in twenty-four hours; notwithstanding they are compelled to admit that an immense power must be generated in some manner, in order to produce these revolutions, and that forces of some character must be applied, or else no movement or activities could be effected. The mind endowed with but limited mechanical ability, will discover at once, that the great positive and negative forces, or the fluid elements of Electro-Magnetism in their passage spirally through a spherical shell at both its axial poles, must be productive of motive power, and that, if these forces are sufficient in quantity, revolutions of the shell or globe must necessarily ensue. We treat further upon this subject in its appropriate place.

It is to be hoped that the wonderful mysteries that have from all time lain concealed within this well guarded open Polar Sea, will soon be revealed to the world; and if we can possibly induce "the powers that be" to appropriate the sum needed to equip an expedition upon the Pacific side, we doubt not that this sealed book may be opened, and the problem that has hitherto eluded the combined efforts of the entire civilized world, may be solved in less than a single year. Let every reader do his utmost to aid this enterprise, and let us inaugurate as soon as possible a Pacific, Arctic, exploring expedition; for when all that lies hidden within the polar circle, is revealed to mankind, then humanity will take another stride in advance.

CHAP. III.

THE IGNEOUS THEORY OR INTERIOR FIRE GLOBE.

It was conceived by the elder Herschell, that our solar system was at one period in its history, an extended mass or spheroidal globe of nebulous matter or gaseous substance, larger in diameter than the orbit of the most exterior planet; that, this mass at some time in the past, and for some unknown cause, acquired motion, or commenced a revolution upon an axis, that in consequence of such revolution, the exterior particles became more condensed, and were thrown off from time to time into vast rings, entirely detached from the great original mass, which by some law coiled themselves up into smaller globes, and in this manner our planetary system has been formed. In consequence of condensation, great heat has ensued, and these young globes have become intensely heated; so much so that all the material of which they are composed, was held in a state of fusion, and although they say the heat was entirely sufficient to melt the most unfusible matter, yet by some process unknown to man these elements cooled and formed into granite.

This theory was elaborated more extensively, by the celebrated French astronomer and mathematician, LaPlace, and hence, it is usually called the Nebulous or Laplace Theory. It has been endorsed by most astronomers, and geologists, and doubtless it is at present, the most popular view of the physical formation of the globes in all planetary systems. This theory has been seized upon by many liberal minds as refuting most conclusively, the Bible history of creation, and it is supposed to be a solution and explanation of very many of the problems and phenomena that exist in the vast domain of nature, which were only mystified by the so-called revealed history given by the inspired Moses.

There is, however, a possibility that both Moses and LaPlace may have entertained incorrect and very erroneous opinions, and possibly both may have enunciated some valuable truths; and it remains for posterity to discriminate between the truths and errors they have left on record, to sift out the grains of wheat and reject the chaff. It is hardly probable that all of truth upon this vast subject will be given to man, until by education, he is brought up to that condition in which he can receive and entertain a just appreciation of the spirit or soul of all things. It is our purpose to glance at this igneous theory, and discover, if possible, how much of truth it contains, and, perhaps, ascertain, whether it does explain all the facts and phenomena that exist upon our globe; and if it is really the ultimatum of all knowledge concerning the physical formation of this grand superstructure; and whether the human mind may not safely venture out, a step beyond this philosophy. It is certainly an open inquiry that may still be made, whether the wondrous architectural skill and ingenuity brought to bear in the production of this marvelous mechanical structure, has absolutely made nothing but an immense bomb-shell filled brim full of intensely heated molten lava; and left it there to cool off during the eternities of the future. These theorists estimate the crust of the globe, surrounding this igneous mass, at various depths, from twenty-five to sixty miles, but probably the mean of the various estimates would be about forty miles.

They bring in support of this view, a great variety of evidences, such as the increasing temperature, as we go downwards into the earth, either in mines or artesian wells. The evident igneous formation of granite; the supposed action of hot water upon the lower sedimentary rocks; the very large extent of territory affected by earthquakes, showing as they say, the cause to be coextensive with the effects. The vast amount of lava, thrown from volcanoes, and the continuous activity of numbers of them from age to age, proving their resources to be inexhaustible, and that they must have a common origin. The foregoing are some of the arguments we are to notice, in reviewing a theory supported by the ablest scientific minds of our age, and that places a vast fire orb within the globe, that contains thirty-four thirty-fifths of the entire material, composing the whole structure. That is, the solid crust upon which we tread with such apparent safety, may contain one thirty-fifth of all the material in the globe, and if the crust is forty miles in thickness, then the interior or liquid fire must be 7,920 miles in diameter. If men can absolutely prove that such are the only principles upon which worlds can be constructed, and that there is no other mode by which they can be formed in a proper manner, set in motion, and made to subserve their purposes, and that this plan reaches the highest possible extent of mechanical skill, then we shall be compelled to adopt this theory, and accept it as correct.

But as long as there must be a variety of ways which competent intelligences might introduce in the construction of worlds, the same as in the buiding of ships or dwellings, we shall be compelled to adopt a less clumsy, and more harmonious view, and one less horrifying to the finer sensibilities that exist in the minds of civilized humanity. We deem it quite sufficient to have been compelled for many long years, to swallow the theological hell, without trying to force down a scientific one of almost equal dimensions. The prominent argument in support of this theory, has been the increase of temperature as we penetrate the earth; generally about one degree in fifty or sixty feet, and this view seems to have been universal, as far as experiments have been made, up to the year 1869.

It will readily be perceived, if the temperature continues to increase at the same rate, then at some depth, all the materials that compose our earth, would be found in a state of fusion, and so far, theorists, without further investigation in this direction, have adopted this conclusion, notwithstanding these mining explorations, and artesian wells have been mostly made upon high lands, and very few to any great extent, below the sea-level. They have found as great an increase of temperature, by penetrating the earth in mountain ranges, and in localities very far above the level of the sea, it having gone up with the same rapidity, as in less elevated portions of the country; so we discover this rapid increase could not depend exactly upon its approximation to any great internal reservoir of heated materials, for it was found that in deep soundings in the ocean, the water was colder, as we approached the sea bottom, and in some instances this has been found five, six, and even seven miles below the sea-level. Prof. Maury marks upon his chart of soundings, one place, 6,600 fathoms or 39,600 feet, and we learn, that no boring had been made previous to 1869, over 2,200 feet, or considerably less than one half mile. While the ocean had given us access to a point 37,000 feet nearer this terrible imaginary furnace, and that tremendous depth failed to present any indications of increasing temperature, but, on the contrary, the warmer water was at the top.

We discover if the law had held good, the whole waters of the ocean would be at the boiling point, and all would eventually pass off, and be held suspended in the form of vapor, as we are told they were in the early stages of the earth's history. The advocates of this theory, have with great care and labor, compiled tables showing accurately, the depth of different mines, and artesian borings, in order to show, as they supposed, conclusively, that such law was universal, but unfortunately, they seem to have forgotten that old Ocean had explored the earth's crust still deeper than the miner, or the artesian borings.

Prof. Parrot has urged this objection to the internal heat theory, and has given the results of most accurate observations upon the temperature of the ocean, showing that it diminishes as we go downwards, rapidly at first, and then more slowly, but Prof. Hitchcock objects to this idea, and concludes the earth's crust to be as thick under the ocean bottom, as under the highest mountain. We see no reason to suppose that the interior surface, if it rests upon this igneous mass, is regulated by the surface bottom of the ocean. There can be no possibility that any such effect would be produced; but the interior would necessarily be smoothed off by the attrition of this heated mass. If the internal heat produces influences in mines, and at the bottom of artesian wells, sufficient to prove its own existence, why does it not exert the same influence under the depths of the ocean? and if so, the temperature would be sufficient under the deeper portions to bring lead and other metals to a state of fusion, and if the heat produces no perceptible influence at the surface in accordance with the nice mathematical calculations of Baron Fourier, then how does it produce such marked effects at so little distance from the surface in mines and artesian wells.

But, since all these estimates have been made, and all these conclusions formed, we have obtained data that has completely overturned all former calculations, and that perfectly corresponds with observations in the depths of the ocean. The corporation or citizens of St. Louis, Missouri, have sunk an artesian well, to the enormous depth of 3,843 1-2 feet, and by so doing, have settled this whole question of increasing temperature, as depth increases; so that all arguments of that character, are perfectly nugatory, and instead of supporting the idea of internal heat, they prove exactly the opposite, and establish the theory of internal cold, or, that the basis of this superstructure is composed of inactive, frozen, negative elements, instead of those that are intensely heated, active and positive. Instead of placing as a foundation the most positive and active materials, that would be constantly making disturbance, the controlling intelligence has placed there, the most inactive and negative, that would lie still, and serve as a basis upon which might be reared a superstructure of the more positive and active elements. We ask the intelligent reader, which of these two plans would display the greater amount of wisdom? or which would you prefer if you proposed to erect a spacious edifice that would require a great outlay of capital and labor, and which you desire should be permanent and enduring; would you make your foundations of uneasy, active, explosive elements that would necessarily be rolling and tumbling about, or would you place under your building, materials that had within them all the properties of inertia, or lying still? I think most architects would choose the quiet materials, and can it be possible that our ordinary mechanics would display greater wisdom than the great Mechanic that has had power and wisdom to plan, and then control the necessary forces and materials that have ultimated in this stupendous world we inhabit, and yet we shall see that this grand blunder is only one of a series, that are committed by the advocates of the great interior fires.

It was found,in this artesian boring, that the usual phenomena of increasing heat attended increasing depth, until they had measured 3,029 feet, where the temperature was one hundred seven degrees Farenheit. If we may suppose the temperature at the surface sixty-seven degrees, this would make forty degrees difference, or an average increase of about one degree for seventy-five feet, however it is probable, if they had made a tabular statement of temperatures, as the boring progressed they would have found a more rapid rise, during the first 2,000 feet, and no doubt it would have coincided with other wells that have been sunk to that distance, in various parts of the world.

It is highly probable that the last 500 feet of the 3,000, would have shown but little, if any increase of temperature, and it is of no little importance, that means should be used at some future time, to ascertain the range at frequent points, from the surface to the lowest level, as this well so materially unsettles a great number of the carefully made estimates of the scientific world. It is unfortunate that more frequent thermometrical observations were not made and noted, but such as have been recorded, prove most conclusively some very important facts, and one is, that the highest temperature of one hundred and seven degrees, was found a little over 3,000 feet in depth, and there can be no doubt, at about that distance, there is a long range where the temperature varies but little; so we may safely conclude that near this point the increasing heat of the earth terminates; a change takes place, and it very gradually subsides; as they found at 3,127 feet, one hundred six degrees or a falling of one degree. No other observation is noted, until at 3,827 feet, the instrument marked one hundred and five degrees, thus the temperature diminished two degrees in eight hundred feet, but we doubt not if observations had been made more frequently, they might perhaps have found a temperature even more than one hundred and seven degrees, above 3,000 feet.

Taking their very meagre record, we arrive at the fact that the temperature changes at a depth approximating 3,000 feet, and from thence downwards a gradual decrease has been actually found of two degrees in eight hundred feet. Now, if we should estimate this declination of temperature at twelve degrees to the mile, we shall discover that about nine miles from the surface, will be found a temperature, somewhat below zero; and doubtless, we should find from thence downwards, the foundations of this globe, in that frozen negative condition that will induce them to lie still; until all the great, destined changes can take place upon and near the surface, that have been provided for in the vast programme of the world's past and future history.

We trust a careful study of the principles presented in this work, upon which globes must necessarily be constructed, will be a sufficient explanation of the foregoing phenomena of increasing heat beneath the earth's surface. We now propose to notice the comparative magnitude of this immense interior furnace of glowing heat. We learn that this crust contains very nearly one thirty-fifth part of the entire solid contents of the globe, and there yet remains thirty-four times as much material to be cooled and solidified, as that which has already passed through this process, and we must necessarily conclude that interminable eternities would pass away before this vast amonnt of fiery materials can be rendered of use, if ever; as all heat must be radiated through the exterior solidified crust, and Fourier has by nice mathematical demonstration discovered, that in consequence of the oxygenated condition of this outer covering, it becomes so bad a conductor of heat, that not sufficient would be radiated to melt ten feet of ice in one hundred years; that is about one inch per annum.

If such is the fact, and this great furnace exists within this comparatively frail enclosure, then it must so exist to all eternity, for it cannot radiate even now, sufficient heat to make any perceptible difference in its magnitude, and if its outer covering should increase in thickness, its radiations must continuously diminish, so we discover that the mass of igneous matter cannot be to any considerable extent progressive, but an eternal fixture. This great amount of valuable world material that might have been so useful in the manufacture of other globes, is eternally locked up within this; and must remain there perpetually, without subserving any of those divine uses, for which matter seems to exist; and to which it seems so universally applied.

These philosophers have been prodigal and reckless in their extravagant waste of materials, out of which worlds are constructed upon higher mechanical principles, by incomprehensible wisdom, and we defy them to tell us, of what possible utility, this great burning mass can be in the interior of the globe, locked up forever, or to show in any manner how it can be of any practical benefit, and further, we say they have not proved that it is there, but merely inferred such might be the fact, in view of certain external phenomena.

The human mind is so constituted in its organism that there are limits to its intellectual grasp; for instance, we have no power that will enable us to lay hold of all this universe at once, not even of this globe; it is too large to be encompassed by the mind's eye, at a single glance. If we wish to get a comprehensive view of these stupendous objects in a brief space of time, we must bring them down and present their forms in narrower limits; and, hence, if we can diminish this globe, and place it before our vision, we can get a clearer view of this whole matter. If we construct a globe, or sphere of eighty inches in diameter, instead of 8,000 miles, then we can see it at once; and we shall find that the relative thickness of the crust of such a globe, would be four-tenths of an inch. We may now choose our material, and form that crust, and place within its hollow, liquid fire, at 7,000 degrees heat, which, says Prof. Hitchcock, is just sufficient to melt all the materials of the rocks. I think we could not find an intelligent person who would not arrive at the conclusion that the shell would soon become a liquid mass also, as its entire contents are only one thirty-fifth part of the fire within.

We may now increase the diameter of our small globe, and make it eighty miles, instead of eighty inches; and we shall then have a shell of four-tenths of a mile, or about 2,112 feet in thickness, which would contain an orb of this intensely heated lava, of over seventy-nine miles in diameter, with this thin crust of solidified granite to resist its overwhelming influences.

Which can we suppose will gain the victory; these terribly raging elementary fire billows within, or this feeble crust that encloses and holds them in check ; and if the great mass of liquid fire is sufficiently heated to hold in fusion the granite, then, of course, it would melt all the granite contiguous. We trust that every one of these philosophers will be compelled to admit that a shell of 2,112 feet in thickness, would be entirely insufficient to resist the influences of such an enormous quantity of the most heated, active and explosive elements in this universe, and all we have to do, is to multiply these numbers by one hundred, and we have our world, 8,000 miles in diameter, with a crust 211,200 feet or forty miles in thickness, with a vast interior globe of intensely heated material, over 7,900 miles in diameter, and thirty-five times larger, in solid contents than the frail crust by which it is enclosed.

It is difficult to conceive of an idea more repugnant to our natures, or one more horrifying to contemplate; it is so much so indeed, that we cannot be brought to suppose that the author of such a structure, so at war with all that is within us, could have produced intelligent beings also, and called all together one harmonious whole. Such has not been our experience, for as far as we have been permitted to look out into the great arcanum, we have found all, beautiful and natural, and in perfect accord with every faculty placed within our own organism, and this is one of the means we have given us, by which we may discriminate and judge between truth and error. Truth is always beautiful and harmonious, because it is a part of ourselves; if we are a part of all, and we must be, in order to be a microcosm. We cannot, if we credit any amount of knowledge or mechanical genius to the builder of this world, suppose for a moment, that this vast interior which might easily be fitted up so grandly and beautifully, and subserve the glorious purpose of producing and sustaining human intelligence; that the great house of all living, that exhibits such Divine wisdom and constructive skill, has been so miserably defaced, and ruined interiorly, by being filled brimming full of incandescent lava.

We pass for the present, a consideration of the supposed igneous formation of the granite rocks, and come up to that period, where it is said in consequence of great internal heat, the earth's surface produced a wonderful prolific growth of vegetation of gigantic proportions, such as enormous tree-ferns, calamites, sigillaria, and numerous varieties that have left their fossil remains on top of the Devonian, and immediately below the coal formation.

There is no doubt but this gigantic vegetation existed; the only question to be considered is, was it produced or in any way influenced by a vast internal fire? was it germinated and brought into existence, and was this enormous growth of those numerous extinct species, induced in any manner by this internal heat? and again, is this enormous growth and accumulation of vegetables and semi-ligneous products, the material from which the bituminous and anthracite coal of a later period have formed? If so, these accumulated forests must, at a subsequent period have formed vast coal pits arranged in such a manner that the woody fibres could not be reduced to ashes, but changed into lignites, then into bituminous coal, and finally much of it by the action of great heat, into anthracite, and some of it into plumbago. Very learned men seem to entertain this opinion, and it might be folly to dissent, but it would seem that some objections may be offered. It appears that this immense flora was found upon the top of a very extensive formation, which is still above another of fossiliferous rocks that had been the residence of organic living beings for untold ages before this growth existed.

Prof. Hitchcock makes the Paleozoic stratifications below it, 68,000 feet in possible thickness, from the top of the Devonian to the bottom of the Silurian, all filled with the fossil remains of animal life; and the difficulty seems to be, not to produce the extensive growth of vegetation, but to obtain the amount of heat from the internal source that would transform these forests into bituminous and anthracite coal, and still permit the existence of vegetable and animal life to continue. As it is supposed that a heat sufficient to produce even charcoal, would not be conducive to a healthy growth of either vegetable or animal organizations; and it is very evident that many long ages previous to the coal period, when the crust must have been very much thinner, these forms of life existed and flourished, as all the paleozoic rocks testify, even to the bottom of the Silurian or Cambrian. There certainly could have been no paroxysms of heat; whatever heat came from such a source, must of necessity, have been uniform and continuous, and the cooling of the crust, and its subsequent changes must have been under such circumstances, steady and progressive; for the same amount of heat continued, with the very trifling diminution, ascertained by Fourier and others. We perceive after we had got the crust so cooled down as to produce vegetable and animal life, it would be impossible many ages after that, to get up a heat strong enough with the crust somewhat thickened, to produce a universal coal-pit, and change all these grand, ante-carboniferous forests of tree-ferns, lepidodendra, etc., into bituminous and anthracite coal. We think in our researches, we shall be compelled to look in some other direction for the causes of the great coal fields that now supply our manufactories, steamboats and dwellings with their required fuel.

What reason have we to suppose after there had been only the necessary heat for many long ages, to sustain the healthy growth of vegetable and animal organized life, that there should suddenly be a rise in the temperature, sufficient to change all of nature's products into anthracite, and thus continue until all the coal stratifications were produced, from 2,000 to 13,000 feet in depth, for such is declared by geological authority, to be the possible thickness of the carboniferous formations. We shall discover also, that while this process of coal-burning was going on, if caused by an internal heat, sufficient to change all this vast amount of woody fibre to coal, such as is found in the various mines, all production of vegetable and animal life, must have been entirely suspended, and have so remained; and this suspension of their existence, would have continued until the temperature became so reduced that they might be able to live and perform their proper functions; for certainly it does not require any great stretch of learning or intelligence to discover that a heat produced by a general cause, that must necessarily be universal upon all portions of the surface of the globe, sufficient to burn a coal-pit, would be very unhealthy for animal or vegetable products, and would render their continuance utterly impossible. As nature in all her great book, discloses no indications of any such cessation of animal and vegetable organic life, we must conclude no such period of suspension has existed in the earth's history.

The so-called sacred historian when he proposed to destroy the inhabitants of the earth, by a great flood, provided as he thought ample means for the escape of the male and female of all the different species of animals, that they might be propagated after the catastrophe. But where could have been found an ark of safety for all these different species that would have rescued them from the melting influences of that lengthy, anthracite-burning period, when caloric reigned supreme, and smoke and blackness covered the wide landscape and all was one dark scene of desolation and death.

Such must have been the carboniferous period, if, this geological view is correct, and if these vast Devonian forests were converted into coal by the influence of the great reservoir of internal heat, and those stirring scenes of life and animation that must have existed during the growth of that immense flora and peculiar fauna were succeeded by universal destruction. If so, nature must have been compelled once more, to reproduce those forms before all the wheels of the great machine could have rolled on smoothly again, in the performance of their great duties. It is extremely difficult upon this hypothesis, to account for those paroxysmal changes of temperature, that produced such widely different results; first, the gigantic vegetable, and the varied animal organizations, then the intensely heated carboniferous, and a little later, the wonderful glacial period, which formations evidently covered a large portion of the temperate zones, and were finally succeeded by a more genial and milder climate that continues till the present time. The most eminent scientific men who have lived, are entirely unable to offer a reason, why so large a portion of the earth, at a particular period, as is conclusively proven, was covered with vast fields of ice, of a great thickness, for very many ages.

In connection with this subject, the reader will do well to keep in view, the great fact, that there are well known opposing elements which mingle with, and permeate throughout the earth, and all its appertainings; that certain of these elements exist from the inmost central portions of this physical superstructure, to the farthest verge of its atmospheric surroundings, all performing their proper functions; that they are distributed where they are most needed to carry out their purposes, and that each one of these positive and negative powers, such as life and death, heat and cold, light and darkness, activity and repose, expansion and contraction, magnetism and electricity, occupy their own particular realm; that the positives have an intimate relationship, one with the other, and are connected together by a curiously arranged affinitizing principle, and that the negatives are arranged upon the opposing side, and sustain a similar relationship one to another. Thus we have cold, darkness death, inactivity, sleep or repose, contraction and electricity, all affinitizing to the grosser molecular structure of the mineral kingdom; their original home, is down in the depths far below life and light, activity and expansion, caloric and magnetism, because it will be seen that the more active and disturbing elements can not with safety be admitted to the interior of our earth; but they must have their abiding place near the superfices, so as not to endanger by their activities, and disturbing tendencies, the entire fabric; for we may easily ascertain where death and darkness hold their court and where sleep and inactivity find an eternal resting place, all locked up in the frigid embrace of a cold, that knows no change; in the rigors of her frozen temperature, there can be no disturbance. We shall see upon investigation, the absolute necessity of placing static instead of dynamic forces, in the most interior portions of the earth, however those portions may be arranged, whether in a solid globe or spherical shell.

Where nature requires all the elements of eternal rest and stability, where the negative forces are most needed which are contented to remain in undisturbed repose through the everlasting ages, that a world may be safely constructed upon them as a foundation that shall prove sure and steadfast, modern science has placed an overwhelming amount of the most active, uneasy, terribly disturbing elements—a huge mass of intensely heated material. We might as well have erected our imposing national capital upon the back of a monster turtle, whose dimensions would equal the State of Virginia, with all the elements of activity contained within him, and then have deposited overwhelming quantities of nitro-glycerine, and other equally powerful explosives beneath its walls, and every where about its foundations, and expected the edifice to be as enduring as time, as to have constructed our earth upon such an uncertain basis as the igneous theorists have placed under its solid battlements and towers.

Hence, in the central regions of the earthy shell, between the exterior and interior portions, eternal night and cold, inactivity and death, hold, and exercise supreme authority, that a grand superstructure may be erected upon them with security, because there can be no possible disturbances in the depths below, that will endanger the fabric. For the spiritual entities that are locked up in the embrace of these frigid material atoms, are enjoying their everlasting sleep, after eternities of wakefulness and activity, and are preparing for their resurrection in the eternities of the future. They are there because they have chosen that position of repose, and do not wish to be disturbed, and it is perfectly safe to build a world upon such a basic element, that has become in the mutations of eternal cycles, the very quintessence of inertia and death. We not only have the analogies existing in the universe, eliminated by thought and patient research to depend upon, in support of the idea of cold, inactive, interior elements in this globular shell, but as we have said, fortunately the energies and activities of the people of St. Louis, have also come to our aid, and by boring a well to such an enormous depth in that city, have conclvsively proved, that, after a depth of 3,000 feet has been attained, the temperature begins gradually to grow colder.

The advocates of the igneous theory, seized with avidity, upon the fact that the temperature increased as we penetrated the earth's crust, thus proving conclusively to their minds, that at a given point, we must attain a heat that would melt the most refractory rocks, and leave all things in a state of fusion. But it appears they have reckoned without their host. Their estimates, unfortunately for their theory, have been based upon entirely too shallow borings, all of them less than 2,200 feet, and they were as ignorant of the temperature below that depth as the schoolboy, and the strongest evidence they brought to bear to prove the existence of the great internal fire, when extended a little farther into the depths of the earth, established most conclusively, the opposite doctrine of eternal, frozen death and inactivity. And there can be no doubt from the data obtained at the St. Louis artesian well, that at the distance of twelve or fifteen miles, the temperature is at least two hundred degrees below zero, the same as it is supposed to be out in the regions of space, beyond the farthest verge of the atmosphere. Hence, we may expect to realize all the changes of temperature, in passing from the interior portions of the globular shell, upwards to the surface, and then to the extent of the atmosphere of our earth, going through the entire strata of organic life, and finding, as we might naturally conclude, the central portions of this extent, most productive of these living organizations; because all the positive, active elements that are required to produce and sustain such living organisms, exist in greater abundance, and are diffused far more extensively, in and through those portions contiguous to the earth's surface. Here is where the positive elements of light and heat exist in their most elaborated and perfected condition, and here is produced life and animation, in all their varied forms; and we plainly see it would have been but a reckless waste of those positive materials to have kept them locked up in the interior of the earth to all eternity.

We will simply observe in relation to these deep artesian borings, and the facts gathered therefrom, that what has in accordance with modern scientific opinions been so universally brought to bear by the advocates of the igneous theory, supporting their views concerning the internal heat, now proves far more conclusively, and far more in harmony with phenomenal facts, the existence of universal, internal cold. Herschell, LaPlace, and others, have placed a terribly unwieldy, unmanageable and turbulent elephant, or a beast with ten million times seven heads and ten horns, within the interior of our globe, and their endorsers, are now saying to this huge beast, "Peace, be still," while they may enter into intricate mathematical computations, and discover what the result might be, of a little activity upon the part of the animal.

We are told by these savans, that he produces all the disturbing phenomena in the form of volcanoes and earthquakes that are known upon the earth's surface, that he produces the wonderful heat of Thermal springs and Solfataras, also the great increase in the temperature of artesian wells, ejects all the substances thrown from the craters, sometimes to immense distances from their mouths, causing all the vibrations and quiverings of the earth, during its most terrific convulsions, and yet they have ascertained that the heat is so firmly enclosed within its boundaries, by the oxygen in the outer crust, that it does not radiate sufficient to melt scarcely an inch of ice, in a single year. If so, then interminable millions of eternities, must pass away before this great monster can be removed, as we must discover that a body of incandescent material over 7,900 miles in diameter, at a heat of more than 7,000 degrees, that does not part with sufficient, during the year to melt an inch of ice, must remain as nearly as possible in a static condition, and eternities might pass away before it would lose enough to be perceptible to the human comprehension.

Hence, we discover that the cooling process, and the consequent formation of granite, or igneous rocks upon the interior surface, is very nearly suspended, for this great mass cannot possibly cool, unless it radiates or parts with its heat, and it cannot form into rock, unless it cools, and we discover by the calculations of Fourier, that this process has very nearly ceased its operations, and that, consequently, the exterior crust has attained very nearly its ultimate thickness, as there can be no appreciable change for thousands of ages to come, and if this internal heat is a fact, and the calculations correct, concerning its almost infinitessimal quantity of radiation, then we may consider the crust practically finished, and that henceforward, all the interior will remain in nearly a fixed condition, and the reflective mind cannot certainly entertain a very exalted admiration for a divine architect who would leave a world in such a condition.

Their theory would lock up within the embraces of the granite bonds, that holds the monster in durance, an amount of material, thirty-five times greater than the crust, or the matter from which it is composed; and there they propose to let it remain to all eternity, in useless inactivity. They say this mass contains nearly all the active elements in the world, sufficiently evolved to produce all the disturbances that are witnessed upon the surface; and yet they can hold it so quietly, that no one could discover that it has an existence. They say that the mineral kingdom has been evolved out of a portion of this same material, yet it cannot produce much more after this, because it is not radiating an amount of heat sufficient to cool any portion of the mass, worth mentioning, and it must necessarily cool before it changes into granite rock.

They say it is primeval, unevolved, homogeneous matter, and yet it is so far elaborated as to furnish all the various substances that are ejected at different times, from the belching mouths of the numerous volcanoes. They also say that this internal, incandescent mass of fire, so intensely active, has existed eternal ages, regardless of the great prominent fact, that all positive, active elements that are in operation, are exhaustive of the forces that produce their activity, that all fires are produced by combustion, which can not possibly exist, without destroying, or dissolving and wasting the supply of materials by which it is fed, and that unless the supply is constant, the fires must discontinue, as well in the interior, as upon the exterior surface of the earth.

Geologists have told us precisely how they manufacture combustible materials from this original, primeval mass in the interior, and how they produce all the substances that have been ejected from the craters; and yet they project forth all these various substances from the great unevolved chaos, under the granite crust, without any evolution or manufacturing whatever; and such are a few of the absurdities of this theory, and it will not be surprising if their exposure should have a tendency to diminish our veneration for minds that can endorse such extremely short-sighted conclusions, and thus make them their own. The reader will doubtless clearly discover by this time that there is no aspect in which this theory can be presented, but it exhibits a sort of unnatural deformity, and seems only paralleled by another unquenchable fire which was built by our forefathers, in which to confine to all eternity, that portion of God's children, who did not look at all things with the same vision possessed by themselves, and we humbly think the day is not far distant, when both these grand delusions, together with that disreputable personage who is said to have exercised a general supervision over the theologically heated dominions, will be consigned to the bottomless pit, and perhaps pass out at the other end, in their journey to oblivion.

CHAP. IV.

VOLCANOES.

Among the various superficial phenomena upon our globe, perhaps, none have attracted more attention than volcanoes; being so prominently marked in their features and characteristics, and sometimes so destructive in their influences, and withall, so difficult to be fully understood, it is not surprising they should have been so carefully studied by men of scientific attainments.

It would appear that it has quite generally been supposed that the igneous theory was the solution of the great problem, and that in these vast internal fires, could be found sufficient cause for all the external disturbances, and sufficient material to supply all the vomitings of those huge mountain throats; and upon that difficult subject at the present, science seems to be at rest; however, there are some persons that are always raising objections to well settled opinions, and thus the world moves onward.

These volcanoes are supposed to be vent holes or chimneys that reach from the surface to the great fire within, contrived for the purpose of safety valves that may permit any surplus gasses or dangerous elements to escape, as there can be no doubt that such an immense amount of active, positive materials in a state of constant surging and ebullition, might produce some disturbances, if pent up for long ages, without any such vent holes. We think no one will hesitate to admit, that a globe of molten lava, that has a superficial area of nearly 200,000,-000 square miles, and a heat of over 7,000 degrees Fahrenheit, and only enclosed by a frail crust of about forty miles in depth, would require at least all the open chimneys that are known to exist in the shape of active volcanoes upon the globe. It is supposed that in earlier times, when the crust was thinner, and the fire orb a little larger, and, perhaps, more active, volcanoes were far more numerous than at the present; in fact, that they numbered hundreds, if not thousands to one, and that vastly more chimneys or vent holes were needed than at present; that the crust has now become so extremely thick, and the internal fire so diminished, that a very limited number of these chimneys will answer all the purposes required, as it will be seen that we have only two hundred and twenty-five of these safeguards left, and they are mostly inactive, except at long intervals; in fact, there are not over four or five continuously active volcanoes upon the globe. Others are in a state of eruption, more or less frequently, varying from a few months to 1,700 years.

It is extremely difficult for us to determine, why this internal globe of fire should be so much less forcible in its demonstrations at present than it was ages since, or why these volcanoes seem to occur in ranges, and leave, such very large tracts of territory entirely destitute of the needed vent holes. It would seem to an ordinary mind, that these safety valves should have been more regularly distributed, if they are used for that purpose, and not so confined to particular localities. Suppose now these amazingly active elements in the interior, should become disturbed directly under Chicago or Northern Illinois, where would they find the most accessible chimney or safety valve; for aught we can see, any explosive element that might be generated directly under that great city, would be compelled to travel to Mexico, or the Aleutian Isles, or to Mount Hecla in Ireland, in order to escape.

It certainly seems to be a question, whether such elements would be willing to go so far out of their way, to accommodate any portion of the outside world. We cannot by any process of reasoning, discover why it became necessary to place Vesuvius, Ætna, and Stromboli, and other volcanoes, all upon so contracted an area while such large extents of territory, embracing very many millions of square miles, are entirely destitute of these escapes or vents, if the cause that produces and renders them necessary, is universal, and comes in immediate contact with the under surface of the thin crust every where alike, upon every square mile of this entire globe.

We cannot help thinking that a supremely intelligent architect, if he had placed within the rocky crust, a universal element of disturbance, that required apertures through to the exterior, for the escape of dangerous gasses, or explosive elements, would have distributed those apertures in a more orderly manner, so that all portions of the globe might be rendered equally safe from exposure to those dangerous elements. But as these chimneys are so partially distributed, so few in number, and so generally inactive, we shall be compelled to concede, they do not subserve any such purpose, and that there is no universal cause of that kind to produce elemental disturbances.

If there is a general cause that produces volcanoes in

accordance with the igneous theory, and these chimneys or craters extend downward entirely through the crust, what powerful influence has resulted in the extinction of the very large proportion of those that ever had an existence? as they are said to number a hundred to one that is now called active. What has closed up these deep vent holes? what circumstance has transpired in the earth's history, rendering it unimportant, that this vast number of ancient vent holes should be still kept open? while all the causes for which they were first opened, are in full and vigorous activity. For what purpose has the fires of those inactive and dead volcanoes been extinguished, and in what manner has this wonderful feat been accomplished?

A partial reply has been made to this query by Prof. Denton, an able geologist, in a recent work, and doubtless he is fully competent to give to the world, the most advanced thought of the scientific minds of the age, upon the subjects of which he speaks in his book. He very gravely tells us, that, as a large portion of the actual volcanoes, are contiguous to the sea shore, most probably those that are extinct were similarly situated, and that nature has at sometime provided some aperture, through which the waters of the ocean, might communicate with the crater, and extinguish the flames. To prove that he is serious, and to make himself more definite, upon this point he says in an article treating upon the general development and harmonious completion of the physical globe, that earthquakes and volcanic eruptions, must ultimately cease to afflict mankind with their convulsive throes, and their terrific explosions, and, that if those great physical disturbances are not quieted by the silent processes continuously operating in the realms of nature, then at some day in the future, the ingenuity and daring of some bold, energetic men will be brought to bear, and they will contrive means that will put a final damper upon the fires of those belching monsters.

He further intimates that he doubts not there are men in New England, to-day, who would for a suitable compensation, undertake to execute and construct a subterranean tunnel, from the Mediterranean to Mount Vesuvius, open that monster chimney, which has so many times vomited forth a portion of the contents of the vast furnace below, to the great terror of the inhabitants, and destruction of the surrounding country, and that they would thus be able to introduce a stream of water of sufficient magnitude to lick up and quench those eternal fires that have from time to time given activity to that famous volcano. Our author must either be serious, or else he is playing upon the credulity of his readers, and as his work has an extensive circulation, it may be well to notice his view of the matter. We are all somewhat familiar with steam boiler explosions and their terrible effects, and have some idea of the cause of these often calamitous occurrences, and that generally, by careless or incompetent engineers, the injector becomes obstructed, the water gets low, and an increasing amount of caloric is accumulated in the boiler, and it is a well known fact that steam boilers are extensive generators of electricity, and it is a fact, which should be known, that electricity will dissolve particles of caloric, and release magnetism, and when you have these two powers confined in your boiler, in sufficient quantities, no amount of iron, or bolts, or rivets, will resist their influences, and you must have an explosion. It would be well if this subject was better understood, and the requisite safeguards placed in all steam boilers which would render an explosion simply impossible.

His theory contemplates a volume of molten lava in the bowels of this earth at a depth of forty miles from the exterior surface, of prodigious extent and inconceivable heat, and he proposes to introduce streams of cold water to the kindly embraces of this enormous mass of incandescent lava through these volcanic chimneys, and gravely says that nature has pursued this method in quenching the fires of those that are already extinct.

He concludes we may safely send down into that huge reservoir of explosive elements, any quantity of the negative power called electricity in its diluted form, as it is found in water, in order to extinguish the remaining volcanoes, thus bringing those antagonistic forces into immediate contact in the bowels of the earth, in continuously increasing quantities; and, if our friend can succeed in accomplishing that purpose, we had better commence saying our prayers, for the whole fabric will be blown into fragments, in less time than is usually occupied in the performance of that interesting ceremony. He is pouring down a constant supply of cold water into this terribly heated furnace, manufacturing, by the commingling of these opposing elements, Electro-Magnetism, with tremendous rapidity, and in this manner, he will have sufficient of those fluid elements which are the most terrible forces in nature, to destroy this globe in a very brief space of time.

It cannot be doubted that by proper engineering, and the requisite amount of labor, a communication might be made between the waters of the Mediterranean and the crater of Mount Vesuvius, of sufficient capacity to let down a large amount of water, and if this crater or chimney continues down and opens into any such vast chamber, as our author describes, we cannot doubt the result either; for in less time than I can pen this sentence, the vine-clad hills, the cities and villages, and pleasant homes of the population of all that portion of Italy, would be torn to fragments, and to say the least, that section of the interior fire orb, would be brought into immediate contact with the waters of the exterior surface, and I leave the reader to imagine the sequel.

And yet, by these means, our learned author concludes the fires of all those numerous dead volcanoes have been extinguished, and for this cause, they have ceased their activity. It is a well known fact that very many volcanoes have made their appearance in the midst of the sea, raising up islands, and producing the usual phenomena, and it will be seen that if the great interior fire is the all-producing cause, then an opening would of course be made between the bottom of the ocean, and the great interior heated mass, and there would be nothing to hinder the waters from going down these chimneys in overwhelming torrents, thus causing an explosive power that would be utterly destructive of all terrestrial things. Can any sane person doubt when an opening is made under the bottom of any part of the ocean, by subterranean disturbance, or by an explosion of any of those dangerous elements that have collected beneath, or from any cause whatever, that the waters do rush in and fill up the vacancy, and that this is the great efficient reason why such disturbances are of such short duration.

Is it possible that philosophers and scientific men who are supposed to possess superior mental abilities, can calculate with confidence to stay such overwhelmingly terrific sourc s of volcanic action, by directing small streams of water into the craters of the few that remain in activity, and also claim that such has been the process by which nature has extinguished the fires of those of the past, that are now silent and dead, which number as thousands, to the tens that still continue active. However desirable it may be, in accordance with the eternal laws of progressive development, which seem to permeate all things existing in our world, and in the universe, that earthquakes should cease to overthrow cities, terrify the people and destroy human life,and, that volcanoes should no more send forth their huge volumes of blackening smoke and lurid flames, and vomit from their bowels the turbid rivers of scorching lava, to the terror and dismay of the surrounding inhabitants; yet, we shall without doubt be compelled to witness their continued operations, until the great producing cause can be removed. If that cause is so vast and wonderfully extensive in its proportions, as to occupy, at the present time, after all the diminution of the past ages, thirty-four thirty-fifths of the solid contents of this entire globe, then the human mind cannot by any possibility, enter into a computation concerning the length of time that must elapse, before the cause of these unpleasant phenomena, shall cease its operations, and its results be no more experienced.

When we talk of extinguishing volcanoes, if it means

anything, it means to quench all those fires, and remove all those influences, of whatsoever nature, that are productive of such effects; it means an entire bar to the operation of all causes that have hitherto ultimated in volcanic action, and then, of course, such effects may be expected to cease, and not before. There is not an intelligent man who stops to reflect, who can suppose nine-tenths of all the original volcanoes have ceased their activity, under any of the circumstances contemplated by the igneous theory; but, on the contrary, they must conclude, that the causes that produced those which are extinct, must have ceased to exist, and that all the resources from whence their surging fires were drawn, have been dried up, and the fountains removed, else they would continue in the same state of activity. If the igneous theory is a truth, the cause that originates the very few remaining volcanoes, still occupies, with its raging, infuriated burnings, an overwhelming proportion of the entire solid contents of the globe, and this cause was but one thirty-fifth greater in volume, when it was one entire volcano from circumference to center, and, can we conceive that this immense mass which must contain all the antagonistic forces, all the explosive elements and furies that exhibit themselves in this living, moving world, and that then demanded the whole exterior surface upon which to expend and exercise their violent activities, can be quieted, tamed down, and rendered comparatively docile, by simply reducing its volume, or contracting its solid contents so very little, and then inclosing the remaining active portion within a comparatively frail and feeble crust, provided with a few scattered breathing holes?

It is evidently great folly and stupidity, to form any such conclusion, for if this universal disturbing cause is only diminished by so small a part, then, there must of course, remain nearly the same amount of antagonistic influences, to exercise their dangerous explosive activities, as originally existed; and they would necessarily require nearly the same amount of room in which to operate; yet, our modern philosophers have closed up and hedged in the internal, monster forces, with fragile bands, and barely allow them to come to the surface occasionally, to get breath through a few chimney tops, and then send them back to repose for ages in the arms of a quiet sleep.

We would not devote so much time to this theory, but for the fact that it has been originated and elaborated by men occupying very eminent positions in scientific circles, and, that it has been endorsed, and advocated by the large majority of the learned of the present day, so much so, that it has almost become philosophical heresy to entertain a doubt concerning its substantial truth. The igneous theory has been for many years before the bar of public opinion, pronounced upon by the great and the learned, and adopted as orthodox—but we have the temerity to consider it, one of the grandest delusions, if not to say humbugs, that was ever presented to the civilized world, in the shape of a scientific conclusion; and we doubt not, the day will speedily arrive, when developments shall be made that will ultimate in the explosion of this fallacy, and that it will only be remembered by future generations as the baseless fabric of a vision, like a thousand other crude notions that have been entertained by our ancestors, during the ages of the past.

In pursuing our inquiries still further in relation to this matter, let us ascertain the nature of those substances, that are usually ejected from the craters of volcanoes in a state of eruption. We are told, and no doubt truly, that they belch forth "volumes of dense smoke, with lurid flames, and ashes in enormous quantities, cinders, scoria, and mud, steam or aqueous vapor, which falls in showers of rain, around the mountain slopes, also large quantities of sand and lapilli, a substance composed of small stony concretions. Rocks of various dimensions that are sometimes very large, are thrown to very great distances, and it will be noticed that these rocks embrace many very different varieties, from the primary up to the later sedimentary formations. Also lava in enormous quantities, and it is somewhat remarkable that the lava is not very thoroughly melted."

Very many instances could be quoted from various authors, showing the wonderful amount of the different substances that have been from time to time, and in different parts of the globe, ejected from volcanoes, but, it is sufficient for our purpose, to show that these vast and varied quantities of material substances, must have proceeded from reservoirs, where they severally had an existence, for, assuredly, they could not have been brought from any place, where such substances did not exist.

It is also argued by the advocates of the fire theory, that if such large quantities of matter, as quite frequently have been thrown from volcanoes, should be taken from the immediate vicinity, or from underneath the neighborhood of the crater, then the mountain would certainly be swallowed up in the vacancy thus produced, and, if no such cases had occurred, the argument would be valid and somewhat conclusive. But, as such cases have happened quite frequently, they prove most conclusively, that the origin of those volcanoes was located at no great distance from the mountain that contained the crater, from which the eruption proceeded. "In 1772, Papandayang, a large volcano in the island of Java, after a short and severe eruption, fell in and disappeared, over an extent fifteen miles long and six broad, burying forty villages. In 1638, the Pic, a volcano in the isle of Timor, so high as to be visible three hundred miles, disappeared, and its place is now occupied by a lake. Many lakes in the south of Italy, are supposed to have been thus formed." Whenever submarine volcanoes have occurred that have subsequently been extinguished, the same result must have followed. The cavity that was made by the eruption of matter from beneath, must have been filled by the super-incumbent waters, and we discover that there must have been some volcanoes that had no connection with a great central body of molten lava, for if so, the bottom of those lakes would have fallen out, and the waters of the ocean would be drained through the numerous submarine chimneys, and we leave the reader to imagine the succession of explosions, that would naturally ensue, until the entire fabric wonld necessarily be demolished, and all things would return to chaotic confusion. If there were no other arguments to present, in opposition to this chimney theory, the one here offered would be quite conclusive.

We may now enquire into the nature of this incandescent material, with which the bowels of our earth is supposed to be filled, and if possible, ascertain whether we can find those several substances that are usually ejected from the craters of the numerous volcanoes. The nebulous theory pre-supposes, as we have said, an original spheroidal globe of cosmical vapor, or world material in the most rarified condition; that, this vast orb might have been 100,000,000,000 miles in diameter, or that it occupied the entire limits of our solar system, and, that by some mysterious means, this vast globe acquired a motion which resulted in periodically giving birth to smaller globes in a singularly unnatural manner. Philosophers speak of our solar system as a family of planetary bodies; they find the great parent in the center, with children and grand-children revolving around, all, more or less dependent, and each one requiring parental influences and assistance, to enable them to perform their proper functions. But, we must conclude that a search through the entire universe, would fail to present to our view, any parents that give birth to their children by peeling them from the exterior surface of their bodies. However unnatural this process may appear, yet, this theory contemplates that the young worlds were brought to the birth in that peculiar manner, and that portions of these vast peelings of world matter, hurried up and traveled more rapidly around the ring than others, or else must have waited for the balance of the ring to arrive, in order to coil up in the form of a globe, which, in process of time, condensed and became intensely heated, and after untold ages, this primeval matter began to cool, and pass through certain changes, and form an exterior crust of granite rock, that continued to thicken as time rolled onward.

Geology informs us that granite rock contains all the elements of all that is found above it, in the secondary, the coal measures, the tertiary, the alluvial deposits, and in the vegetable and animal kingdoms; that all have been evolved from this igneous granite formation which was first evolved from the primitive, homogeneous, incandescent matter contained within the enormous cavity that is bounded by the rock-ribbed crust of the globe. If we dare venture down into the huge reservoir of fiery material, and take a survey, what shall we find there, that is usually vomited forth from the flaming, smoking crater? We may examine carefully every corner of this vast Cyclopean furnace, and not find a vestige of any of those substances that come to the surface of the earth in such untold quantities, during the activity of the various volcanoes; neither flame nor smoke, ashes, cinders or scoria can be found in any one of the deep recesses of this fire orb, although it may be nearly 8,000 miles in diameter, for all these several substances are but the result of consuming combustible materials; and, there can be no such materials in the homogeneous mass of unevolved matter, that is said to exist in the earth's hollow, because it still remains in its unelaborated condition.

If we enquire into the nature of combustible materials, we shall find that they are those, that are subject to being consumed by fire; shall we find any such in this great central reservoir? If so, why have they not been consumed by a heat that may be 10,000°. The materials that will produce flame, smoke and ashes, are comparatively few in number, and those substances must pass through interminable processes of elaboration from the granite rock, before they can be produced. You cannot burn granite and cause it to produce flame and smoke, as would so much hickory, wood, or bituminous coal. Yet granite may contain within itself the latent element, which, when developed, may ultimate in material that will produce flame, smoke, ashes, and cinders. But how many long ages must pass away, before this elaboration will take place, that may result in coal, wood, or peat, oils, sulphur, phosphorus, or inflammable gasses.

Flame and smoke are both but particles passing off in the decomposition of combustibles, acted upon by that great solvent, heat; ashes are but the earthy residuum of those materials after they are dissolved, or all that can be dissolved by the intensity of the heat produced in their own consumption. Cinders are the result of mingling such residuum with foreign mineral substances not in the great mass of homogeneous matter, which has never as yet been elaborated into granite rock; then, neither of the above articles, that are belched forth in such quantities by volcanoes can be found in all this huge receptacle, because all these substances are the result of evolution, or certain processes of development, that are carried forward in the great laboratory of nature, as will be readily discovered by the intelligent reader. We might as well undertake to extract the full grown chicken from the new laid egg, as to extract the materials that are usually vomited from the craters of volcanoes, from this supposed mass of incandescent, primeval, latent material. All the elements of the full grown chicken may exist in the egg, in a latent, unevolved condition, but it must pass through processes of incubation, before you can find the bones and feathers and muscular fibres of the matured fowl; so must all primeval material pass through multitudinous processes, before it arrives up to the condition of substances which are thrown forth by volcanic action. If you cannot find the substances above named, how much less liable shall we be, to find vapor in sufficient quantities to fall in copious showers of rain, around the mountain, or mud, a mixture of earth and water, for certainly neither mud or aqueous vapor could exist within the limits of a vast reservoir, filled with latent world materials, heated so intensely. Yet mud is ejected from these craters in vast quantities, and there are so-called mud volcanoes that vomit forth little else, and others from which issue a bituminous substance, that ultimates in asphaltum, an inflammable material that would hardly remain a great length of time, in this universal reservoir of incandescent heat.

We need not pursue this reasoning, for it is a self-evident fact, that the power that is generated beneath the earth's surface, sufficient to belch forth all these various forms of matter, with such overwhelming force, must originate in the vicinity of the materials that are ejected, and further, that this vast explosive force must necessarily be backed up by something permanent, otherwise these projectiles that sometimes are thrown from the mouths of the craters several thousand feet above their summits, could not be acted upon with any such tremendous power. For example, Cotapaxi, nearly 18,000 feet high, has projected matter 6,000 feet above its summit, and, at one time, it threw a stone one hundred and nine cubic yards in volume, to the distance of nine miles. There can be no doubt, that the explosive power that projects the great rock from a volcano, must act in the same manner as the forces that drive the ball from the cannon, or the shell from the mortar. In all these cases, the explosive forces must be backed up by a permanent resisting mass of solid material, entirely sufficient to receive the recoil, otherwise this force could not be communicated to the projectiles; hence, the breech of all firearms, or that part behind and surrounding the explosive substance, is made of great strength, and such of necessity must be the case, in order to impart the entire power of the explosion to the ball projected, and it must be conceded that, whether the projectile is a shell sent from a mortar, or a great rock from the crater of a burning mountain, the cases are perfectly analogous, and the forces must be applied in a similar manner.

In either case, you must first find the projectile, and then apply the forces in such a manner as to make them effectual in sending it to its destination. Hence, when an officer wishes to bombard a city, he not only procures the gunpowder and the shells, but he must provide a suitable receptacle, in which to explode the powder, before he can think of sending those missiles into the town; and, we perceive, if a rock of such dimensions, was thrown nine miles from the crater, then the explosive force must have been brought to bear, in a manner analogous to the mortar or the cannon, or the rock could not have been hurled such an immense distance. It will be seen at a glance, that the vast exploding power that projected that rock, and all other materials that are thrown from these craters, must be backed up by substantial masses of matter, sufficient to receive the necessary recoil, in order that the power may be imparted to the projectile. Suppose the rock in question could have been found among the primeval materials of this vast interior fire globe, forty or fifty miles beneath the mountains, and an explosion should have occurred, of sufficient magnitude, to have thrown that missile to the top of Cotapaxi, and nine miles farther, making a distance in all, of sixty miles. I leave the reader to guess the result of such a paroxysm in nature, for somewhere in these vast internal regions, that terrific force must have recoiled, and reacted with a power equal to that which hurled this vast missile against the resistance of gravitation, over sixty miles, and after such recoil took place, the next business would have been reconstruction.

The annexed diagram shows a section of the earth's crust upon a scale of forty inches or one half inch to a hundred miles. It represents the crust as forty miles in thickness, and the craters of the volcanoes reaching through the entire distance, into the supposed mass of fiery, unevolved matter below. Thus at a glance we get an idea of the igneous theory concerning volcanic mountains, belching forth smoke from a grand reservoir where no smoke exists.

The reader will now have discovered two prominent difficulties in relation to volcanoes, based upon, and connected with the igneous theory; first, the materials cannot be found in the great mass of primeval, incandescent matter that is supposed to exist within the earth's crust, which are projected from the volcano; and secondly, no power could be generated that could possibly throw out such quantities of matter with the usual force, all that great distance, without destroying the entire fabric, as the necessary conditions in which forces are applied for the purpose of throwing projectiles, such immense distances, cannot exist in an open space of such magnitude, filled only with an incandescent fluid, except by an extravagant waste of the powers so applied; as they would be expended in all directions. Hence, it is clear that volcanoes must have their origin amidst the great fires that are kindled, to produce the smoke and flames that belch forth from their summits, and they must burn where they can act upon the kind of matter that is ejected from the craters; for, if ashes are found in large quantities, there must be some combustible which, when burned, will leave such earthy residuum, before it can be thrown out, and so, of all other materials that come forth. If vapor or mud is ejected, there must be some causes that will produce those articles, and place them in the way before they can be vomited from the crater.

It will be further observed that if the origin of all volcanoes, is found in one general reservoir of homogeneous matter, enclosed within a thin crust of rocky formation, and, that all the matter ejected from the craters in all portions of the globe, came from this grand reservoir, then, of course, volcanoes could never vomit forth but one kind of material, whatever the character of that material might happen to be—but the great fact that they have brought up from the depths below, a variety of substances, proves most conclusively, that the variety does not come from one general reservoir of unevolved matter, but on the contrary, that all these different substances come from diversified localities, and that they have been produced near the locality of this crater.

Although these various materials have been thrown forth in vast quantities, yet, cavities have already been discovered beneath the earth's surface, sufficiently capacious to contain a very great proportion of all that has been ejected by any single one of these craters, and, that there may exist cavities of huge dimensions, in the vicinity of the large volcano, ramifying in different directions through the bowels of the earth, overarched by vast rocky concretions, there is no good reason to doubt. Although Mount Ætna may have thrown out a quantity of matter, from time to time, five, or six, or ten times its bulk. There must have been under the island of Sicily, and the adjacent sea, an abundance of material to meet this enormous demand, and so of every other volcano, for it is not necessary that all this material should be extracted from a point, directly underneath the crater. For forces that are sufficient to eject it from the top, are certainly sufficient to bring the matter to the cavity from whence it is thrown out. Combustible or coal formations are found in veins or stratifications; as these burn out, avenues are found through which lava and other substances may be urged forward by the continuous forces generated in the rear. It will also be noticed that materials of this character which are brought to a state of fusion, will expand and greatly enhance their bulk, so that they might easily fill all the crater below, and rising above the mountain top, exude from the mouth, or be thrown with great violence by explosive forces that are most naturally generated in the depths of an active volcano.

Although the ridiculous aspects of this absurd theory concerning volcanoes, might be pursued to a greater extent, we have doubtless said sufficient to satisfy the reader that it is a mere assumption, and unsupported by any well established facts, or sound analogical reasoning, and we proceed to show, since neither the materials thrown up by volcanoes, nor the explosive forces that project them forth, can possibly exist in this vast interior, that there is ample room for both to be produced within the confines of this hollow, spherical shell, whether it be but forty or even thirty miles in thickness. It then becomes necessary not only to offer reasons why these phenomena are not connected with any vast interior fires of such magnitude, but to present some rational causes for their comparatively superficial locality. We have discovered already the absolute necessity of constructing the foundations of this globe, upon which the entire fabric rests, of the most inactive and quiet elements, instead of the most active and explosive.

We have shown that such material has been introduced, as will endure the unlimited ages it is designed to exist, and that the element is negative coldness, or materialized electricity, divested of all magnetic or positive influence, and consequently in a state of perfect rest, and instead of being in a heated positive condition, it is in a frozen negative state, devoid of the least symptom of activity: this shell is built up in this manner until the depths, or the inner foundations are made secure, and it is then that more positive materials are added, or rather that more positive elements are mingled with the material. Hence, we begin to find causes that may produce disturbances, but those disturbing elements by no means go down to the foundations, else the whole fabric might be endangered, thus we see the necessity of confining such influences to a limit that will not endanger the security of the entire structure.

If we may suppose this shell or spherical globe is perhaps thirty-two miles in thickness, each half would be sixteen, and the interior eight miles of each half, may be formed of cold negative material that would remain forever in undisturbed repose, leaving eight miles in depth upon both the exterior and interior portions in which to introduce the positive, active and more disturbing elements that cause all these wonderful, superficial phenomena. Doubtless in very many places, far underneath the surface of the earth, causes exist productive of heat and fire, but, as we have said, if fire continues to burn for any length of time, it must have something combustible on which to feed, as it can no more exist in the depths of the earth, and produce ashes and cinders, and melt the solid rock into lava, unless there are combustibles to feed those flames, than it can upon the earth's surface, and when those materials are exhausted, the fires must necessarily be extinguished, and if it should so happen that a sufficient supply of combustible matter is at hand, a volcano might be the result, because this positive element must necessarily find vent, and in doing so it would be very apt to carry with it any loose materials that are found in its way.

Here we find the perfectly natural, common sense cause, why so many volcanoes have become extinct; in the exhaustion of the combustible and inflammable materials that originally fed the fires that produced them. In other cases the cavity that was formed underneath, has been filled with water, and the fires have been extinguished in that manner.

It might be considered difficult to find combustibles, contiguous to the earth's surface, that would be sufficient to furnish the many volcanic fires with the requisite fuel, to keep them in activity from age to age, and produce all the marvelous effects that many of the burning mountains exhibit; however successful we may be in furnishing the different kinds of matter that is thrown from their fiery mouths.

We admit the necessity of supplying the continuous demands of Ætna, and Skapta Jokul, of Cotapaxi, and Popocatapetl, and all the other two hundred and twenty volcanoes of modern times, with the requisite fuel to feed their eternal fires, within the narrow limits of six to eight miles from the earth's surface, or that portion of this hollow sphere, to which we say the magnetic or active disturbing element is confined, as we aver that below that distance, all is cold and inactive, and there is not sufficient positive elements to produce any of those terrible phenomena, but that all of matter is slumbering in the arms of frozen and torpid death. Hence, all activities must originate nearer the surface where such elements can be found, and it might be proper for us to inquire what materials, scientific minds have brought to light, that might contribute towards a supply of those vast internal fires.

It will be recollected, however, that but a very limited number of volcanoes are constantly active. Stromboli, upon one of the Lipari islands, has been observed for at least 2,000 years in a state of activity, probably longer by far than any other volcano of this class, but the lava never flows over the top of the crater. In Lake Nicaragua is a volcano constantly burning, and Vilarica in Chili is never quiet. Popocatapetl which is nearly 1,800 feet high, has been pouring forth smoke ever since the conquest of Mexico, and also Kilauea in the Sandwich Islands, seems to be continuously active, as far as observation has extended. With these exceptions, perhaps all other volcanoes are only active at long intervals varying from a few months to many hundreds or may be thousands of years. So it would appear that the causes that produce their occasional paroxysmal activity, might be exhausted, and then again supplied by further accumulations of combustible and inflammable materials which upon ignition again produce similar results.

It cannot by any means be supposed that earthquakes or volcanoes are mere mishaps or casualties, that they occur outside the great programme of events by mere accident that was unforeseen by the minds who were actually responsible for the projection and construction of the earth. These phenomena must have been perfectly understood, and are as necessary in working out the great purposes of the architects, as the diurnal and annual revolutions, or as day and night, and the changing seasons. There is evidently as much demand for them, as any others with which we are acquainted, and they cannot cease to exist, until all the purposes for which they were designed, have been accomplished to the fullest extent. Doubtless the wisdom that contrived machinery upon so vast a scale, was abundantly competent to furnish all the means requisite, and engines appropriate to the production of such wonderful exhibitions. If nature upon the exterior of the earth's surface, did not make demands upon her internal resources, then most probably, this means of supplying those demands, and of transferring those resources to the surface, would not have been brought into activity. For we may be assured, that, whether the cricket chirps upon the hearth, the sparrow twitters upon the branch, the light nings flash, or the thunders roll in the distance, the earthquake rends the solid globe, with its terrific throes, or the volcanic explosion comes to the surface freighted with its unwieldy mass of lava, of smoke or flame, all is in obedience to some great design, and for the accomplishment of some exalted purpose; and it is idle to suppose that these phenomena will cease, until all their purposes are accomplished.

We find opposing elements everywhere, as far as we have traveled and explored the universe of causes and effects. You may realize the positive and negative, the male and female, heat and cold, light and darkness, fire and water, caloric and vapor, magnetism and electricity, and thus on to the end of the chapter, if we can find an end. These antagonisms exist, coming into belligerent, and amicable contact, the one with the other, and thus producing the varied activities that are working out the great problem of the eternally progressive existence of inorganic as well as organic material forms; of atoms as well as globes, of the animalculæ and infusoria, as well as the highest forms of organized living intelligences, working in, and permeating all that is active from the least to the greatest. Can we conclude that these antagonistic elements do not exist beneath the earth's surface, within the limits of six or eight miles, in sufficient quantities to produce all the superficial disturbances that have ever occurred, or that ever will occur until the great problem is finished? Let us go down into the secret chambers among the rocks of different ages and formations, where have dwelt the terrible forces that can move a world, and if we can discover forces of that character, will it be difficult to find those that may cause the earth to belch forth in various places, and from time to time, with powerful throes, the dense smoke, the lurid flames, and the material contents of the great womb where these powers are generated and brought into activity?

It is said that out of sixty primary elements that exist in the mineral kingdom, the one-half of all that composes the ponderable globe is oxygen, an invisible gas, the supporter of life and combustion, that enters so largely into the composition of water and atmospheric air, and all things else that constitute the earth; so we perceive that one-half of that portion of the globe that man has become acquainted with, is a gas that none ever saw, tasted or smelled. One quarter of the shell or crust is supposed to be silica, the base of sand quartz and flint. Thus we have three-fourths of the material of this globe, as science teaches in these two elements, and the greater portion of the other fourth is composed of fourteen other elements, among which, hydrogen, nitrogen, carbon, phosphorus, and sulphur, are prominent. Take these simples and compound them in different proportions, in connection with the others of the sixty that exist in smaller quantities, and you have all the solid and gaseous substances of which the earth is composed as far as it has been explored, in the same manner that any other combination of simple substances produce a compound. We have in these various combinations of simple elements, all material forms, and all the active or positive, and negative forces of which we entertain the least knowledge, all combustibles and all explosives, all gasses and chemical compounds, all fluids and solids mingled and commingled in all possible proportions and forms. All the combined influences of gunpowder and nitro-glycerine, and all other explosive materials, that have ever yet been invented or can be found; for most certainly, nothing of that nature has been produced upon the earth, that does not exist in some form within its hidden recesses.

What is gunpowder? what were those little harmless looking black grains that were poured down the throat of the swamp angel five miles from the city of Charleston, and whose dissolution released a power that followed the unwelcome messengers over the whole distance into the very midst of that devoted city, carrying dismay and dread in their pathway, and producing destruction and terror upon their arrival? They were a composition or mixture of sulphur, niter, and carbon, in the form of charcoal. It is a well-known fact, that the earth is abundantly supplied with all these and other explosive elements and gasses, and, all having proceeded from the negative, are permeated with electricity in an inactive condition, ready to be conjoined with positive magnetic forces where the occasion may require, in precisely the same manner as gunpowder when it is set on fire or nitro-glycerine when exploded. The Electro-Magnetic currents permeating all the active portion of this earthly sphere, there is no difficulty in exploding these elements when the demands of nature render it necessary, and it cannot be doubted, that the supply is fully equal to all the requirements that can possibly occur.

In addition to this we have immense store houses of combustible materials that have been produced by the activities of the positive elements, and of course, must be contiguous to the earth's surface. We may appeal to Geology, and ascertain what discoveries have been made concerning the past, by giving attention to the unuttered language of the rocks which seem to speak so plainly and graphically, that we may well listen with great interest to the tales of bygone centuries. The secondary or stratified portions of these silent instructors, teach us that their primitive ancestor has been torn asunder piece-meal and dissolved by the jarring elements which acted as so many solvents, and were able to disintegrate the solid granite. They teach also, that the particles of which they are composed, have been gathered together in the ocean depths, and sought repose upon its bottom until they have accumulated in the process of innumerable ages, in many instances mountain high! und subsequently some terrific forces in nature, have raised them from their quiet resting-place, and exposed them to the view of inquisitive men who have given them names according to their age and condition.

The reader not versed in these subjects, need only consult Prof. Hitchcock's able elementary work for all the data he may require upon this subject. This work is a compilation of the views and observations of the ablest authors who have written upon this department of human knowledge both in Europe and America. We learn from the various sources of information introduced into these pages, that the bottom of the earlier sedimentary or Silurian formation may possibly extend eight miles beneath the earth's surface. We also learn from this and other sources, that eminent geologists, since the recent discoveries of petroleum, have entered into extended investigations, in order, if possible, to ascertain the origin of that wonderful production of the rocks, and, very many of them have determined, satisfactorly, that the secondary formations have been the store house in which the coral insect has deposited its rich treasures, for thousands, if not hundreds of thousands of ages, during the period of their accumulations upon the bottom of the ocean.

Prof. Denton remarks that they existed and performed their immense labor from the bottom of the Silurian to the very top of the Devonian, and left their rich treasures scattered in various places, through the entire depth of these sedimentary deposits, and authors of high standing inform us that this might have been for more than eight miles, thus we have the testimony of the ablest geologists who live, or have lived, and thus we find above this, a coal formation that may be another mile or more in depth, that is, the coal may exist in layers or stratifications alternately with shales or underclays, for that or even a still greater distance. Now, if we look about us, we think we may find a sufficiency of explosive and combustible and inflammable material, to produce all these volcanic and thermal phenomena, without resorting to a vast interior fire globe for the original cause.

Prof. Denton who has taken great interest in the petroleum subject, says: "The oil bearing rocks are of great thickness and vast extent, from the base of the Silurian to the top of the Devonian, is, we know, veritable oil territory; the oil bearing corals being found in all the limestones of these formations. As these rocks underlie fully one-half the continent, the possible oil ground is of immense extent; we shall burn it for fuel as well as for illumination. Steamboats will cross the ocean by its aid, and locomotives run more swiftly than before, nor does the free flowing wells give us any idea of the amount of this material which the earth contains. Many limestones and sandstones are saturated with oil. Bituminous shales abound from which twenty to sixty gallons of oil may be distilled from a single ton. I saw one bed of petrolenm shales partly in Utah, and partly in Colorado, that on a moderate calculation, contained forty thousand million barrels of oil. A bed of bituminous shales, thirty feet thick, underlies Tennessee, and contains much more oil even than this."

We cannot suppose that this little worker of the past ages, has so industriously filled up these deposits, in this portion of the world, to the neglect of all others. If the limestones of the Silurian and Devonian periods in America, where observations have been made, are so impregnated with coral oil, shall we not conclude that the same fact exists wherever limestones are found under similar conditions? and may we not well suppose that formations of this character which are still under the depths of the sea, undisturbed by any paroxysm of nature, are equally well supplied by this oil product of the coral insect? As we have already ascertained from actual observation, and are compelled to conclude from analogy that such immense quantities of petroloum exist upon various parts of the globe, we may enquire what connection this oil may have with other combustible materials.

It has been quite clearly proven from observations that the vast quantities of oil that are deposited below the coal measures, cannot be a production emanating from coal, but it has not been proven that petroleum may not have something to do with the formation of coal, as it is conceded in very many instances, the bituminous properties in the oil, have been changed into that substance. Although it may be supposed that large quantities of the stratified coal formations, may have been of vegetable origin, yet that fact by no means precludes the possibility that coal may also be an animal product, for if you find bitumen or some other elements that by certain processes, may be converted into coal, in the vegetable, and find the self-same elements in the animal, why not by a similar process convert the animal product into coal also?

Here we may be permitted to quote in support of this idea: "Although it is generally the product of vegetation, it is not invariably so. In Albert county, New Brunswick, there is a large fissure in places seventeen feet wide which is filled with a jet black shining coal. It has been worked to a depth of seven hundred and fifty feet, and apparently continues to a much greater depths. This coal is now acknowledged to be solidified petroleum, and is therefore as I think an animal product. All petroleum coal that I have seen and heard of, occupies veins, generally perpendicular instead of horizontal beds. There is one in Ritchie county, Western Virginia, another in Scotland, several in Cuba, and others which I discovered partly in Utah and partly in Colorado on White river. The coal of these can scarcely be distinguished from the Albertite of New Brunswick. In the same region is a bed of highly bituminous shale, equal to Cannelite, which I found at various points, indicating that it extended over twelve hundred square miles. The bituminous deposits of this country, are not all discovered yet. We have sleeping servants under the ground that future generations must waken."

All this would indicate that the bituminous properties in the animal oil, is the great source from which nature has drawn her supplies in order to produce the inexhaustible deposits of coal that in her great laboratory is working out her grand designs. She may have made use of the bituminous properties in both the vegetable and animal worlds, to accomplish her beneficent purposes, and supply the later ages of humanity, the requisite amount of this much needed article. If the quantities that geologists suppose have originated from the enormous vegetable growth of a single period, are so extensive, what then must be the magnitude of those deposits of coal that have had their origin in the bituminous properties of this animal product which has been accumulating through the interminable ages that have passed away, since the commencement of the Silurian deposit. The gigantic semi-ligneous products of the age just anterior to the coal measures, had comparatively a brief existence. They occupy but a single page upon the great unwritten history that the rocks reveal.

But these little industrious workers of the deep, have been silently plodding during the vast cycles of ages, from the commencement of the secondary period; living and dying, building up their calcareous cells, and depositing their modicum of oil, and giving place to a succeeding generation, for a lapse of time too extended for human computation; and wherever these deposits have been made and subsequently buried beneath superincumbent stratifications, contiguous to shales and clays, this becomes possible coal as well as oil territory. It is quite evident that all vegetable coal formations if they really exist, must be limited in their extent, because this enormous growth from which these coal deposits is said to have been formed, is limited to a very narrow geologic period. All was produced since the old Red Sand Stone, and all terminated with the carboniferous deposits. It will be at once discovered that from this source alone, coal formations would be of limited, and narrow extent, and we should be very much troubled to find the ashes and cinders and other igneous productions that have been thrown out from the various volcanoes in different portions of the world.

Vesuvius when she waked up to activity in the year 79, vomited forth a quantity of ashes and cinders that accumulated foot by foot upon the surrounding country, until the beautiful villas that adorned the neighboring slopes, together with the two famous cities, Pompeii and Herculaneum, were entirely lost to view, and they thus slept for a period of sixteen centuries before their resurrection.

Tomboro, a volcano on Sumbawa, one of the Molucca islands in April, 1815, during a period of remarkable activity, ejected a quantity of ashes that strikes the mind with perfect astonishment in view of the vast quantity of combustibles that must have been consumed in order to leave this overwhelming amount of residuum. The roofs of houses at forty miles distance, were crushed in, and rendered uninhabitable by the weight of ashes that fell upon them. It has been calculated that sufficient ashes fell upon this occasion, to have covered the entire states of Maryland and Delaware, two feet in depth, or they would have made a mountain twice the size of Mont Blanc. Many other volcanoes which we need not mention, have thrown forth from time to time inconceivable quantities of those substances that can only be produced by the actual burning of combustible materials, and, that cannot be accounted for upon any other principle.

We feel the utmost confidence in expressing the opinion that scientific men will be compelled, at no distant day, to furnish combustible materials, to produce the ashes and other substances that are erupted from these various craters, aside from the great central reservoir, and they will find the so-called vegetable coal deposits are too near the surface and entirely insufficient in quantity. But far beneath the coal measures it has been discovered by observation, may exist interminable caverns of solidified petroleum, or wide extended beds of bituminous shales, or clays equal to cannelite or any other coal for burning, entirely sufficient to supply all the demands of all the volcanoes that ever did, or ever will exist. Although we modestly express an opinion that petroleum has had very much to do in the formation of a large portion of the coal deposits that seem to be of vegetable origin, and of comparatively recent production, however that may be, there must, without doubt, exist inconceivable quantities of coal that are exclusively the product of petroleum; deeply buried and scattered all through the Silurian and Devonian formations, under the earth and under the sea. The palpable reason why we are not better acquainted with the exclusively animal coals, is the fact of their lying deeply hidden by the superincumbent stratifications of a later period. It will be seen that we are abundantly able to furnish all the requisite combustible materials, to keep all the volcanoes in the world in activity, and make the above concessions to scientific conclusions; but personally we utterly ignore the idea that any considerable amount of bituminous or anthracite coal, has ever been produced without the aid of animal oil or petroleum; for it is utterly impossible to convert wood into coals without the aid of heat or fire, and then we have only charcoal or lignites, and they must remain such forever, unless saturated by some more powerful bituminous product than exists in wood; and it will be remembered that the gigantic flora of the Anti-Carboniferous period, was only a kind of herbaceous production, a semi-ligneous material, not as well adapted for burning, even into charcoal as the trees of our modern forests.

When this matter is thoroughly understood, we shall ascertain that most of the coal is but shales and clays saturated by the gasses arising from burning petroleum, or else by the petroleum itself, and the probable reason why we find so little of this oil in the immediate vicinity of coal beds, is that it either lies far beneath the coal deposits, or that it has been exhausted in their formation. It is no surprise that we do not find in the coal fields, the exact aroma that arises from petroleum in its crude state, as the peculiar smell must have been modified, and overcome by this mixture of shales and clays, and subjection to magnetic and electric action, during the ages of the past. And, as we have been told, that wherever we find limestone, from the bottom of the Silurian to the top of the Devonian, it is possible oil territory, we also perceive that where those deposits of oil are underneath or contiguous to shales and clays, it becomes probable coal territory. This silent process of forming coal, must have been in activity from the interminable ages of the past, and deep beneath the ocean bed, the same work is going forward to-day, as it has been during all the vast periods of the sedimentary deposits. Perhaps the reader may begin to get some faint inkling of the vastness of the store houses which contain the combustibles that have supplied the fires of the volcanoes in all past time, and that will continue to furnish their supplies in the future, for the self-same processes of manufacture are still in activity.

This crust or shell whose exterior surface we inhabit, is by no means solid, but vast cavities may be found, some of which have apertures that reach the surface, and may be explored for very long tortuous distances; and it is quite possible that the smoke that issues from some of the active volcanoes, may originate in the smouldering combustible situated hundreds of miles distant from the crater, and that it finds its way to the surface through the windings and turnings of the secret chambers that have been burned out in the ages of the past. Suppose now that these passage ways should by some means, become closed up while the fires were burning, gasses would necessarily accumulate that must find vent, and fearful disturbances would doubtless ensue. That there are great unknown cavities beneath the earth's surface, is proven by the fact that sometimes, volcanic mountains have sunk into the depths below, and at different times, cities and towns, and islands have also disappeared, as Port Royal in the West Indies, Lisbon, Caracas, and others, and it is quite evident those places could not have sunk, if there had not been some opening below, to have received them. If the earth or rocks beneath those towns, and islands, and mountains, had been solid, and there had been no cavities into which they could have fallen, it is by no means probable that the earth would have opened a simple fissure, sufficiently large to have swallowed them.

We trust it will from a careful perusal of the preceding pages, become quite clear to the reader, that volcanoes when they have exhausted the fuel requisite to cause their activities, feed their fires, melt the large quantities of lava, and produce the ashes and other substances which come forth, must cease to burn and become extinct. He will also discover that the requisite amount of fuel must necessarily be provided before such wonderful results can be produced in any portion of the material realms. It would seem hardly necessary to present this simple view of the subject, had not our philosophers apparently forgotten this natural principle, and undertaken to build and keep in activity a raging fire within the bowels of our globe from age to age, where no particle of fuel of any description, could have existed since the time they supposed it was first kindled. We have devoted all the space we can possibly afford to this subject, and find it by no means exhausted, but we doubt not other minds will seize upon the few ideas presented, and elaborate them to an extent that may ultimate in throwing an increasing flood of light upon this hitherto difficult matter.

CHAP. V

EARTHQUAKES.

Earthquakes have been of such frequent occurrence and so destructive and wide-spread in their influences as to receive a large amount of attention from scientific minds, and it would seem that those who have had time and favorable opportunities for this line of investigation and for extended research into the various physical phenomena of the earth, ought to be able to give us a clear and lucid understanding of the causes that are prominent in the production of such terrific superficial disturbances. But we find this subject enveloped in darkness and doubts, quite similar to others of a like character. Scientific opinions are entirely unsettled, some minds adopt one theory and some another, and a treatise upon earthquakes by the learned, will give the reader little more than a lengthy catalogue of those that have occurred from time to time, in various parts of the world, their locality, time of duration, the direction of the waves of motion or vibration, the amount of buildings shaken down, and general damage done to the cities or neighborhoods where they have occurred, the number of lives destroyed, if any, and all the various minutia attending the particular catastrophe, and thus on, until the reader is surfeited with these lengthy details; while the mind is still left entirely barren of any knowledge of the general principles or causes that produce such fearful disturbances.

Even that great master mind, Von Humboldt who has rendered such efficient aid to modern science by his learned contributions, confines himself in his lengthy treatise upon earthquakes to a description of the phenomenal phases, and scarcely ventures an opinion concerning their producing causes, or any of their varied operations, beyond the scrutiny of his own vision, or of those from whom he received his information. Deeply as he had penetrated by his researches, into the mysteries that abound in the realms of nature, he was evidently entirely inadequate to give the world the philosophy of those terrific disturbances, and contented himself by observing and noting their visible phenomena.

We learn that many of the paroxysms are very extended and wide-spread in their influences, and hence, it is concluded that the causes must be deep-seated and very extended also. Our friends who endorse the fire theory, have seized upon this fact, and claim that an earthquake that exerted a vibratory power over a field of such vast extent, as the one that sunk a portion of the city of Lisbon in Portugal, must have a cause as wide as the effects produced, and as they know of none except the great fire globe within the earth, they necessarily conclude the cause must originate in that. But a query might arise here, and we might ask with propriety if our friends may not prove too much; for if the earthquakes of Lisbon or Guadeloupe, were produced by a cause so universal as to occupy the whole globe, except this thin crust by which it is enveloped as a kind of mantle, then what should have hindered those earthquakes, and all others from being universal also, and shaking the whole fabric into ruins.

Can they tell us why there should be any boundaries to a superficial disturbance anywhere upon the earth's crust, where they claim that the cause in which this disturbance originates, is so overwhelmingly universal that it contains thirty-five times the solid contents of the entire superficial crust, upon which it is exerting its powers? We are led to conclude that the grand difficulty will be to give a reason why any earthquake should be limited in its extent, if the producing cause is homogeneous and universal; why one side or any one portion of this vast furnace should manifest activity sufficient to produce exterior vibrations, while all the other portions lie in repose; or why if this universal cause which lies equidistant from all portions of the exterior surface, is the all producing origin of physical disturbances, they are so limited in their extent as to be felt in quite severe shocks in one city, and entirely unknown a hundred miles distant. It is not unfrequently that we read of vibrations of the earth in San Francisco, or at some point upon the coast, or in the adjacent Sierra Nevadas, and we know nothing of any such disturbance in Sacramento; and such is the case in any portion of the world where slight earthquake shocks are of frequent occurrence, and it will become our igneous friends to give some explanation upon the point before their theory is fully established.

The conclusions of these learned men are really very curious; one author considers "The crust to be brimming full of molten lava, and that it is ready to gush out upon the least contraction, and proves by figures which are unfailing guides to truth, that if the crust should contract 1-12,350 part of an inch, it would be sufficient to force out the matter of a volcanic eruption." Another popular author says, "There may be large cavities between the rolling mass and the superincumbent crust, and from contraction or some other cause, vast impending rocks of 100,000,000 tons in weight, may become detached and fall into the boiling flood below, creating such a terrible commotion in the molten mass, as to be experienced upon the exterior surface in the form of a fearful earthquake." It would almost seem that the author meant this for a grim jest upon a very grave subject, but we cannot doubt his sincerity. Which of these two shall we believe, the one who says the crust is so brimming full that the least contraction would cause the matter to ooze out and produce volcanoes, or the one who tells us there are very extensive vacancies between the molten mass and the superincumbent rocks.

If we are bound to adopt the igneous theory, we are inclined to accept the latter view, for if this is the grand source of all volcanic eruptions, the vast quantities of substances that have been thrown out since the formation of the crust, must necessarily have produced very extensive vacancies; as, the overwhelming quantities of ashes that have been vomited forth from time to time, must have required a largely multiplied amount of combustibles to produce them, and the vast and continuous clouds of dense smoke would prove, that inconceivable masses of material have been burning during interminable ages to produce this, together with the flames and other elements that have escaped, and, we must conclude in that case the vacancy beneath the crust must have assumed very enormous dimensions. We further discover, if rocks fall from the superincumbent mass, by the force of gravity, then all materials detached from the crust, would be forced as nearly as possible to the geometrical center, which, in that case, would be the center of gravitation, and there would necessarily be a continuous vacancy between the crust and the liquid mass in the interior, or in other words, the molten lava would by gravitating force, cluster around the geometrical center, and remain entirely detached from the superincumbent crust.

However small the vacancy might be, it would be compelled to equalize itself upon all portions of the liquid mass, which could but hang suspended to the grand center of gravitation; and again, if these tremendous detached portions of granite may fall into the great heated mass, it would be interesting to know how the author disposes of them after they have fallen. We do not wish to be too inquisitive, but this would seem to be a legitimate inquiry, and we should be glad to ascertain whether they are fused with the general mass, or float upon the surface, or sink to the bottom which would be the center. We are disposed to think the specific gravity of granite rock, greater than any homogeneous mass of molten fluid, that can possibly exist in the interior of the crust, and we think our author must arrive at the same conclusion, consequently, it would not float, but sink, and this might interpose a difficulty in the early formation of the infant crust

It cannot be supposed that a crust of a magnitude as immense as our globe, could have all formed at one time or have been continuously connected, so as to have been a self supporting arch, but that it would have been cooled in detached parcels, and if we admit that by contractions and solidifying, granite rock attains to greater specific gravity than the original fluid, then, of course, it would sink to the bottom, and either melt and fuse again, or else the solid portion of the mass would form in the center, and the whole theory would destroy itself.

It was very reasonably supposed that earthquake shocks being realized over so large an extent of territory simultaneously, must have an original cause as wide as the effect produced, and they evidently could think of nothing but the great internal fire that was commensurate with such fearful results; so modern science very generally points to that as the original cause of all these superficial disturbing phenomena. As our ancestors and very many at the present day, charge all the seeming evils humanity endures, in consequence of their own irregularities and disobedience, upon an imaginary, ill favored individual they call the Devil, whom they consider either ubiquitous, or else a wonderful traveler, and have looked upon him as a cause entirely adequate to the production of all the fearful miseries that are so endured, and yet it is impossible to trace out the connection between these unhappy effects, and the personage upon whom they are charged. So, when scientific men learn that an earthquake occurred at Lisbon, which sunk a portion of that city, and extended over into Africa with sufficient violence, to destroy cities upon that side of the Mediterranean, and, that the shocks were felt across the Atlantic, and over an extent of territory many times larger than the European continent, and they learn of another at Guadaloupe in the West Indies, extending its influences north to Charleston, and south to the mouth of the Amazon, it becomes incumbent upon them, to find a cause somewhere as extensive as the effect produced, and no other that seemed adequate being apparent, they resort to the great fire orb in the interior, and find one that will cover the whole ground, and quite likely if it existed it would cover too much ground for the safety and permanency of this planet.

We think, however, aside from this imaginary interior molten mass, we may find inherent in this spherical shell, powers entirely adequate to answer all its purposes, and enable it to perform all its multitudinous labors, even to give it propulsion in its orbital and axial revolutions; as we cannot conceive that any other planet can possess a surplus of such forces, and bestow them upon our globe for its benefit. If we find forces of this character in abundance, in and upon the earth, we may not be surprised that they are entirely sufficient to produce all the superficial tremblings and vibrations that have ever yet occurred. It can by no means be doubted that forces that will move a world at the rate of 1,000 miles per hour upon its axis, and 68,000 miles per hour in its orbit, certainly ought to be sufficient when properly applied, to cause a little trembling, and vibrating motions in its crust, and even produce extensive cracks and fissures in its surface.

It is quite possible there may be many elements in the depths below the surface, that are needed above, and, if we would have the meat we must crack the nut in which it is contained, and if there is anything within the earthly shell that is required at the surface, then it must be brought there regardless of consequences. If men build cities in the way where the workmen are engaged in arranging and modifying the elements in this unfinished world, then the cities must experience the natural result. That this world is in a very unfinished condition, no person who looks upon it with an intelligent eye, can entertain a shadow of doubt. If we take a survey of its exterior superficies as it appears to-day, we shall find nearly three-fourths covered by one wide waste of waters, and a vast extent of the portion that is above their level occupied by sandy plains, arid deserts, and craggy, inaccessible mountain cliffs, or in a climate so rigorous as to preclude the possibility of producing sustenance for any number of inhabitants, else under the blazing sun of the tropics where only the more inferior and stupid of the races of men seem to flourish.

We shall find but a small portion of the area of the earth's surface in a genial, temperate clime, blessed with a fertile soil that is capable of yielding an abundance of the fruits that man needs for his sustenance.

When we come to take an actual survey, we discover but a very limited quantity of the 200,000,000 square miles that constitute the superficial area of our globe, that may be considered desirable as a residence for intelligent men; hence, some powers must be engaged in improving and preparing the unfinished portions, so as to extend as rapidly as necessary, the capabilities of the earth for sustaining increasing numbers of inhabitants.

Men seem to wander out into the mazes of darkness, and establish in their own minds many an imaginary hypothesis, in order to furnish causes for well-known facts, and they use great multitudes of technical words for the purpose of satisfying themselves and others of the truth of their opinions, and our libraries are occupied by very many books called scientific, that in process of time become little better than useless rubbish, to say nothing of the everlasting accumulations of theological productions that are continually being superseded by more intelligent ideas of the natural and spiritual realms.

After Dr. Harvey discovered the fact of the circulation of the blood through the arteries and veins, he could doubtless have explained in comparatively few words, phenomena in the physiological structure, that had puzzled the brains of the learned Doctors for ages, and upon which they had perhaps written many useless volumes. It may be possible that men will yet ascertain that there exists a fluid circulation in the physical structure of the globe, perfectly analogous to that found in the human system, and it would seem very probable the human organization had inherited all its powers and functions from this great parent, the earth. If we should find this to be the case, then many of the puzzling phenomena now so embarrassing to the student, may be rendered plain and quite comprehensive; and with comparatively few written pages, a system might be established that would harmonize with all of the known facts and principles in the great and universal realms.

Earthquakes and volcanoes very frequently seem to act in concert, and possess a sort of sympathetic relationship for each other, and hence they have been attributed to one common cause that is considered sufficiently extensive for the production of both. It must, however, be admitted that in their effects they are entirely dissimilar; the one causing the earth to vibrate and rock suddenly with violent shocks, sometimes opening its crust into yawning chasms that admit towns and islands, and portions of country into their depths, while the other usually expend their fury through burning craters, throwing out during their activity, a variety of mineral and other substances, and they are, no doubt, generally produced by causes quite dissimilar and remote from each other. As a cause in the human system productive of vomiting, might not either be attended by pneumonia or nervous affection, and the cause of paralysis might not produce vomiting, yet it is quite possible that a patient may be afflicted by two or three difficulties at one and the same time, and great activity in one, might seem to relieve the system of the violent effects of the other. It is an acknowledged fact, the most difficult part of the physician's duties, is to diagnose his cases and ascertain precisely the true cause and nature of the maladies that afflict his patients; so we need not be surprised, if the learned Doctors who attempt to feel the pulse of our old mother the earth, when she groans or quakes in consequence of internal disturbances, should experience still greater embarrassments, in ascertaining the exact causes productive of her complainings. These causes lie very deeply hidden beneath the reach of their exterior vision, beyond all the processes of experimental observation by which they obtain their deductions, and upon which they base their most carefully formed opinions; they are dark, uncertain, and quite liable to lead them astray from the truth.

We may be quite sure as we have remarked that neither earthquakes or volcanoes are mishaps or casualties, or oversights, but that they are all in the original programme; they occur as all other phenomena must take place, in accordance with original design, and the forces that will produce them, may be found in abundance where they originate or in the vicinity of their occurrence. They are evidently employed to assist in working out the grand purposes of those powers and principalities who seem to exert a controlling influence over all earthly things. There cannot be any more chance work connected with these phenomena than with the operations of any other portion of the realms of nature. It is not by chance that spring and summer, autumn and winter, succeed each other in the periodical revolutions of the earth, or that the lightning flashes are beheld in the heavens, and their reverberating explosions are heard in the distance, that the forked erratic chain descends towards the earth, and sets on fire our dwellings, and prostrates the riven tree to its foundations. By no means; these and other like phenomena are simply working out great purposes in nature's laboratory, and may occur to satisfy the requirements or imperious demands that nature in one part of her domains, is constantly making, for elements that may be found in another.

If the old dame upon the surface, requires to replenish any of her exhausted resources for the use of the vegetable or the animal race, or for any other purpose, all that is needed in such cases, exists in the mineral kingdom; for every etherealized element by which we subsist, came from thence, and perhaps deeply buried within the dark recesses of our earth, there may be essential materials existing among the grosser atomic particles that are absolutely necessary to furnish nature's wants above the surface. It may be oxygen, or nitrogen, or carbon, or some other life-giving essence that is partially exhausted, and we discover the means are amply provided, by which these life essences can be obtained in continuous supply.

The reader may have already learned from the preceding pages, that the original elemental material of which worlds are constructed, must necessarily be found in the most inactive condition, and that such material must be the essential element of all negative properties existing undisturbed by positive forces, for as we have said, when positive forces and elements are introduced, and enter into the negative, then all becomes active, and it can no longer remain a chaotic mass of primordial atoms, because activities have commenced, and henceforth it becomes progressive, and subject to continued change.

We ascertain that the highest form of exclusively negative fluid matter in existence is called electricity, and that when matter is resolved to its first principles or original chaotic state, it becomes one mass of atomic electricity; cold and inactive, and this cold, dead, primeval fluid substance is the material from which our globe, and all other globes are manufactured by the immortal ever living mechanics who are competent to control the forces, and atomic particles that ultimate in the construction of such stupendous fabrics. Thus we see, if all is produced from electricity, that negative element must predominate everywhere throughout the entire structure, but we must keep in view, that negatives are entirely inactive, unless acted upon by positive elements, and electricity without the aid of the great positive element, magnetism, is perfectly quiet and docile, and only when the two powers are conjoined, is any active result produced.

Now, it will be perceived that the negative elements pervade all from the center to the circumference, from the foundations of the earth to its surface, and from thence to the limits of the atmosphere, but, in an inactive state, only so far as the positive element extends. Where the positive forces extend their influences, we may expect to find those and all other elements in existence in a state of activity, and of course down in the depths of Belisma, where these positive powers do not penetrate, all is stillness and locked in the frozen embrace of death and night. Here we find a permanent foundation, upon which we may establish those terrible powers, and a point beyond which they exert no influence, in this manner giving the positive activities, down in the depths of the earth, a permanent negative basis upon which to rest, which cannot by any possibility be disturbed or endangered.

It is a well understood fact that there are Electro-Magnetic currents, running from north to south, or in longitudinal curves from those two points everywhere around our earth, in its atmosphere and hence the direction of the magnetic needle. We must suppose those currents exist beneath the earth's surface, down to the lowest depths of all activity; for, what else produces any activity, down in these deep recesses, but the great positive and negative elements acting in conjunction, and thus, you have the combined energies of the two great powers that are able to move worlds upon their predestined journeys through the regions of space; and do we need any other forces to produce all the various phenomena that men have witnessed upon the earth's surface? It would seem not. But, we have in addition, another force finer and more powerful still, the offspring of the great positive and negative, male and female pair, called aura or the aural element, and this diffuses itself in every place where the two parents exist, interweaving its etherealized threads at right angles across the Electro-Magnetic threads or currents, forming a beautiful and all-potent web, composed of warp and woof of the most powerful elementary essences that exist in the universal realms of nature. These numerous webs that permeate the active portions of our earth, and atmosphere containing within themselves all the essential elements of strength and power, are the bands and bars that hold all things in the active portions of our globe in a permanent condition, and that prevent the general tendency to dissolution.

Explosions of the Electro-Magnetic elements are not of unfrequent occurrence in the atmosphere, as almost every one has witnessed in the lightning's vivid flash; and at times these explosions are very disastrous in their effects, not only destroying great numbers of human lives, but they do immense damage to buildings and other objects in their destructive course, and not unfrequently cause very sensible vibrations of the earth. They have been known to expend their fury upon the mountain cliffs, tearing asunder huge rocks, and hurling them with terrible force to the plains below. Not long since an occurrence of this kind was witnessed in the highlands, upon the Hudson river, by which large quantities of rocks were torn from the brow of the mountain by the force of the explosion, and scattered upon the river below, to the great hazard of some small vessels that were passing at the time.

It will be remembered that the Electro-Magnetic currents are passing through the exterior portions of the earth's crust, precisely upon the same plan that they are through the atmosphere, and if we have explosions that are accompanied with serious consequences in the atmosphere, why may we not have explosions beneath the earth's surface, that might from the attendant circumstances result in still more serious effects, as we may very clearly see that an explosion in the atmosphere above the earth's surface, may have the room to expend its forces, and be attended by comparatively trifling results, while a similar explosion confined below the solid crust of the earth, and deeply buried beneath the superincumbent rocks, might be terrible in its consequences. Let us now inquire if we cannot come to an understanding of the real cause of so-called electrical concussions, whether they occur above or under the earth, and in this inquiry the question naturally arises: Is it the Electro-Magnetic elements alone, that cause the explosion? or whether these elements may not be combined with others of an explosive character, causing the detonation and scattering these forces in every direction from the point where the concussion or explosion occurs. We express the opinion that the Electro-Magnetic forces in a state of activity, unattended by any other explosive element, are silent in their operations, and never accompanied by any detonation whatever, and hence when the reverberating thunders occur, they may be partially produced by the ignition of some of the explosive elements that are found in nature's great laboratory, and not entirely by the agency of the Electro-Magnetic elements acting in a separate capacity.

One method of destroying the ships of an enemy that are approaching the harbor of a maritime city, is to place a number of torpedoes in the channel or as nearly as practicable to the track the ship must take, and the explosive elements of the torpedo may be ignited by establishing artificial Electro-Magnetic currents or wires between them and some convenient place upon the shore where may be arranged a galvanic battery, and thus they use the Electro-Magnetic current for igniting the torpedo, the same as these currents ignite the explosive elements in the atmosphere, and in the earth, which cause the detonations, and assist in producing the vibrations and the attendant destruction. Nitre, sulphur and carbon in appropriate quantities, will produce that explosive element called gunpowder, and we find all those elements in the mineral kingdom, scattered almost everywhere, and from thence their etherealized elements are passing into the atmosphere, and whenever essences of such a character are combined in suitable quantities, either in the earth or above the earth, they are liable to be exploded by the Electro-Magnetic currents; or wherever any explosive materials or gasses exist, with which these currents come in contact, they are liable to ignition and explosion at any time, so we readily discover that there may be in nature's workshop, abundant causes for explosions and disturbances, and it is no marvel that they so frequently occur in different portions of our globe.

When we take into consideration the extreme violence of the Electro-Magnetic concussions, exploding in the atmosphere, where there is ample room for all the fury and marvelous strength of these forces to expend themselves, and, that under such circumstances they cause severe tremblings and quakings of the earth, we may not be surprised if a similar explosion, pent up in the depths below, should produce effects greatly multiplied, and cause all things to tremble, and vibrate for a great distance. We may recollect that these concussions both in the atmosphere above and in the earth beneath, are produced by the two great forces that contain all the power of all other forces below them; they are the concentrated essential elements of heat and cold, of light and darkness, and of all positive and negative powers from which they are eliminated, and if nature in working out her grand purposes, has anything of large import to perform, she must call upon these two great powers; otherwise she certainly would call upon the child to accomplish that which would require the strength of the full-grown athletic man.

Caloric is superior to fire, because it penetrates where fire cannot go, and performs duties beyond the ability of the inferior, grosser element; its particles being finer and more powerful; magnetism is superior to caloric for the same reason, and operates in a field that caloric does not enter. So is steam more powerful than water, and exerts its influences in a manner that is impossible with the aqueous element from which it proceeded. Electricity is entirely superior to steam, as we have before remarked, and here you have the two great elements in nature, that may accomplish all those feats of strength and power which we behold with such astonishment, and why should we travel out into the realms of the unknown for powers that are so plentifully dispersed wherever they are needed, and what forces can you find in any portion of the broad universe, that will prove their superiors? If you wish to burst the steam boiler, you will be compelled to call upon them for aid. If you desire a first class thunder storm, they are the forces that are called into requisition, as no explosion of any character, can occur without their assistance, and suppose an earthquake is necessary, we may be fully assured that a proper disposition, and manipulation of these elements, will produce as grand a specimen of such phenomena, as the most ardent admirer of the sublime and terrible in nature, can possibly desire.

We discover then that these two elements being superior to all other physical forces, are the only powers that can be called into requisition with certainty in the production of great physical disturbances; yet it is possible that even their powers may be enhanced by other agencies, and as we have noticed by coming in contact with, and igniting and exploding other elements.

We apprehend that spiritual essences which have been released by a dissolution of grosser material particles, cannot by any possibility, when they demand escape to the surface, be confined in the depths beneath. We conclude if the earth was a solid, and composed of granite to the very center, and an explosion should take place at that point which released such essences or ethe-realized matter that requires exit, then such essences or forces would come forth, even if it caused the destruction of the whole fabric, and as forces and elements of that character do exist contiguous to the earth's surface, we may well suppose that we have upon different portions of this globe, powers amply sufficient to produce all the disturbances that have ever occurred.

We might explode a few hundred pounds of gunpowder in the atmosphere, a thousand feet from the earth, and the effect would be comparatively trivial, but place that amount beneath the earth's surface in an extended cavity, and ignite those explosive materials by an inconceivably powerful Electro-Magnetic battery, we then might find the results to be very terrible. When we take into consideration that such elements exist in vast quantities in the bowels of the earth, together with all the inflammable and explosive gasses, that large cavities may be found in which they are stored away, and that the Electro-Magnetic currents are permeating every portion of the crust, for several miles in depth, we need not be surprised that we have occasional tremblings, and quakings upon the surface, and that sometimes they are attended by very serious disasters. Neither need we be surprised that islands are often times thrown up from the deths of the sea, for we are contemplating powers that are equal to any such emergency; powers that are brought to bear in the propulsion of worlds in their orbits with such terrible velocity, and that first gave momentum, and serve to continue the activities of the machinery of not only our solar system, but all the solar systems in the broad universe.

There is little need of traveling beyond the realms of universal nature, and searching after far fetched causes for the production of the grandest result that has yet occurred. All we require is to become familiarized, and form an acquaintance with the spirit or soul of those things that are scattered with such profusion all around us, and which we have been so apt to overlook in our investigations and researches after truth. It is difficult to discover how an intelligent man can stand and witness the terrible operations of the Electro-Magnetic forces, behold them make an attack upon a sturdy oak of the forest, and in the twinkling of an eye, rend it from its topmost branches down to the roots in a thousand fragments, scattering them to the four winds, and still be at a loss for natural forces that can produce the occasional vibrations of an earthquake.

But, as we are called upon to offer some reasons why earthquakes are at times so extended in their influences, as those spoken of in previous pages, we confidently reply, that none have as yet been more extended, or shaken more territory, than is occupied by the Elcctro-Magnetic currents, and if there is any wonder, it is that so many of the shocks are so limited in their extent, for we find these elemental currents running from the north to the south pole unbroken, and that these wires are interwoven by others of the aural element that are crossing at right angles, making a complete web of interwoven filaments that extends to all portions of the globe, and that there are very many of these webs both above and beneath the surface of the earth. They are the real bolts and bands that hold the entire superstructure together, as we have said, and that prevent the dissolution of the mighty fabric. Suppose now, we produce a derangement of any portion of the Electro-Magnetic wires, or bolts and bars that bind the material elements of the globe together; are we not liable to extend the vibrations out upon the currents or wires? the same as an electric shock may be communicated upon wires to any given distance, thus transmitting messages across the ocean or around the globe. It is quite possible that disturbing forces may be entirely sufficient to break and tear asunder these nervous net works of the physical globe, and produce all their disastrous consequences upon the surface.

Thus we discover that the disturbances do not originate in the coarse, granitic and earthy particles of our globe, but in the essential elements of the mineral kingdom, in the spiritual essences of the whole fabric; and when such is the case, the grosser material must, of course, experience the natural results. If any of the bolts and bands that hold the structure intact, and prevent its dissolution, are disrupted or sundered, we may not wonder that certain portions of the great crust or shell should show signs of disruption also, and present fearful cracks, and that cities and islands should be swallowed up in the cavities beneath. We trust the reader may discover that we have ample powers within reach of the earth's surface to produce all the disturbances that have ever occurred, and not only that, but to raise all the mountain ranges that are found upon the surface of the globe, for if these elements that are superior to all other physical forces, will not accomplish the most stupendous work that can present itself to human observation, then we shall be compelled to call upon feeble, puny children, to perform the labors of full-grown giants, for all other forces that can be found in nature's great laboratory, bear such a relationship to the super-eminent positive and negative elements which contain within themselves all the essential powers of all there is to be found in this mundane sphere.

We are not compelled to resort to an interior imaginry power to produce the vibratory movements of the earth, during these shocks, for it is utterly impossible for an intelligent mind to discover any rational mode of application of powers existing in such a form, and generated in such a mighty cauldron, that would produce results of the character that have been experienced upon the earth's surface, in the shape of earthquakes, with all the various phenomena that usually attend those physical disturbances.

It does not seem to be pertinent to our subject to give an exposition of all the minutiæ that attend the phenomena of earthquakes, as in support of our hollow globe theory, it is simply necessary to disconnect them with any great mass of internal molten lava and show that we have other powers sufficient for their production. It is entirely sufficient for our purpose to present some leading ideas in connection with those remarkable telluric disturbances, leaving the minute particulars of this mighty problem for those who have the requisite qualifications as well as time to devote to subjects of this character.

We may say in conclusion; when we arrive at a clear

and comprehensive knowledge of the relationship existing between the universal animal economy, and this physical globe from which all their powers and peculiar confirmations are inherited, we may obtain a more intelligent view of many of the marvelous occurrences in nature, that are so mystified at the present. Every animal must certainly derive all its peculiarity of construction with every element in its nature, from the earth, and if it is provided with a nervous system that permeates every muscular fibre, then the physical globe must have something of this character, for it assuredly could not have imparted to the animal, what it did not possess itself in an eminent degree.

Then we think it will be clear, that this great physical structure must also be endowed with a mighty nervous system permeating every portion of the alluvial and sedimentary covering, which lying contiguous to the exterior, enwraps the granitic frame work in the same manner as the bony frame work of the animal is covered by a complete envelope of fleshy or muscular fibre.

If any little disturbance of this nervous network in the animal or human structure, is attended bv tremors, why should not similar disturbances of the fluid elements in the physical globe be attended by similar results? We trust by a careful consideration of these fundamental principles, the reader may clearly understand many of the remarkable phenomena that have so puzzled the minds of eminent scientific observers, and we also trust that a perusal of the succeeding pages will throw a flood of light, not only upon the subjects already noticed, but very many others of great interest to reflective minds.

CHAP. VI.

MATERIAL AND SPIRITUAL FORCES.

The positive and negative, the male and female elements exist everywhere, and permeate all things throughout the entire universal realms. These elements pervade the mineral, the vegetable and the animal kingdoms of our world; they exist in all the complicated machinery that has been brought into activity, in the production af our earth, with all its varied appurtenances. Aggregations of material particles in any form, cannot be generated and produced, unless preceded by the active union of these two counter elements. The imponderable agents and forces cannot be brought into activity, and perform their allotted functions, unless they contain within themselves the positive and negative, the male and female elements. But for a continuation of the forces generated by these counter elements, our world would cease its revolutions, day and night would no more succeed each other, motion would resolve itself into inactivity, and rest in the quiet embrace of eternal death. It is evident these elements permeate all things visible and invisible, that they have existed in, and are inseparable from the fountain of all spiritual essences and material particles; they are a part and parcel of the great whole of spiritual and material existence from which all things visible and invisible have emanated, and been produced. Hence, there can be no material particle, or no elemental, spiritual force in the natural universe, divested of those male and female elements, and in all our researches after proximate truths, and inquiries in the great fields of nature for the laws by which her varied departments are governed, and the innumerable processes she has made use of in her laboratory, in developing so much that is grand and beautiful, we must keep the idea constantly in view, that these counter elements diffuse themselves throughout all things, and have so done from all eternity. Whenever we lose sight of this self evident fact, our minds are liable to be clouded,by mists, and wander off into the regions of uncertainty and doubt.

Perhaps one prominent reason why philosophers and scientists have sometimes failed so signally in arriving at the real truth concerning facts and phenomena that present themselves to view, may be the prevailing ignorance, and lack of comprehension concerning the spiritual realms, where the causes are found that precede all known effects, for evidently, the prime causes of all facts and all phenomena originated in the spiritual, or the so-called immaterial, and have existed before the results were made known to mortal vision. Hence, it is important if we would reason upon,and understand clearly those things we do see, that we should by some means form an acquaintance with the realm of causes, that we cannot see, and become familiarized with the spiritual essences in which all these causes lie hidden.

Children sometimes ask questions that older people cannot answer, and they most probably made inquiries many thousand years in the past, that taxed all the mental powers of their elders, the children of a larger growth. There was evidently a desire upon the part of some persons in the long ago to answer the queries, and solve some of the difficult problems that would naturally present themselves to inquiring minds. Reflective minds have early learned to inquire who made the world and themselves, and how and why they were left to drift about as waifs upon its broad surface, and those perhaps who have been more matured, have vouchsafed a reply, and said that God our father, made it in six days, together with all the other worlds, and then made man from the dust of the earth, and a woman from one of his ribs, and told them to multiply and propagate their species, that the earth might be inhabited, and we find ourselves here as the result of that act, upon the part of God. But the mind still unsatisfied, queries who is God, and who made him and endowed him with power and ability to build worlds, and people them with animals, and men and women? And the inquirer has been put off with the remark that hidden things belong to God, and revealed things to man, and that it is wicked to ask questions that are beyond our understanding, and that we must be satisfied with what is given us to know.

We claim, however, that it is not impious, nor does it manifest any want of reverence for superior or divine authority, to institute any proper inquiry concerning matters, in which we have a direct and personal interest, for every person must have such interest in the causes and various forces that were brought into activity in the production of this marvelous world and its multitudinous inhabitants. So every question is pertinent and legitimate, which if answered correctly, would throw light upon this great subject, or in any manner, lead to a solution of the great problem of life with all its possibilities. Therefore, if this God made us, and is our Father, and he introduced us into this world as his children created in his own likeness, why should we be deprived of the privilege of making some inquiries in relation to our Father and Grand-father also, or any of our ancestors with whom we hold a direct personal relationship? It must certainly be a legitimate inquiry why our father who was a builder of worlds, did not transmit to his posterity whom he formed in his own image and likeness, the same powers he himself possessed, also, why he has not given us as children, some information of a rational character, upon the extremely interesting subject of our origin and final destiny. We claim it as an inherent right existing within us, to make any and all inquiries concerning our ancestors, as much as it would be for our father to inquire concerning his, and we doubt not humanity in the coming ages, will exercise this right to the last verge of possibility, and push their inquiries and researches in all directions, and use all available means in following out their investigations in any manner that would tend to illuminate the mind concerning the great problem of their own existence.

If we can find the birth place of primal causes in the material realms, then we need go no farther, but if not, then we must trace existing effects back to their original spiritual antecedents, in order to arrive at the necessary essential elements that will enable us to bring some of the problems presented, to a satisfactory solution. We of the present age are still propounding the same very apposite questions, and asking from whence all this panorama of magnificent effects that we behold spread out before us in such multitudinous and beautifully varied forms. Still the same unsatisfactory answer comes from the theological world; God made them; and the philosopher groping in an immense field of mazy darkness, vainly endeavors in the material realms to ascertain the more spiritual causes that have been productive of such grand results, and so each succeeding generation in their turn, offer us a new set of opinions in relation to many of the facts and phenomena of which the human vision takes cognizance.

We have noticed the existence of certain elemental forces, or spiritual essences that are positive or negative, male or female in their character, and that these forces may exist separate from the gross material particles, and we trust it will be found that all aggregations of matter are produced by such pre-existing superior forces, and that these primal causes have been brought into activity in molding all forms or accretions of materialized atoms. The forces which pre-existed and gave form to the accretions of materialized particles, being invisible to us, may be properly termed the spirits or spiritual essences that exist in all forms of matter, through which they express themselves to our vision, and if such forces may exist separate and independent of the visible, material forms, then it follows that such forms or aggregated atoms do not add to the original power of the pre-existing spiritualalized forces. Thus we see all forms or aggregations of matter must have had a spiritual essence which acted as a pre-ordinate cause for the production of the form, and if so there must have been a spiritual essence or form to the globe we inhabit, containing all the forces that now exist in the structure, for as we have said, the aggregation of the particles composing the globe, has not added to or diminished those forces that pre-existed, because they are eternal essences and were brought into activity before the globe was formed. Hence, we discover that the particles which compose our world, have taken their respective places in accordance with certain forces that have pre-existed, which are essentially spiritual in their nature, and being sublimated and finer than gross matter, they are more powerful and exert authority over such particles, and we trust we shall find that magnetism and electricity are essentially spiritual forces, although they may be a sublimation of material atoms, and that these two great positive and negative powers were brought into activity, by union and contact with each other previous to the grosser materialized formation of our mundane sphere.

If we admit that material atoms are eternal entities, we may well suppose that the more etherialized essences that may exist independent of the grosser atoms, are eternal also, which being spiritual, must be a part of the great fountain of spirit existence, and as the projectors and builders of our world, must have been spiritual beings who could not come in direct contact with grosser substances, they of necessity must have made use of the spiritual forces that now seem to permeate the entire material globe, for the purpose of attracting and giving form to the more materialized elements. Hence, there must have been previous to this visible, material globe, a spiritual structure of the same form, and similar dimensions governed by those spiritual forces that have exerted controlling influence in giving form and dimensions to the gross material of which our globe is composed. In other words, if our world was the production of intelligences in a spiritual condition, they must have used such materials as they could handle and control, and with which they could come into contact; they must of necessity, at first, have constructed a globe from spiritual materials, or from those finer essences that pervade all things, and which being more powerful and active, exert a controlling influence over the grosser material atoms. Spiritual workmen that cannot well handle the granite or bricks and mortar that compose our buildings, or the massive stones of the pyramids may do much better, they may handle and control the more powerful essential spiritual elements; they may use for the accomplishment of their purposes, the etherealized essences of the mineral kingdom, and produce their vast spiritual superstructures, and then time and the positive active forces will accomplish all the rest. They may build their spiritual world in the first place from aura, magnetism, electricity, caloric, vapor, oxygen, hydrogen, nitrogen, carbon and all other spiritual elements; they may make a complete nervous network or skeleton of such materials, and no human vision could discover that any such world was in existence, although it might contain all the forces and powers, and movements, that it ever would contain, after this nervous elemental framework should be completely clothed with inactive and gross material particles. It contained all the life essences before and when it became materialized, it only added just so much of death, that life and death and all other opposing elements, might find therein a dwelling place, for those opposing elements, as we have said, are a necessity, that all things may be kept in activity. There must be life and death, cold and heat, light and darkness, love and hatred, joy and sorrow, pain and pleasure. Each element must have its opposing force, each positive must have its negative, and each male its female, or all things would stagnate, become torpid and die.

So we perceive that the spiritual pre-existed, and the material followed as a sequence, and is entirely dependent upon the spiritual for the form in which it is presented, and, that this form cannot to any considerable extent, be dependent upon gravity or centrifugal force, for its production, as both these forces are entirely subordinate and dependent, the one upon motion, and the other upon aggregated particles for their existence, as they do not act independent of these concomitants. There can be no such thing as centrifugal force, until you first give some body of matter a tangential motion; it is generated in this manner, and without such motion, no force of that kind can exist, so it is by no means an independent power, and gravitation is also entirely dependent upon aggregations of material particles, and without such, there is no gravity, it is but the symbol of inactivity and repose or death, and depends for its existence entirely upon the negative principle called *vis inertia*, or the power of lying still. We shall learn that both these forces are subordinate and comparatively feeble in their character, and they have had little to do with producing the configuration of our globe, as neither of them could by any possibility come into activity, until the configuration was a well established fact. If gravitation and centrifugal force were the primal causes that ultimated in the graceful curves and outlines of this physical globe, they must have been brought into activity before the material formation existed, but as we find these two powers are entirely dependent upon the pre-existence of matter and motion, we shall be compelled to look for causes that existed earlier, and are more potent in producing results, and in our researches we shall, no doubt, find the above named forces acting in a less important capacity, of which we may speak hereafter.

It would seem that a clearer understanding of the great fact that all the great forces and powers, the laws and principles that exist and permeate through all material forms in this universe, are essentially spiritual, and only express themselves to our vision through the material forms, will enable us to look in a proper direction, and open to us the great fountain of universal causes, and that philosophical minds illuminated by this grand discovery, will arrive at conclusions with vastly less labor and study, and with increased assurances when thus found, of their correctness and greater proximity to real truth. Reasoning from the material plane, we are continually involved in the mists and shadows and clouds that are thereunto attached, because we are only in the realm of effects, where men have been pursuing their researches with but partial success, very far away from that diviner region of more spiritualized causes that exist entirely beyond the material sphere.

We come now to a more minute consideration of those elements or spiritual essences that seem to permeate the material or mineral kingdom, and the relationship that seems to exist between the grosser and more etherealized substances that may be found attached to the globe we inhabit. In pursuing our researches in this direction it would be well for us to learn that all the more ethereal essences are eliminated from grosser matter, by a dissolution of the particles in which they have existed. If we wish to obtain the alcoholic essences from the grain, we must bring some solvent to bear sufficiently powerful to separate the spirit; this is usually done by distillation, and caloric is evidently the solvent that is brought to bear. A somewhat similar process will release the essential oils or spirit of all known vegetables. Caloric or heat is also a solvent that will release vapor which is the spirit of the waters, by a dissolution of the aqueous particles or globules. It also seems to be very well understood that the spirit of the man or woman escapes by a dissolution or decomposition of the material particles of the physical, or to say the least, those effects quite speedily follow the departure of the spirit.

We may very properly term the more refined essences and elements that exist in connection with the earth, the spirit or spirits of the grosser materials found in the mineral kingdom, and as all essences and elements, primates and ultimates, simples and compounds, have existed in the granite, it will be understood that some of those refined essences hold a near relationship to this original formation, and may be very properly termed the spirits of the granite, which have been eliminated by a dissolution of the gross particles of that primary rock. It will doubtless be conceded by most geologists that at some period in the earth's history all was granite, and that the sedimentary deposits could not have been formed unless some powers or forces had been brought to bear sufficient to tear those rocks in pieces, and dissolve the atomic particles of which they were composed. Such being the case we very readily discover that this operation would have released those finer essences or gasses that we may term the spirit of the rocks. If all existed in the granite originally, then it is plain that all must have remained there in an eternal prison house, unless the atomic particles of the granite could have been entirely decomposed, and when that took place, then of course, all essential elements might readily escape.

Chemists have found over sixty simple substances that have emanated from this source, during the inconceivable period of time since this decomposition commenced, and geologists have found immense deposits of stratified rocks several miles in depth, which are the direct result of this dissolution of the original particles of granite. It will be noticed that a large proportion of these simple elements that have made their escape from the dissolving granite, are but sublimated essences that cannot be seen, or tasted, or smelled, and that are not recognized in any manner, by our unaided sensuous nature; they are but simple gasses or the spiritual essences of the mineral. Such are hydrogen and oxygen, nitrogen and carbon, and those gasses or essences evidently bear the same relationship to the mineral kingdom, that certain forces existing in the animal economy bear to the material substances of which their organisms are composed, and all this seems to occur for the very good reason that the animal organism has inherited all that it possesses from the mineral, and it certainly could have inherited no characteristic from the parent, unless the parent had such to bestow. Hence, we discover the close relation existing between the two, and we observe if the animal or human are endowed with spiritual essences and attributes, the earth from which these peculiarities were received, must possess something of an analogous character also, and we are driven to the conclusion, that our mother the earth, is endowed with a spiritual as well as material nature, and that the positive and negative, the male and female forces are essentially the spiritual powers that gives the great superstructure, life and activity, and enable her to perform all her varied functions.

If the mind should revert back to that period in the earth's history when all the elements and essences with which it is so beautifully clothed and enveloped at the present time, were contained in the primary granite, we would, of course, behold naught but one wide spread scene of desolation and death. No mountain ranges had yet appeared, for the accumulation of antagonistic forces were yet insufficient to produce such stupendous results. No atmosphere or water, for no nitrogen, oxygen, hydrogen or carbon had yet escaped from their prison house, and without such essential ingredients, neither of those important elements could be produced. We might have beheld one wide extended plain where undisturbed harmony held universal control, and nothing would have greeted the vision but a smooth continued surface of unbroken granite, undisturbed as yet by the belligerent powers that were destined to produce such fearful revolutions in the future.

Those powers had up to this period expended their forces in materializing and solidifying the etherealized elements that had been accumulated and placed in position by the spiritual mechanics and workmen who had been engaged upon this grand superstructure. But the great positive and negative forces were increasing in their influence and strength, and evidently preparing for the mighty struggle.

Had some of our modern conservatives stepped upon the arena at this geologic period they would doubtless have cried out to the jarring elements, "Peace, be still," let all things remain quiet and harmonious, and do not disturb the fair face of nature or waken her from her slumbers. But as progressive development is an eternal attribute of nature, that has ever kept even pace, during all her multitudinous changes and modifications, those mighty positive and negative powers continued to accumulate until they were able to rally their forces, and march forward in the terrific work of dissolution, and until the exterior portions of this rock-ribbed shell succumbed to the general devastation, and the smooth surface of the old granite formation was rent and torn asunder, ground to powder, and left in one wild state of disorder and confusion. Out of this death and wide spread destruction came forth a new and higher life and animation, for the spiritual essences so much needed upon the surface, began to be set free that they might ultimately unfold into this grand scene of beauty and glory that is presented to our vision at the present day.

As a result of this apparent universal ruin, we find upon the earth's surface, many remarkable sublimated elements, among which are fire and water, the one positive, the other negative; they seem to occupy positions directly opposite to each other, and never come in contact unless they enter into a mortal combat; they fight to the death, and the weaker is always compelled to yield to the stronger whenever they come together. Philosophers have talked learnedly of fire, but they have simply told us of its effects, without giving us much information concerning its constituent essences. The child very soon learns that fire will burn, and it would seem that science had advanced but little farther. We may call it the lower positive element, and a coarse diluted form of magnetism, while water may be considered the lower negative element, and the most diluted form of electricity. The one so little understood, yet so powerful and destructive in its operations may be considered a positive or male spirit of the mineral and the other composed of two invisible gasses combined with electricity, may be termed a negative or female spirit eliminated from the same source. The two elements seem to be scattered profusely upon the face of the earth, open to the inspection of every intelligent mind.

Water is very inactive, quiet, and harmless, unless acted upon, and in conjunction with more positive forces, as gravitation, heat, or perhaps atmosphere. Either of these forces may produce violent agitation, and activity in the watery element, and render it extremely powerful and destructive. It is gravitation combined with this fluid, that produces the mighty cataract and the rushing torrent. Heat conjoined in sufficient quantities with water, renders it a solvent for much of the mineral kingdom, produces violent ebullition and activity, and it becomes destructive of all forms of organized life, while without these combinations, it is quiescent and harmless, and is the natural abode of untold billions of living organisms. But from this element which is found at the bottom, or is the least active of the negative forces, may be evolved a power higher and altogether superior, that is denominated aqueous vapor, and we find that it is produced by a dissolution of the particles of water, for as vapor is produced, the water disappears, hence, there must be a solvent, a superior power positive in its character, that can act upon water in such a manner as to eliminate this more sublimated element called vapor, which when evolved, is so much more expansive and powerful in its nature, for vapor when found in conjunction with the requisite amount of caloric becomes exceedingly active and forcible. It has risen entirely above gravitation, become superior to that subordinate force and knows no up nor down; it has become an etherealized power independent of all more materialized elements and acts upon them in a manner that renders it of immense value to the human race.

It is said that steam or vapor at a given heat, seeks to occupy 1,800 times the space required by the water from which it was evolved, and that all its force depends upon this power of expansion; but we are compelled to conclude that steam not only acquires the power of expansion in consequence of the sublimation of its particles, but an increased activity and power by its conjunction with the positive element, caloric. We think there is an important principle involved here which when properly understood, may throw much light upon some subjects that seem to need illumination, and perhaps we may claim the indulgence of the reader, if we are somewhat prolix in our exposition. The purpose is to show the intimate relationship existing between so-called spirit and grosser materials; that they are not only very nearly connected by indissoluble ties, but, that the two are essentially one, existing in different conditions.

It is very plain that if steam or vapor has been evolved from the water, and it is a more sublimated and powerful element than the latter, then some force must have acted upon the particles of water, in order that this change of condition could be produced, and it will only be necessary to examine the processes by which this common result is obtained, to find a solution of the whole matter. We have learned that the two opposing elements, fire and water, cannot be safely brought into immediate contact, as they enter into a conflict that must terminate in the subjugation of the one or the other. So water may be placed in an iron vessel or boiler, and the fire introduced to a suitable apartment underneath, and we perceive the iron is a perfect safeguard between these two contending parties; they cannot possibly injure each other, and no result would follow, but for the fact that from this so-called fire which cannot enter into the boiler, is evolved a more sublimated essence denominated heat or caloric; an element whose particles are so diminished and minute, that the solid iron of the boiler presents no barrier. They walk through the insterstices between the particles of this integument so impervious to fire or water, as an army might walk through a thickly wooded country or the narrow streets of a city.

It is this more sublimated, essential element, caloric,

that enters the steam boiler, and becomes a solvent for the particles of water, permitting the escape of this powerful element which is now performing so vast an amount of the necessary labor of humanity, and contributing so largely to supply their accumulating wants. We shall discover that the negative elements depend upon, at least, two conditions for their power and activity, the one is the fineness of fluid particles, or the extent of sublimation, and the other the joint action of the positive element or force, as steam divested of the positive element, becomes cold and inactive, it gradually condenses, and returns to the original condition, from which it was evolved, having lost the positive or active element by which it was enabled to enter into the higher, more etherealized state. We find that vapor nearly devoid of the positive element, caloric, is quite inactive, and steam after it has performed its labor, and mingled with the atmosphere, becomes inactive also, because it has parted with the spirit that aided in producing its power and activity.

We may here notice that we have found two powers or forces of a positive character, and two of a negative all evolved from the mineral kingdom; and, as we eliminate steam by a dissolution of the particles of water, so we may by dissolving the particles of steam, obtain another superior force, evolved therefrom, which is but the sublimation of the particles of vapor, and is the great negative force known as electricity. This may be a term familiar to every one though not fully understood by any one; for, it may well be doubted whether there is any living electrician who perfectly comprehends all there is to be learned in regard to that subtle element which is now brought into daily requisition in a variety of ways in promoting the interests, and subserving the purposes of enlightened humanity. Upon the other hand by a dissolution of the sublimated particles of caloric, we produce another more spiritualized positive element called magnetism, the counterpart of electricity, and the essential, sublimated element of heat, while electricity being directly opposite in its nature, and negative in its character, is the essential element of cold. We now perceive that these two are the great, all powerful elements or forces, the one positive, the other negative, superior to all other forces or essences that are more gross and materialized, and consequently occupy a condition of inferiority, and that one or both of these sublimated forces dwell in all things in and upon the earth, and exert as occasion may require a superior power and controlling influence over all terrestrial objects.

We may discover in the diagram illustrating some of the ideas presented in this chapter, in relation to the positive and negative forces which rise, one above another in spiritualization and power by a sub-division of particles, that caloric becomes a solvent, capable of disintegrating the globules of water, thus permitting the escape of the higher element, vapor or steam, and that magnetism also acts in a similar capacity upon the vapor, and thus assists in the evolution of the great negative force, electricity. On the other hand, we may learn that either vapor or steam are powerful fire annihilators when properly applied, and exert positive authority over that more subordinate element, and that electricity exercises the same authority over caloric, and that in both instances, the higher elements are evolved, thus caloric is generated in the one case, and magnetism in the other.

What now are the operations that have been going on in a steam boiler, that finally culminate in an explosion? a process which seems to be so little understood at the present time, for occurrences of that kind are by no means unfrequent, and certainly men would avoid them if they comprehended the subject, as somewhere there must be a remedy, and at some time the danger of explosions must comparatively cease to exist. It is found that electricity is generated in large quantities in the steam boiler, as well as steam, and that element has power to dissolve the particles of caloric, and thus generate magnetism. It will be seen that when the boiler becomes super-heated, the great positive and negative powers have been evolved, and all it requires is a sufficient quantity of those fluid elements; as the strongest boiler that was ever constructed, would be entirely incompetent to resist their united force, so we think that science will sometime reveal the fact that Electro-Magnetic forces produce the explosion, and then engineers may apply a safeguard that will effectually prevent such a catastrophe. It has been proved by experiment that a boiler will generate electricity much more rapidly when insulated or placed upon some non-conducting material; and, in this manner the aural element has been produced by artificial means, from magnetism and electricity thus generated in the insulated boiler. It has also been demonstrated, that steam admitted into a receiver or chamber, and cut off from the boiler, when heated to 1,200° Fahrenheit, parts with all its electricity, and that it cannot be condensed, as it becomes simply hydrogen and oxygen in their original condition, which may be changed to water, or condensed in the same manner as any other suitable proportions of the same gasses, namely, by the action of a current of electricity. So we discover, that water cannot be produced, unless it contains the requisite quantity of the electric fluid, and we may very properly say, that electricity is the great negative spirit of the waters, and it is also the spirit that aids in giving force and power to steam. For experiment has proven that you cannot increase the expansive power of steam, after you have attained 1,200° of heat, and further that steam and electricity are both powerless and inactive, unless conjoined with the positive elements, caloric and magnetism, for it requires both positive and negative, male and female to produce results.

We discover, that spiritual essences all through the natural realms, are released from grosser materials, by a dissolution of the particles, or what we may term the death of the material, analogous to that separation which takes place at the death of the human body, and which permits the spiritual essence to take its departure, and leaves the material form to dissolve, and affinitize with the particular elements to which it belongs, so the positive element or that spirit which brings power and activity to the steam, departs when it has performed its labor, and passes from the cylinder into the atmosphere.

The mineral kingdom from its earlier or primeval condition, has been constantly disintegrating, and changing form and releasing the more ethereal elements with which we are enveloped, and which we require to sustain life. The earlier granite formations must have been acted upon by the elements, magnetism, electricity, and the various essences in the form of fire, air, and water, and dissolution has to a wonderful extent taken place, and hence the earth has progressed from a lower to a more advanced and spiritualized condition, and hence it is changing form at the present by the same universal law, and will until all of matter, becomes more etherealized, and less gross than at the present. How far this spiritualization of matter shall extend, we leave the reader to ascertain by his own reasoning, but we say, if progressive development is a universal principle, and all things come under the influence of this law, and we are convinced that original gross materials have been refined and purified to a certain extent, then we may expect that this work will go on through the eternities of the future, and each one can form his own conclusion with regard to results. It would certainly appear, taking this view of the subject, that all gross material substances would, at some period become refined and spiritualized by processes that are now in active operation, but we leave this problem to those who desire to pursue the subject.

We require in order to produce that explosive article called gunpowder, seventy-five parts sal-nitre, ten of

16

sulphur, and fifteen charcoal which is nearly pure carbon, and as a result of this mixture, we have manufactured a granular substance that seems to possess, latent within itself, active elements of a wonderful destructive character. It is said to have an explosive force of at least, 1,500 atmospheres, and that a cubic inch produces 236 cubic inches of elastic fluid, and I believe science teaches that this power contained in the powder, depends simply npon the expansion of the particles, but here a question arises as to the force that causes the expansion of the particles, contained in the elements that constitute gunpowder. Would the fire that burns these black grains produce that result, if there was no other element brought into activity? Would fire produce any such result upon charcoal or sulphur or sal-nitre, separate under ordinary circumstances? by no means. Then it is evident that these materials acquire a peculiar power by being mingled, they did not possess when separate, that the necessary manipulations in the manufacture, or some other cause, has magnetized these particles, and given them a positive spirit which may under proper conditions when let loose by combustion, unite with electricity, and cause the particles to expand to their utmost tension, thus producing all their marvelous effects. So we shall perceive but for the life energies of the two great positive, and negative elements which were roused into activity, no explosion would take place, and hence we say, that the spirit of the gunpowder passes out at the time of the explosion, or the dissolution of the atoms of which it was composed.

Science will object to this idea, and claim that a given quantity of powder may be exploded under a bell glass, and that all the elements of which it was composed, will remain without any diminution of weight, and that it may be commingled by a little manipulation, and exploded again and again, thus demonstrating that nothing, or no elementary spiritual force has left the mass by the explosion. In replying to this objection, we say, that science, before it can demonstrate the fact that no spirit has left at the explosion, must collect and re-explode the powder, *ad infinitum*, without any loss of material or force, and when that is done, and not till then, will it be proven that no spirit or essence departs at the dissolution of explosive materials. It would then also, be proven, that those materials contain forces that are inexhaustible, and with proper apparatus for saving them, they could be applied eternally without being replenished.

We simply say the power that carries the cannon-shot to its destination, and produces the attendant detonation, has gone forever, and cannot be restored to that same material, but there are plenty of the same elements left, that may enter into and take possession of the residuum of material, if it can be collected, which will perform the same office.

Thus, we think it will be plain that the two great positive and negative forces mingle with all inferior powers in nature, and they are constantly brought into activity in performing our labors, and executing our purposes. But for magnetism and electricity, steam would have no expansive, active force, because it would have no life, and gunpowder and other explosives would possess no such terrible powers, because there would be no element to excite the astonishing activities, at the dissolution of their material particles, and it is evidently the existence of these grand spiritual forces within the particles of steam, and explosive materials and their escape at the time of their destruction that produce all the wonderful effects.

We have in our researches, seemed to arrive at one prominent fact, and we may observe in all the realms of nature, that life, activity, and power increase in intensity, as material substances are more sublimated or become refined. Thus coarse particles like granite rock, or anything of a similar character, are apparently inanimate and inactive, and seem to lie in the embrace of death, but as you ascend in the scale by dissolution of these coarse particles, releasing the more spiritualized elements, such as the gasses that constitute air and water, you find more life, activity and power, and so on as you go up towards the great positive and negative powers that stand at the head of materialized, elemental forces. Yet the original granite rock contains all that there is in the universe, and if our world to-day presented nothing but one mass of granite, as it might have done in some of the ages of the past, it would nevertheless contain all the forces and elements that can now be found within its precincts.

Hence, it will be difficult to find the dividing line between material and spiritual substances, if there is any such line, and tell where matter terminates and spirit commences, or which is matter and which is spirit. For we shall find whether we call it matter or spirit, it is one and the same indivisible element, the spiritual is material, and the material is spiritual undergoing change, and ascending upwards by virtue of the law of eternal progress. The higher or more sublimated existing in and permeating the particles of the lower, the lower being acted upon, and controlled by the superior power of the more spiritualized essences that dwell in them, which are released when the particles of the grosser are dissolved.

It might be interesting to notice briefly some of the uses of the various forces, and observe how they have been made subservient in supplying the wants of humanity, for we dwell in the midst of these spiritual essences, a combination of which enters very largely into our physical bodies, as it will be perceived devoid of them, we could not be sustained in life for a single hour; they are all necessary to our existence, and contribute in a variety of ways to our support. As a mechanical power the atmosphere has been made use of since the first windmill was erected, and successfully applied to grinding and preparing food for our ancestors, they were the only mills used by the inhabitants, and this uncertain power is still applied to many purposes, although it is gradually giving way, and being superseded by superior forces that are more constant and reliable. Wind may be considered a low grade of mechanical force, yet it doubtless, subserved the perposes of our forefathers for a long period, both in Europe and America, before water was called into requisition so extensively, and before the use of steam was known; but this is too fast and practical an age, to wait for the uncertain and fickle winds.

Water is entirely superior as a power for the propulsion of machinery, because it is more constant and reliable, and very many large cities are built, depending entirely upon this power as a basis. Immense manufacturing establishments are operated, that give employment to thousands of people, simply from the fact that water is a fluid element possessing a certain amount of activity, and that by the aid of gravity, it seeks repose upon the lowest possible level. We discover then that gravity ascends the scale of materialized, elemental forces, as high as water and atmosphere, and no higher, as we find steam and caloric act entirely independent of this so-called power, which seems rather an inherent property that is attached to all gross matter.

In this age of advancement, men have resorted more generally to the sublimated particles of water, or vapor in a heated condition, thus being excited to great activity; and steam becomes the grand motive power, used by mechanics in the propulson of a very large proportion of the machinery applied to many purposes; because the apparatus for the generation and application of this superior force, can be introduced under almost all circumstances, whether upon land or water, stationary or in transit. It may be placed in the boat or upon the railway, used for navigating the waters of the river or ocean, or for dragging the ponderous train across the continent. The farmer, the manufacturer, or the mechanic, may call upon this force to aid in accelerating their labors in an endless variety of ways, and find it a ready assistant in the performance of a vast multitude of arduous duties, and were civilized humanity to be deprived of the use of this great force, by any possible circumstance, unparalelled distress would necessarily ensue, and perhaps no greater calamity conld visit our race. We have now become exceedingly dependent upon this power for the production of a very large number of the necessary articles that are required for human consumption.

We trust we shall find after careful research, that the real active elements, the soul or spirit essence of steam, is the Electro-Magnetic force, and that devoid of these two superior elements, it becomes inactive and lifeless. Engineers well understand that the power of steam dedends upon its activity, so we perceive that in the application of this power, we are only using the great positive and negative forces diffused with the particles of steam, and that more than probable, the time is not far distant, when we shall be able to make an application of those great powers independent of this adulteration or combination with vapor, and that the large amount of machinery will be propelled by Electro-Magnetic force, and this event only waits until men can learn to generate these fluid elements with sufficient economy, and render them no more expensive than steam or other mechanical powers. This power is already used extensively for very many purposes; men have learned to subdue these all-powerful elements in such a manner, as to make them obedient servants in the performance of many of their requirements; they compel them to go and come, and do their errands, and carry their messages from continent to continent, and transact their business. Through these agents they hold ready converse with their friends in distant cities, buy and sell merchandise, pay their notes, transfer their property, money, or stocks, and attend to all manner of transactions. After having done so much already, what may we not expect in the future, when men shall have a better knowledge of these universal powers, and the means by which they may procure their aid more economically, and control them more successfully?

We have learned that all these forces are composed of fluid particles, and that their power and activity depends upon their sublimation or fineness, and that we have not yet reached the extent of etherealization of matter, by any means, but that the particles of magnetism and electricity, are capable of subdivision to an inconceivable degree; each time generating forces that are superior and more spiritualized, until somewhere in the realms of the spiritual, material atoms attain to their last limit of divisibility, which limit is entirely beyond the comprehension of the human mind. In fact, it is extremely difficult for us to comprehend that matter may be sublimated to that condition in which it has the power manifested by the Electro-Magnetic elements, yet having witnessed their power and learned that they are particled substances, we may conclude that still higher elements also exist, produced in a similar manner, by an elimination from the lower, and that the superior forces are fluid particles likewise.

Aura is evidently an element that bears a very close relationship to the above named forces, and being far more sublimated in its character and finer in its particles, it acts in various capacities, where the magnetic and electric fluids would be powerless, as we discover that the latter forces have duties to perform in the physical organization, but they can by no means perform all the duties required. They may assist in the digestion of food, in the circulation of the life currents, in the production of the required animal heat, in the separation of those elements that need to be exhaled and ejected from the system; in one word they may perform those coarser, less refined operations and processes that are continually carried on in the animal economy. But there are higher duties which require attention that call for more refined and etherealized powers, and it has long been understood that the human organization was pervaded by an element variously called nerve aura, odic, or odylic force, which occupies the brain, and the whole system of nervous network that permeates and extends to the remotest corners of the physical body, carrying messages back and forth, and doing the bidding of the monarch that sits upon the throne of his power, in the frontal portion of the cerebrum.

For the information of the curious in such matters, we remark that this is one of the very materials from which nature manufactures those spiritual forms and organizations with which we enter that sphere of existence, that is one step in advance of our own, and we discover that this spiritual organization composed of aura, and other refined and etherealized elements is within us now, and it is this which constitutes us living, sensuous beings, and which will live when we cast off this outer covering, throw away the bark, and retain only the spiritual form. Thus we are permitted to take a philosophical and comprehensive view of the great change called death, and all the fears and terrors that we have entertained upon that subject, may at once be dismissed, as the change is only in the outward and visible, while there is no change whatever in the interior, spiritual or more refined organizations. Men will some time learn that the spiritual realms are as natural as the material, then all fears will cease and there will be far less servile bondage in our world, and less reverence for a self-constituted priesthood.

This etherealized essence which is the offspring of the Electro-Magnetic fluid, or generated by the male and female forces existing in the positive and negative spiritualized elements, as we have already remarked, frequently displays its glories in the polar regions of this hemisphere, and when it exhibits itself to any considerable extent, the various Electro-Magnetic phenomena are very much influenced, and telegraphing can with difficulty be successfuly performed, showing the very close interrelation between the different elements. It is the higher development of this etherealized fluid that enables the more distant or exterior planets, and the interiors of all globes to enjoy a sufficiency of genial light and warmth to supply all their needs in the absence of solar influences.

There is but one more elemental fluid of which we have any knowledge, that is exhibited upon the broad face of universal nature, which is more refined and sublimated than aura, and as we have treated upon the latter in some other portions of this work, we may proceed to a brief consideration of what we have termed in the absence of all other names, *empyria*, which like all elements and powers below this in refinement, is the direct offspring, or an elimination from the one which is next in order below. It has proceeded from the aural fluid essence, and is still more etherealized, and refined in its particles, because there are offices to be filled and duties to be performed in Nature's vast realms, that are entirely beyond the ability of any of the forces heretofore named, and hence one that is superior, and more sublimated than all, must be called into requisition. It will be necessary for the student of nature to observe, in the consideration of this most refined and important of the forces, which display their varied activities throughout the universal domain, that the positive and negative, the male and female, are kept distinct until we pass the Electro-Magnetic, and arrive at the aural element, where we find a fluid so refined and exalted that both these principles concentrate, and are entertained within its embraces. That is, at this point of refinement, the positive and negative converge, and after this condition of sublimation is attained, both male and female will be found to exist in a single fluid element, and hence aura being both positive and negative, may engender other and higher forces that in their evolution require the male and female principles; because aura is in possession of both, and so is empyria this more refined offspring. It is this element that exists in the white light, and reflects itself through the solar spectrum in the form of the primary colors. This element alone being superior to all others that come under our observation, is able under certain conditions, to impress itself in the full blaze of the mid-day sun upon the particles of atmosphere, and display those beautiful scintillations beheld in the many colored rainbow.

If we look abroad at nature's realms, upon our own earth, we shall find vast multitudes of living organizations, for it would appear that globes are of small consequence, unless they are peopled with such forms of life. This would seem to be the highest purpose for which they can be projected and brought into existence, as the smallest animalcule, being a living organization, is superior in this respect to the largest concretion of inorganic material. Hence, the emiment Jewish teacher esteemed a single living soul, of more value than the entire inanimate world, and we are compelled to acknowledge the wisdom of his teaching, and we cannot doubt that the intelligence and power that is capable of bringing a world to a condition suited to the existence of living organisms, can also find the means of producing and animating those organisms, without resorting to any miraculous or other than natural processes.

If by the use of forces acting upon materials in existence, a world of vast proportions may be formed, and developed to a condition in which animal life can be sustained, then we may well suppose that the same intelligence could find the requisite forces to produce the animal life, without going outside the boundaries of the universal realms, or resorting to any powers but those that are simple and natural. And we must necessarily conclude that life and animation are produced by simple and natural processes, by the application of laws general in their character, and not in each particular case, by the special intervention of some supreme power, or infinite intelligence.

We have discovered in our previous researches, that various effects are produced upon this earth, and that when such is the case, there must be forces in existence, adequate to their production, that the plastic hand of nature has been continually at work in bringing all things by which we are surrounded, and which are so grand and beautiful, into their present condition, and each of nature's great powers or forces that we have noticed, has acted in a separate and distinct capacity. Now we behold another group of phenomena that occupy a prominent position, and which are grand and sublime in the extreme; they are living, moving, breathing, animated evidences that somewhere in nature's great laboratory, is to be found an exalted power that is entirely adequate to their production. These phenomena are connected with the life element that exists in the natural realms, and permeates all the varied organized living forms, and this sublimated, most spiritualized fluid that diffuses itself through all nature, engendering the wonderful principle and power of life, is *empyria* more refined in its particles, and eminently superior in its power, to all the elemental forces known to exist upon the earth.

We have called the reader's attention to the fact, that in the materialized organization of our globe, there is a region of death, inactivity and darkness; that out of this, by an application of positive elements, come life, activity, and light, that gradually and progressively, the gross material is sublimated, producing the finer, and that the several natural forces assume powers and activities, in accordance with the sublimation of the elemental fluids. Thus rising upon a graduated scale through the grand pyramid of positive and negative powers, each one having its own distinctive duties to perform, the one higher than the other, until we rise up to this most etherealized essence of which we are now treating, and whose province it is to infuse life, animation and activity into all forms of matter that come into the proper conditions, and are susceptible to its influences.

Caloric can evidently produce results superior to fire, and magnetism has powers far exceeding caloric; on the other hand, steam has more power than water, and electricity still more than steam, and all these forces seem to act in very different capacities, and each one no doubt performs an entirely distinct set of duties. The aural element being far more refined and sublimated than those mentioned, also has its proper sphere of operations and certain legitimate purposes to accomplish, and we discover in the realms of nature, particular fields in which these several forces must be brought to bear, in order to perform all that is necessary in the great mundane work shop. But we still discover around us amidst this universal machinery, a higher work that is being performed daily, at all times and in all places, by some other power that must act in this superior capacity, and we are driven to the conclusion that nature is provided with a force entirely adequate to the accomplishment of this higher, and still more important labor. We discover that organized material forms are continually being impregnated with the life element, and no person that opens nature's great volume and scans attentively her pages, can deny the fact that in her domain there must be a force which operates in this particular department.

We have written at some length upon these different forces in nature, endeavoring to show their positions and relationships in the great laboratory, their different values and proportionate powers, and also their several appropriate spheres of action; and we trust the reader, if he does not find this matter clearly set forth in these pages, will look out into nature's open book for himself, where he may observe the whole machinery in active operation, and where he will doubtless discover in the varied departments of this earthly sphere, that certain labor is to be performed, and certain results are to be produced. If so, particular agents or forces must be provided to do this work, and produce the several results; and these varied operations are being carried on continually, in the most harmonious manner. As, for instance, the springs which are the sources of our rivers, and are found in the more mountainous regions or the uplands, must be supplied with the requisite amount of water, and caloric attends to this duty; he descends to the lower parts of the earth, where the vast bodies of water are found, enters into the constituent elements of the fluid particles, and performs his official duty of destruction and dissolution, which permits the vapor to ascend and float away in fleecy clouds upon the denser atmosphere, by whose currents they may be wafted to the mountain side, condensed in a colder stratum, and descend again in the form of rain or snow, thus continually resupplying the waters of the mountain streams.

If we wish an agent that can pass through the apparently solid iron of the steam boiler, and become a solvent for the fluid particles within, thus generating steam, caloric or heat will perform this feat to our satisfaction, but it cannot by any possibility attend to the duties assigned to magnetism. It can by no means form itself into longitudinal currents that will govern the magnetic needle which guides the mariner to his destination; nor can it generate those frictionizing undulating processes that produce light; neither can it combine with electricity, and cause the vivid flash and the glaring forked shaft that sometimes carries destruction and death in its rapid march. The Electro-Magnetic elements must unite, in order to produce this marvelous result, together with an extensive group of phenomena, both above and below the surface of this globe. If an earthquake is necessary, and we cannot suppose they occur unless they are, there are no other powers that can be relied upon with any degree of certainty for the production of such a result, and the important duties of these powerful elements are so extended and various, that it would be impossible to present them in this connection, even if we had the ability; but we may be assured that devoid of the great positive and negative forces, this mundane machine could not have been put in operation, neither could it be run for a single hour.

The aural element also has its own particular province which cannot be filled by any other power; its own separate duties to perform that renders the appointment of an agent entirely inadmissible. It enters those realms where magnetism can scarcely approach, and you will find this element displaying his wondrous powers upon a scale of unequaled grandeur, in the frozen regions of polar night; and no power but this can make those brilliant displays under such peculiar conditions, and burnish up the Arctic skies with the richly painted glories and splendors of the Aurora Borealis. Neither can any other force enter into your physical system, assume the delicate duties it performs there, and go and come at the bidding of the monarch that sits upon the throne of your intellectual kingdom, for it is well-known we cannot lift a finger or raise an arm or a foot, unless this ethereal and powerful element is called into requisition. We know also, when by any disorganization or derangement of the wires or system of nerves upon which this force travels and performs its varied duties within us, that we begin to suffer, and so continue, until a harmonious circulation is restored by a returning healthy condition of the nervous conductors or passage ways upon which this active energizing element is wont to travel.

We have already discovered still higher duties in the natural realms, for some still higher power to perform, and consequently, that higher power must exist, in order that those necessary duties should receive proper attention. It is a well-known fact that by the action of the galvanic battery, an influence may be brought to bear that will produce activity in the limbs of a dead frog, or of a dead man, although the nervous activities thus produced, are extremely transient; however, from the fact that motion and apparent animation is produced to any extent whatever, we must conclude that the nerves are permeated by something analogous to the vitalizing fluid, or activities could not have been excited.

And, if by artificial means, this life element can be manifested in the least possible degree, in an organized body where it had been entirely extinguished, then it is a matter of no surprise that in nature's great laboratory there may be a power amply able to diffuse this element through all suitably organized forms of matter, at the proper time, in the entire vegetable and animal world. Nor is it surprising, where we discover forces equal to the performance of all other duties below this, that a power should be provided that may produce this grand result, and permeate organized forms with the required vitality and animation.

We trust the ordinary reader whose opportunities for scientific acquirements have been limited, and for whom this work is more particularly designed, will be able to comprehend, that wherever in the great domain of nature, duties are to be performed, effects to be produced, or results accomplished, there may be found in all cases adequate forces for the performance of those duties, and the production of those effects and results, and that there must of necessity exist such a power in this particular department. Hence, we find this most sublimated essential spiritual element, upon the very summit of the grand superstructure of positive and negative forces, whose potency is not only sufficient to infuse vitality into animal organisms, but under proper conditions, make an exhibition of its existence in the fluid atoms of white light, and paint their constituent elements in vivid colors upon the screen, or upon the atmospheric particles in the overarched canopy, in defiance of all the powers of the mid-day sun.

This life dispensing element has its grand insignia in the rainbow, and whether this beautiful phenomenon officiates as a remembrancer to the covenant making Hebrew God, or subserves other important purposes, it may and doubtless will at some time, convey the information to intelligent humanity, that life and vital essences shall always permeate organized, materialized atoms, until all spiritual entities have passed through their varied forms, and until all material substances shall be exhausted in the performance of their important duties. For if it can be proven that any given amount of gross material has been etherealized, and contributed its finer essences in building up and constituting those spiritual beings who have lived, and passed away to inhabit higher realms, then we may conclude that more and still more of the material world shall be applied in the same manner If we pursue this train of reasonimg it would seem possible that our globe at some period in the eternities of the future, might become so sublimated and expanded into spheres, as to render the whole a suitable abode for spiritual beings. Thus all things may continue in their progressive existence, attaining higher and still higher conditions, during those cycles that know no termination.

We apprehend that we may be entitled to the indulgence, and, possibly, commiseration of the enlightened reader who has followed these pages thus far, if we should modestly express an opinion, that in all cases where we have spoken of spiritual elements, essences, and fluid particles, we should represent them as being permeated by spirit entities, and that the positive elements are diffused by real spiritual existences in a state of activity, while the negative are a mass of such entities, in a condition of inactivity or rest; and, that the dazzling splendors that we behold in the sun, are but its spiritual spheres inhabited by inconceivable hosts of shining spirit intelligences, so innumerable as to defy all attempts at mathematical computation, and that the solar spots depend simply upon the evolutions and change of position of the incomprehensibly numerous armies of spiritual beings that inhabit the spheres of that central orb.

The learned Dr. Dick had a conception of the same

idea, as the reader may learn by referring to page 104, Celestial Scenery, in his great work. The eminent author could not conceive how evolutions of such immense magnitude could take place so rapidly by any of the ordinary forces that had come within the reach of human comprehension. He evidently entertained a vague idea that the marvelous display of rapidly changing spots upon the sun's surface, or in its apparent atmosphere, might possibly be caused by the influence of spiritual, intelligent beings. We feel perfectly safe in making the assumption that this view of the subject is far more rational, and will furnish the world a clearer and more intelligent exposition of those strange phenomena, than any that have yet been presented; for what but spirit intelligence with their wondrous activities, could perform evolutions so rapidly, and upon so grand a scale, as exhibited in those vast, moving spots upon the solar surface; many of which evidently larger than our globe, have changed positions, and disappeared in a very few hours. Then we may rationally conceive that the solar spots are caused by the temporary absence of portions of that shining host who inhabit the spiritual spheres of the monarch of day, and that in consequence of that absence, the human vision penetrates through to the dark electric body within their realms. We may also discover that each one of the millions of orbs that exhibit their splendors in the sidereal heavens, are surrounded by illuminated spiritual spheres, thus enabling them to send down their scintillations of light which penetrate through the dark regions of interminable space, and come in contact with our vision. This fact alone is the grand reason why we behold the universal displays of stellar glory, that prove such a prolific source of enjoyment to contemplative minds, not only presenting vast fields for study and research, but filling their whole interior natures with admiration and reverence for those powers that have been competent to establish this magnificent and orderly arrangement of heavenly bodies throughout nature's universal realms.

The rapid transitional movements of the Aurora Borealis, would also indicate the marchings and countermarchings of intensely active, spiritual beings; and we will barely suggest that this view might to a certain extent, throw light upon that mysterious phenomena. Those persons endowed with clairvoyant vision, have no doubt, beheld vast armies of such living beings performing their varied evolutions in the atmosphere or heavens above, and it is not very surprising that such exhibitions should occur many times, previous to some terrible earthly conflict. Hence, they have been considered as portentous of war, and as human wars are not mere accidents, but are all planned in the spiritual spheres, with great precision, it may possibly be, that in the management of these human conflicts, they find it necessary to practice some of the various military evolutions that are sometimes presented to the inner vision of the clairvoyant, and it is possible also, that the conditions of the atmosphere in the polar regions, are such that a faint outline of the movements of spiritual beings, becomes visible to our material eyes.

However all this may be viewed, we are compelled to admit that those beings who exist in the spiritual, and are more sublimated and positive in their natures, must possess great activities, and that they are doubtless busily engaged in some deparment of natu re's realms and if they are not employed with the merry dancers of the Aurora Borealis, they must be somewhere else employing their time and making themselves useful in the universal laboratory of nature where so much is to be accomplished. For, as we have before stated, every mechanical operation must be performed by mechanics, and if these spiritual workmen are able to adjust the materials in such a manner as to produce a beautiful world, and manipulate the essences necessary to construct the delicate eye of the animalcule, then they may safely undertake any other mechanical performance required in nature's extended workshop. We need not look far, before we shall find very numerous mechanical contrivances so intricate in their character, that the human mind can form no very distinct conception of the necessary appliances that are brought to bear in their production; or the manner in which the materials are aggregated that gives them their peculiar forms.

When we behold the beautiful outlines of the majestic oak, or more graceful elm, we may well wonder how their material particles have been built up into such appropriate and symmetrical shapes, so that each limb and branch, twig and leaf, occupy their proper places, and we may very safely conclude that some intelligent power has had the supervision, and attended to the disposition of the multitudinous atoms of which the tree is composed. The devout religionist says in his solemnity, an infinite God has watched over and supervised all this; that, by his all-seeing eye and the might of his wisdom and power, he is able to accomplish the minutia of all this immense labor upon all worlds. We think, however, by taking a more intelligent and harmonious view of this subject, we shall be led to conclude that all this multitudinous labor has been performed by an infinite host of spiritual beings who must necessarily have an existence, and who are continually working out these important purposes in the various departments of nature, and that real spirit entities have been thus engaged from the earliest periods of the history of all worlds.

Then, if it is conceded that all these curiously contrived mechanical structures, both in the vegetable and animal kingdoms, are built up and generally supervised by competent spiritual mechanics, it will certainly become necessary that the mechanics or workmen should begin their labors at the time of the commencement of the structure. We then perceive it quite possible that some of those natural forces or elemental powers which seem to be engaged in certain departments, may be real spirit entities who are busy in the construction of the animal and human forms from the time of their conception, until they arrive at maturity, and are placed in full possession of every function that properly belongs to a perfect animal or human organization.

If the most simple mechanical production requires skill, care, and intelligent labor in the adjustment of all its material, how nuch more then, shall such intelligent labor be required in the construction of the most intricate and complicated piece of machinery that has ever been produced in our world. For, by the most careful scrutiny of the anatomist and physiologist, who employ a lifetime in the study of the various functions of the animal or human structure, it is still impossible to arrive at a complete understanding of all that is contained in this complex piece of mechanism, and to acquire a knowledge of the manner in which the various materials have been aggregated, and brought together in their peculiar forms and organizations.

Strange as it may appear at first view, we are driven by a process of reasoning, to the conclusion, that invisible essences which we call elemental forces are pervaded by spirit entities, performing their activities and wondrous labors, and that intelligent beings, perhaps extremely diminutive to our vision, are absolutely engaged in building up the mechanical structure of all infantile living forms in the dark recesses of their temporary uterine abodes, and that it is thus prepared to enter the active scenes of the outer world, where an independent life awaits its coming. But, whatever these workmen are able to do in preparing the structure for its entry into the more active scenes, they are unable to confer upon it in that condition the independent physical, vital principle or element which the infant receives after coming in contact with the exalted empyrial essence which exists in our atmosphere, and which alone can produce individualized life and animation in any organized being.

All of life that the unborn infant can enjoy before the birth, must be entirely dependent upon the mother; it has none separate from her. If the mother dies during her pregnancy, the infant dies also, and never in any case does it obtain an independent, living existence until the lungs that have been prepared for that purpose, are inflated with the atmosphere, and the whole system is diffused with that essential element which has power to bestow life, with all its various phenomena upon the organization. Hence, we may discover a sort of inspired truth in that passage, whoever may have been its author, which says, the power he calls God, "Breathed into his nostrils the breath of life, and man became a living soul," as it is absolutely necessary that the act of breathing should take place before he can become an independent, living being, because the vital portions of the physical system must come in direct contact with the vitalizing life giving element, before the power of life can be received, and the whole machinery can begin to act for itself in any such individual capacity.

How singular that modern science is just now revealing to us the great fact that the air we breathe, the water we drink, the food we eat, are but one living mass of animalculæ and infusoria, and that divested of these, they would contain none of those life elements, or recuperating forces so necessary in sustaining our continued existence. We now may have said upon this subject of natural forces all that is pertinent to the matter we have in hand; yet we have, probably, scarcely entered the wide fields that may yet be explored by succeeding observers.

The few scattering suggestions we have made, may perhaps arrest the attention of other minds who will have more time to pursue these inquiries, and who will be able to present them in a far more lucid and satisfactory manner. We doubt not it will appear quite evident to the intelligent reader, that men have hardly as yet entered the portals that lead to the grand fountain of knowledge, that science and boasted philosophy are but puling infants, that the most eminent men with their highest attainments, are still wandering amid a maze of uncertainties and shadows. Although they may fancy they are now prepared to enter the great temple and grasp the most profound principles, and gain access to the entire realm of causes, yet in the future they may be overwhelmed with the fact that many of their former well built fabrics have been crushed out of existence, by newer and fresher demonstrations of truth. For we cannot suppose by any means, that scientific research has reached that point where it may be said, "Thus far, no farther shalt thou go," or that the numerous opinions formed by scientific men in the different departments of learning, are all absolute verities.

We must conclude that change, whose sacrilegous hand is continually making its mark upon all things, will enter the sacred temples erected by the most eminent minds, and lay her destroying hand upon the highly revered and long cherished ideas of these votaries, and trampling under unhallowed feet, their most brilliant conceptions, will build entirely new fabrics, and establish new theories upon the ruins of the old; and thus on, until man arrives at that period in his development, when he shall be able to obtain a clear and comprehensive understanding of truth, as it exists in the very *soul* of all things.

CHAP. VII.

GRAVITATION.

Gravitation, to which allusion already has been made, would seem to require more than a passing notice, for as a power or force it has received a large amount of consideration from scientific men of great eminence, and when the discovery was made, that such a power had an existence, and operated in accordance with fixed laws, science seemed to take a long stride, and marched on thence forward with more rapid pace. But, we are of opinion that gravity has been rated too high in the scale of those forces that appear to have been brought into activity, and exerted so prominent an influence in the production of all visible, tangible things that exist; that more, very much more, has been placed upon the shoulders of gravity, than this subordinate, dependent comparatively inactive power is able to bear.

We think it will be ascertained that gravity can hardly be considered to exist as an absolutely active, elemental force, but rather a concomitant of the grosser forms of matter, and that its power is entirely dependent upon the existence, and regulated by the density or peculiar quality of the matter over which it seems to exert an influence. Gravity as a force evidently has no attachment to, or affinity with, or power over material particles that become more etherealized than our atmos-sphere, and although it seems to act with such potency, upon grosser forms under certain conditions, yet if it may be termed an absolute force, it occupies but a low and very subordinate position.

We have remarked, that upon this elemental structure, the physical globe, all material substances were more or less active in accordance with their grossness, and as we have said, gravity only keeps company with the more gross particles, and it will be seen as activity ceases, gravity usurps its authority and assumes control; for this sluggish force keeps little company with the more active elements. It has little control over the atmospheric particles, scarce any, over vapor cold, in its heated condition, none, and caloric is entirely beyond its reach. But when we travel into the realms of inactivity, and the nearer we approach the state of quiescence, we call death, the nearer we get to the realm where gravity holds his universal reign, because, in this gross department of nature, this force seems to exert its influences, and affinitizes with the elementary substances. So when we approximate conditions of matter which is more etherealized, gravity exerts no control; its domain evidently finds an impassable boundary, and its power, a limit beyond which it cannot go.

We discover then, that this great power only assists those gross material substances over which it exerts a controlling influence, to find that repose and rest they seem to require; for, being composed of the more inactive elements, all they require is inactivity and rest; and it becomes the duty of this force to carry all such material forms directly upon a straight line, to a position as near as possible, the bosom of the great mother earth where they may find the quiet and rest they seem to need. This we conceive to be the great and prominent duty of the wonderful force called gravitation; and, it was acting in the performance of this duty, when it brought down the apple that arrested the attention of the great philosopher to a consideration of the subject which resulted in his very extended theory in relation to the movements of the heavenly bodies. His theory, however, will most likely be modified and corrected by other philosophers, when the proper time arrives. It will be discovered that gravitation is not in possession of any such reciprocal influence, operating so extensively between the different planetary bodies, and that all these movements are governed and controlled by no such subordinate power, but by real, active, positive and negative elemental forces that are competent to extend out, reciprocate and affinitize with forces of the same character, existing upon other worlds.

We behold the fluid particles of water, under the control of this force, gravity, rushing in the mountain torrent down the declivity, and leaping from rock to rock, until they find a position in the more placid river of the valley, and still under this control, they urge their way onward to the bosom of the mighty ocean. But this same water is evaporated by a higher power, its fluid particles are dissolved, and the vapor is taken from the arms of gravity, and carried off upon the currents of the atmosphere, to condense again upon the mountain tops, and again fall into his embraces. So we see different forces are necessary, each one acting in its own capacity, thus maintaining a kind of equilibrium, in order to preserve the beauties and harmonies of nature, and carry on that everlasting round of activities requisite for the continuance of all terrestrial things.

We are informed by science that the plastic hand of gravitation, aided by centrifugal force, has had much or all to do in rounding out our globe into its present form, and in shaping its curves and appropriate outlines; that by an eternal law it has rounded the earth in the same manner as it renders globular the dewdrop which may be suspended from the tip of the leaf. They say nature's great laws operate with equal force, whether in the forming of worlds or dewdrops; but in relation to this, we observe that, if you add another dewdrop to the one already suspended, gravitation instead of rounding out both, carries them to the ground, and very materially interferes with their globular shape. Now, what this force would have done with the earth under like circumstances, is impossible to tell because our globe in a plastic or fluid state, was never so attached to the tip end of a leaf, or placed in such condition, as regards this element, as was the suspended dewdrop.

Again, it would appear evident that if gravitation exerted a controlling influence over this great accretion of material atoms composing the earth, which formed it into a globe, and if it controls the dewdrop, and forms that into a globe also, and the law is so universal as to reach the two extremes, then it ought likewise to form all accretions of fluid or plastic materials, into globes. But, this is by no means the case; for, in every instance where gravity exerts any control over fluid or plastic materials in any considerable quantities, upon this earth, it universally flattens them or gives them a plane upper surface.

Gravity is evidently but a puny, feeble arm of those universal Electro-Magnetic forces that pervade all nature, which is provided for the purpose of reaching out and conducting all ponderous bodies that are gross and inactive, and inclined to rest, to a place upon the bosom of the earth, where they may repose until acted upon by some other superior power. It simply acts in this subordinate capacity, and here may be found the limits of its influence. Gravity is no traveler, who rushes from planet to planet, and from world to world, drawing the heavenly bodies from their predestined courses, and forcing them onwards in their great journeys, but, on the contrary, he is a very quiet, stay-at-home old gentleman, who never ventures from his own domain, or travels off to reciprocate or change work with his far-off neighbors upon some distant orb. Philosophers have called upon the gravity belonging to the moon, to come to the earth, all that long journey, and do for us the very opposite thing that could be performed by the gravity attached to our planet, and they have endeavored to send our gravity out to the neighboring planets, and there make him perform services that he utterly refuses to do at home.

It is very plain that this power here upon the earth, does exert its influence over all substances that come under its control, in such a manner as to keep them still and quiet, it presses all things down to the earth, and expends its power in preventing any movement. It would hold the waters of the ocean as quiet and still as the night of death, if there was no other force to produce an agitation. It would hold all nature in solemn stillness and stagnation if there were no other power to make things move, and it cannot be denied by any intelligent man, that the only office which gravity performs, is to place all substances under its control where they may lie as quiet as possible, and that it holds them in their positions, with all the power in its possession. This power never exerted the least influence in raising or removing in a lateral direction any ponderable body, not even so much as the weight of a feather, or the most infinitesimal dust in the balance. But philosophers suppose they have succeeded in importing a gravity from the moon and the sun, that performs wonders in that respect. It not only in the opinion of some of the learned, provides the momentum that propels planets in their orbits, by operating in conjunction with other tangential forces, but by a reciprocal attraction, acts in a manner that confines them to their pathways, and holds with a steady arm, the whole machinery together. Not only this, but the gravity that comes to us, all the way from the moon, they say, reaches down the right arm of its power, and to a certain extent, drags the mighty waters from their ocean beds, and causes periodical tides from three to forty or fifty feet in height, according to conditions and circumstances. It is fortunate for their theory, that the moon has this quantity and quality of gravity to spare, for we certainly have not upon our earth, a sufficient quantity, nor any of the kind that can produce such wonderful results. Our gravity as we have said, is by no means a disturbing element, but would, were there no other forces superior, hold all moveable things in eternal quiet and repose.

Hence, the necessity of importing a peculiar quality of gravity from the moon, which has power to produce the disturbance and agitation in the waters of the mighty deep, and exert its influence in regulating the ocean tides.

Both Newton and Compte, the one a believer in God, and the other an Atheist, assumes that *vis* inertia, gravitation, and motion, are the three essential elements in the orbital movements of the planetary worlds; but the one supposed these fundamental properties, or states of matter, were under the control of a governing mind, or a supreme power and will; and that these causes were proximate, while the other could perceive no evidences of such a controlling power, and conceived all causes to be ultimate. The one was compelled to call upon the controlling influence, or governing mind to produce momentum, while the other involved all things, in the irremediable darkness of Atheism; each of these philosophers have their adherents and followers.

Dr. Dick, who says of the planets and their motions, "That the law of gravitation pervades and governs the whole," remarks that, "The laws of motion originally impressed upon all the bodies of the system, continue to operate as they have done from the beginning," and also, "That unless an immaterial power continually re-excited motion in the material universe, all motion would stop in a very short time, perhaps in less than an hour" and further represents that "A presiding Divinity is continually exerting his attributes, and impressing every part of that universe to which he gave existence." Prof. Hare, the great American philosopher and chemist, who though a confirmed skeptic, embraced late in life, Spiritualism, and wrote extensively upon the phenomena and philosophy, endorsed to the fullest extent, the views of Sir Isaac Newton, thus acknowledging, that gravitation was only a proximate cause, and that it was not by any means sufficient of itself to produce the movement of the heavenly bodies, and that it required continually from first to last, the eternal activities of a God behind this force, in order to enable it to produce the planetary movements, and continue the varied evolutions of the universal worlds.

While the system of Compte has the darkness of Atheism to contend with, in addition to its inefficiency, that of Newton requires the re-excitation of motion, or a special operation of Divine power to act upon that force which he had instituted to perform this part of his labor. This shows that he whom they denominate the Infinite architect, was unable to construct a self-moving machine, or one that would generate the requisite forces for its own propulsion, but, that he has left the machinery in that imperfect condition, in which it requires his constant and unremitting attention to keep it in motion, and that *vis* inertia, gravitation, and motion, are not sufficient, unaided by Infinite power, to move the worlds.

It is not a very difficult matter, here upon our earth, to find self-moving machines, that are able to generate the power within themselves, by which they perform locomotion. We find men and animals walking about the streets, and performing labors by virtue of powers that exist within them. We find also that men have constructed locomotive machines and engines that travel upon the land and the water, and they move in obedience to forces that are generated within themselves; they carry their own power with them, and do not depend upon extraneous forces. Can it be supposed that men bring to bear mechanical ability superior in this respect to that introduced in the construction of worlds, or use powers for propelling machinery contrived by them, of which the builders of this world had no idea, or do not all mechanical principles have their origin in the globe upon which they exist?

Again, can any mechanical forces be brought to bear in the construction of the animal organization, by which they perform locomotion, that was not perfectly understood, and which might not have been introduced in the structure of this globe for similar purposes. We may look around us where we please, and we shall find none of the numerous self-moving machines that are found everywhere upon the earth's surface, propelled by that force we call gravitation; for, on the contrary, that is the very power which all self-moving machines are compelled to overcome.

We think it will appear quite evident, that both Newton and Compte have signally failed in arriving at well founded conclusions concerning the forces that are brought to bear in producing the varied movements of the planetary bodies. The former, after all his philosophic deductions, and mathematical reasoning, only found proximate causes that were entirely unable, unless acted upon by Divine power to accomplish the desired result; while the latter taking a materialistic view of the subject, considers the same causes as ultimates, thus making an application of material forces in the movement of material objects, independent of any intelligent adjustment of the particles composing the objects moved, or direction of the forces brought into activity in the propulsion. The one seems quite as far from arriving at a solution of this great problem as the other. For we cannot conceive that an intelligence endowed with sufficient ability to build worlds, would undertake to propel them in their orbits by proximate or insufficient forces; neither can we conceive that worlds would build themselves, that the atoms of which they are composed, could be aggregated in an orderly manner, and that the forces by which they perform their movements, could be collected and applied independent of intelligent direction.

We think upon due reflection, it will be plain to every thinking mind, that the forces alluded to by these eminent philosophers, cannot by any possibility be productive of such grand results. How can the positive school of philosophers pretend that *vis* inertia, gravitation, and motion, are ultimate causes, when they are each one dependent upon gross matter for the simplest manifestation they ever produce.

Certainly, when we obtain forces which are able to exert a potential influence in the production, formation, and subsequent movement of a world, we shall be compelled to find those that may and do exist independently and previously, to the gross material of which the world is composed. We must find those forces that preceded in their activities, and rendered it possible that the so-called *ultimates* of the Compte school, could have an existence. *Vis* inertia, gravitation, and motion, are acknowledged alike by both schools, to be but states or conditions of matter; hence, being dependent upon matter for their manifestations, they must be subordinate in their character, and by no means, enumerated in the list of original causes, but in accordance with the Newtonian school they must be considered proximate or secondary. As, we plainly perceive, there can be no *vis* inertia, unless there are first gross particles of matter that lie still; until there are larger accretions for them to rest upon. Gravitation cannot exist until there is a mutual relationship established between two material bodies, one apparently exerting power over the other in consequence of superior size and density. Motion is evidently the positive of *vis* inertia, and being but a state or condition of matter, can only be produced by real, absolute elemental causes that exist independent of motion or matter.

In view of this reasoning it will be quite impossible that gravitation has had anything whatever to do in giving momentum, or in guiding and directing the orbital course of this or any other planet, or that it has exerted any very extensive influence in producing the form, or curving the outlines of this globe. But by a careful inspection as we have said, we shall doubtless find it comparatively an inconsiderable power, and that it only acts in the absence of those elementary forces which are entirely superior in their character. Gravitation is evidently confined in all its operations to the most inactive and gross matter, and is by no means a disturbing element, but, rather in every instance where it exerts entire control, produces quiescence and repose. Doubtless, if there was no other force upon our globe, superior to gravity, whether of that peculiar kind belonging to this world, or an article imported from some other planet, all things upon the earth would most surely rest in eternal stillness, and universal death would reign supreme.

When particles of material take their respective places in organized forms of life, either in the vegetable or animal world, if they were acted upon only by this force, they would, as a matter of course, descend to the bottom, and all forms would be built upon the principle of stratification, being far the largest at the base, and the tree or the animal would necessarily be formed with enormous roots or feet, in proportion to the upper parts of the structure. In fact, the vegetable and animal world would present little more than innumerable stratiform concretions, as all such organizations have been elaborated from materials in a fluid state. But, we ascertain forces entirely superior to gravitation, are actively engaged in arranging the molecules in the vegetable and animal organisms, and in placing them where they are severally required. There are systems of arterial and venous passage ways leading to the remote corners of the animal structure, and an apparatus for generating the positive and negative forces, that by an application of those propelling powers, the necessary fibrine and other materials may be transported through those avenues, to all the various parts, giving to each its portion in due season. There are also, channels of communication in all the different vegetable formations, from the tip of the roots to all the various twigs, through which the fluids are forced that form all portions of the structure, and the great power of this formidable element, gravitation, is set at defiance in all these varied processes.

It must be evident that superior forces do operate in the vegetable and animal economy, for the distribution af all molecular particles, in such an admirable manner regardless of the principles of gravitation, as we observe in the fully developed organized forms of life which are scattered in such profusion around us, upon the surface of this physical globe. There must then exist an abundant supply of those superior forces, and they must be a part and parcel of the earth upon which these organizations are found, and from which they are constantly drawing a supply of the necessary powers which they severally require, to aid in giving them their proper forms, and in sustaining their varied activities. Hence, it will be plain, that the physical globe must be the great reservoir, and contain the great fountain of those superior positive and negative forces that are the prominent producing cause of all organized forms and activities upon its surface; and if so, then it had an abundant supply of those forces to produce its own form, to round out its own curves, and finish its own beautiful architectural outlines, also, as well as to furnish it with all its varied activities; its movements, including its axial and orbital revolutions. The scientific world must soon become acquainted with the great fact, that it is the superior forces that control and move, attract and govern the heavenly bodies in all their evolutions. For this subordinate power, gravitation can have no more to do with the formation of globes, and with their various movements and revolutions, than it has to do with the formation of the lofty oak of the forest, or the wild horse that roams over the plains, or the great army that is marshalled by its generals and officers upon the field of battle, or with any other of the activities that exist upon our physical globe.

We have been taught in this work that all material aggregations and molecular organizations, had pre-existing spiritual forms, and those forms whether small or great, may contain within themselves, the spiritual forces that will place the material particles where they are required, and thus they assume by these forces, the dimensions and outlines of the original spiritual existences, whether it be a world, a dewdrop, or an animalcule beneath our vision. Each spiritual form has inherent within itself, the forces to attract the grosser materials by which it manifests itself to the material eyes of men; and the spiritual world while invisible, contained all the inherent forces that have attracted and placed in position all material particles of which it is composed, and it had these forces before gravity could reach it, for that element can only be found, where there are gross particles upon which it may act.

Now, let it be understood, that we do not propose to interfere in the least degree, with the very accurate and extended mathematical demonstrations of Newton, Kepler, Galileo, or any other philosopher; we only propose to show that those mathematical calculations, arrived at by such arduous labor, are applicable to other and higher forces that do exert a reciprocal influence between the heavenly bodies. That such a sympathetic cord exists between these orbs, that each one acts or reacts upon the others, no one can doubt; we only propose to show that those philosophers have mistook the power, and that it is Electro-Magnetic influence instead of gravitation, that produces this interchange of action between the different heavenly bodies in this system, and in the universe at large.

Cohesion, molecular attraction and gravitation seem to be different manifestations of the same force, and are all evidently designed to hold in place the material particles that superior forces have established in their several positions, and brought into close proximity; they all seem to act to this end and this alone, and beyond this single purpose, they evidently exercise no control. It would be impossible for us to say how far out into the regions of space, and beyond the confines of our earth, gravitation might extend its influence, and it is also impossible for any one to prove absolutely, that it does extend any influence beyond the limits of the atmosphere. For it must be conceded there is a limit somewhere, between this and the nearest planetary body, a boundary beyond which no material substance would be attracted to the earth, and we doubt very much whether this power extends beyond the limits of the fluid particles of air by which the earth is enveloped, but we leave this problem to be settled by some one in the future who can give it their attention.

If gravitation acts upon matter for the sole purpose of holding all things in their places, it follows that the largest body of matter would atract all things, within the circle of its influeuce, to itself, and that it would exert a power over smaller bodies in proportion to its size and density, and that this attraction would exist, regardless of its shape or formation. As we plainly discover, this power aided by cohesion and molecular attraction, would hold an aggregation of materials together in one form as well as another, and that it would act upon all substances on the surface, in a general direction, at right angles with the plane of such surface, without regard to the location of the substance acted upon, or what might be the particular form of the body exerting the attractive influence. We understand then, that there is no particular geometrical center of attraction with gravitation, any more than there is with cohesion, but that the force lies in the general direction of the largest accumulation of particles, as is proven by pendulum experiments in the vicinity of mountains. Hence, as far as this force is concerned, it makes no difference what the shape or form of the body may be, all substances that are upon its surface, will be held there with all its power, whether the body may be a solid globe, and have but an exterior superfice, or a spherical shell with both convex and concave surfaces.

All ponderable substances seem to be attracted to the nearest portion of the large body of matter, by an inherent power that exists in this increased accumulation of particles, evidently by positive and negative, affinities existing between the smaller and the greater, and wherever you may be upon the surface of a spherical shell, you are upon the upper side, so far as gravity is concerned, as much as you would be upon the exterior of a solid globe. In this case, the antipodes of those who dwell upon the exterior, would be the living organisms who inhabit a locality upon the interior or concave surface directly opposite. We need scarcely remark that the old Newtonian theory which taught that the grand central attracting point to which all things upon the earth must necessarily gravitate, was confined to the geometrical center of the globe, is gradually being superseded among very many scientific men; and the more common sense view that the power exists in, and is confined to the gross material particles of the globe and its appurtenances, as presented above, has been adopted in its place. We most assuredly can find nothing attached to the geometrical center of our globe, that should make it the central moving point from which this force should proceed, any more than there is to any other point in space.

We have learned then, from the preceding pages, that gravitation must necessarily be an element that permeates all ponderable bodies or material particles, and as a fluid element, it must be of the most sluggish character, nearly destitute of activities, or of any power that will produce motion, except in a single direction, which motion seems to be only designed to ultimate in *vis* inertia, or entire cessation of the activities super-induced by the conditions of two ponderable bodies of vastly different dimensions. It would appear further that the element which seems to act upon the smaller body of matter, causing its fall directly to the large one or to the earth, must exist reciprocally in the smaller body also, so that we may, with similar propriety, call this force the propulsion of gravitation, as well as the attraction of that element.

The real forces, *vis* inertia or gravitation, evidently cannot be confined to the particles attached to the earth by cohesion, but they must exist equally in those substances which are detached and separate, and which seem to be attracted with such power. They must exist conspicuously in the ponderous material that presses itself with such power upon the bosom of its mother, as well as in the mother herself, hence, we are compelled to conclude that "attraction of gravitation" is to a certain extent a misnomer. For we perceive if this power was not reciprocal, but confined in its operations to the body of the globe, distinct from all detached particles, it would, of course, act extraneously upon those particles, and independently of their conditions, and the question would then arise concerning the charactor or quality of those bodies that would first become subjected to an extraneous force.

Accept the hypothesis of distinctive attraction, and we shall, no doubt, be compelled to conclude, that it would, like the wind, exercise the strongest control over the lighter, more buoyant fluid particles; and that these together with every mote that occupies a place within the circle of its influence, would be attracted directly to the earth's surface, and nothing of that character could rise above its immediate contact. So we discover if the attractive force was in the earth alone, it would exercise no more authority over a leaden bullet, than it would over a piece of cork, or any other material of the same dimensions, because the force exerted would not depend upon the conditions of the matter acted upon, as the power exists in the earth, and outside the material particles which are attracted, and in that case, all substances of the same dimensions, would have the same weight.

But we discover that all substances do not have the same density and proportionate weight, and that the power of gravity is to a great extent, dependent upon the character and condition of the substances over which it exerts its control; hence, we see clearly that this elemental power must also exist within those substances, and that it is a propelling as well as an attracting force. But as such, it is so nearly allied to inertia or entire inactivity, that it only propels in a single rectilinear direction towards the point where rest can soonest be obtained, where it lays its heavy hand on all substances under its control, and there it would hold them forever, unless some extrinsic force superior to itself, should remove them from their position. Hence, it will be clear, since gravity is not a distinctive force, existing in the cohered body of the earth exclusively, attracting all things to itself, but a force found in all substances subject to its control, in accordance with the peculiar properties and conditions of their particles, that there may be a great variety of substances and fluid particles of such a character as to be entirely beyond the control of this elemental power. This could not be the case if it was an absolue attractive force, and existed exclusively in the great body of the earth.

There is now, no difficulty in discerning why refined material particles, or the so-called imponderables, are not acted upon by this element, as, although they are composed of material atoms, they are of too sublimated a nature to be seized upon by this subordinate power.

The atmospheric particles, although an entire column is said to have a weight of fifteen pounds to the square inch, set at defiance this marvelous power, rise above its influences, and impart their weight or pressure laterally or upwards with the same force they do downwards, or towards the earth. Place the hand upon an aperture in the bottom of an exhausted receiver and the pressure would be the same as if upon the top, proving that gravity has not the least control over the fluid atoms of this combination of nitrogen and oxygen. The atmosphere not only exists independently, and operates regardless of this element, but it enables a variety of other material substances to do the same thing, by giving them a resting place within its bosom, holding them in its own arms in defiance of this power that is said to move worlds in their orbits, and guide them in their predestined courses. Thus, we see the particles of smoke and flame ascending upwards with impunity, and the fleecy clouds lazily floating in the sunshine, or rushing to and fro in the gathering storm, all manifesting perfect indifference to this power, and not so much as saying, By your leave, Friend Gravity. It can hardly be doubted, that aerial navigation is a fixed fact, that must transpire, and be utilized in the future, and perhaps at no distant day. This certainly cannot ultimate, if gravitation exerts the all-potent influence represented by the old school of philosophers, for powers which they have placed in this element, can by no means be overcome by any mechanical contrivance that human ingenuity can invent.

It will be observed that an extraneous force that acts upon ponderable bodies upon the earth's surface, always exerts its strongest influences upon those which have least density, or that are least controlled by the force of gravity, hence, the winds always affect and remove the lightest and most refined substances first, and then others of greater density and weight, as its powers increase, and gravity would quite likely do the same if it was an extrinsic force, existing entirely outside the substances acted upon.

Our philosophers as we have remarked, have long supposed that lunar and solar gravity have exerted a wondrous influence over the fluid particles of the waters contained in the ocean, and this power must, of course, have been exerted in direct opposition to a similar force existing upon the earth. Hence, the gravitating forces they import from the sun and moon, must come into immediate antagonism with the same forces that properly belong to the earth, and it would appear that our little neighbor, the moon, has entirely the best of it in the conflict. There would seem, however, to be much doubt whether the moon has a sufficiency of this elemental force to send out and compete so successfully with those powers that exist upon our own planet, and if our exposition of this matter, is in the least degree correct, then the old established theory concerning tidal phenomena, must be materially modified, if not entirely superseded, and one more in accordance with the harmonies of nature built upon its ruins.

La Place, the great French mathematician and astronomer, pronounced it one of the most difficult problems in the whole range of celestial mechanics. So we perceive that the present theory concerning tides, is by no means well established in the minds of eminent philosophers, and doubtless, when the subject is carefully and critically examined by scientific minds that shall rise up in the future, it will be found to present a very clumsy and ill-shapen appearance. The moon is said to exert an attracting influence over the waters of the ocean that compares with the same influence exerted by the sun, as three to one. Notwithstanding the sun is supposed to exert a controlling attractive power over the whole planetary system, embracing the primaries and all the secondaries, which holds them in their orbits and imparts continuous tangential forces to the entire machine; yet somehow our philosophers have given this little satellite an attractive force on our tides, three times as great as the central sun which, they say exercises such supreme authority in that respect over the whole system.

This superior influence exerted by the moon as regards the tidal phenomena is supposed to depend upon its proximity to the earth, being so much nearer than the sun or any other planet; hence, the duty of presiding over, and to a very great extent regulating the tides, has been assigned to this little satellite.

However, it must be admitted that the moon is not quite so near the waters of the ocean as the earth itself, and whatever power of this character it has to spare, must travel out from home 240,000 miles, before it can come in contact with those bodies of water situated upon our globe. Now the earth, being about fifty times larger than the moon, and supposed to be possessed of gravitating power somewhat in proportion to its size, and proximity to the waters of the oceans, that rest upon its bosom, it would become absolutely necessary that this force coming from the moon, should neutralize all the corresponding power existing upon the earth, before it could exert its influence in producing the phenomena of the tides in any such manner. If the earth and the moon unite together in producing phenomena upon either of their surfaces, they must do it by some power that can be mutually interchanged, and not by forces that would directly antagonize. And unless the moon is in possession of a superior article of gravity that is fifty times more forcible and efficient than our own, it would be perfectly impossible for our little neighbor to produce the ocean tides by gravitating attraction.

The moon is said to be 39,000 times nearer the earth than the sun, yet the sun is 70,000,000 times greater than the moon, and of course, would exert a proportionately greater attractive influence, and it will be seen at a glance, without a resort to figures, that the difference in distance could not give the little satellite such a preponderating attractive power, and enable it to exert a force so much greater than the sun over the waters existing upon the earth. Again, if the moon exerts this predominating influence over the waters, three times greater than the sun, why does not the same influence prevail upon the land, and why does not the moon assume a proportionate authority in defiance of the sun's power which seems to control not only the earth's movements, but the moon's also, as well as all other planetary bodies?

It would seem very unnatural to suppose, that there was a simple force of gravity in our little moon, that operated to such an extent upon the watery element of our globe, when that same force cannot be discovered as operating in any other department of nature. Again, if this force of gravity existing in the moon, really produces such sensible influences upon our oceans, what would be the influence that the gravitating force going out from the earth, would produce upon the waters of the moon? For, as the earth is nearly fifty times larger than the moon, and the gravity of that orb raises our tides quite generally six to eight feet, then the gravity of the earth which is so many times larger, acting upon that planet, would raise her tides proportionately higher, or from three to four hundred feet, thus destroying all possibility of living contiguous to the water, or building maritime cities when that planet comes to be inhabited.

We are forced to the conclusion, in viewing this matter in its various aspects, that the established theory in relation to tidal phenomena, is a dynamical error, and that they are not produced by any such cause, but by forces that are entirely superior to gravitation, and that in this as well as in so many other departments of nature, the great positive and negative forces have been called into activity to produce these, as well as a great variety of results that have been ascribed to subordinate causes.

Fire and gravity, as it would appear for some time in the past, have been common pack horses upon which our savans have piled all sorts of burdens, until these jaded animals are entirely overloaded, and although they are excellent in their particular sphere, they serve no good purpose, when called upon to carry loads they are entirely unable to bear, and to traverse those realms in which they do not properly belong. If they desired to run the entire machinery of a solar system, and prevent the numerous planetary bodies from deviating from their predestined orbits, they have called into requisition this feeble, puny force, and delegated it to perform all this wondrous labor, and a power that only wishes to be still, they have kept running hither and thither through the universe, accomplishing the most astonishing feats, during all the ages of the past, and would impose upon him still greater labors in the ages to come.

Fire has also been called into requisition by the philosophers of a later period, and placed in a very conspicuous position, and made to perform most astonishing labors in the construction of worlds; so much so, that the present most popular theory concerning the formation of the physical globe, is termed the igneous or fire theory. These savans have managed somehow to keep those raging fires burning, from the very earliest periods of even the sun's history, without any abatement or cessation, and they tell us it is now raging with inconceivable fury in the bowels of our own earth and within all the planets, and, in accordance with their ideas, it seems likely to continue burning on forever. They conclude by computation that this fire occupies more than thirty-five out of thirty-six parts of this globe, and in some inexplicable manner, they have been enabled to keep this positive element in active operation, without furnishing one particle of combustible material to replenish its exhausted resources. This we must admit is the most astounding feat that philosophy has ever performed in the whole range of celestial and terrestrial mechanics, if it has been successfully accomplished.

There is, without a shadow of doubt, some sympathizing power in this universe which acts reciprocally among the different planets of our solar system, which power performs all, and perhaps still more in regulating their movements, than philosophers have ascribed to gravitation. Great and important duties are evidently to be performed in this department of nature's realms;

duties of the most stupendous character; and hence, forces must necessarily be brought to bear, that are commensurate with the magnitude of the labors. If we should take a complete survey of the extensive and complicated machinery of the broad universe, we should, perhaps, find no department that would require more exalted physical powers than must be applied in giving momentum, and in regulating the axial and orbital revolutions of the several planetary bodies. If we can find in our researches any one physical force that is superior to others, that, certainly, must be the one which would be called into requisition in the performance of such super-eminently arduous labors.

If gravitation is the most exalted element that can be found, if it exerts a dominating influence over all other physical forces that have an existence, if it stands supreme at the very summit of all the various powers in nature, then, this must be the field for its most sublime operations; for certainly the human mind is incapable of contemplating a more important position in which any such power can be placed.

But, if we should ascertain that there were other superior forces over which gravity exerts no control, and compared with which it sinks into insignificance, and is but a puny infant beside a stalwart giant, then let this feeble power at once and forever stand aside, giving place to the great positive and negative elements, Electro-Magnetism. We have here, powers abundantly competent to enter the arena, and perform all the astounding duties required at their hands; for, if the worlds cannot be moved by these tremendous forces, it will be in vain to look for others of lesser magnitude to accomplish the mighty achievement.

When the mind contemplates the great fact that all the stupendous globes in our planetary system, are moving in their respective orbits with a tremendous rapidity, ranging from 250 to something over 1,800 miles per minute, the one being the velocityof Uranus and the other of Mercury, and, that Jupiter, which is over 1,400 times larger than the earth, travels at the astonishing rate of 500 miles per minute, we may well conclude that no secondary forces can perform all this immense labor. We shall perceive, also, this power must be positive and absolute, and have its existence entirely independent of the huge masses of matter placed under its control. If we find *vis* inertia, gravitation and motion, to be simply effects produced by original caus es, and dependent upon those causes for existence, we shall, of course, find them entirely incapable of acting in this capacity, because they are secondary, and negative to those more exalted powers that must be called into requisition in the performance of the most wonderful labors that can take place in the physical universe.

It will be observed as a principle in the realms of nature, that all positive forces when applied to the performance of labor, are continually exhausting their own resources, and need constantly to be recuperated, and this must be true, whether we bring power to bear to propel a steamship, a manufactory, or a world. The forces applied must be unfailingly replenished, or the movement of the machinery will be suspended, and we may rest assured, if there was no method of continually generating the forces requisite to move the worlds in their orbits, they would cease their motions as readily as the steamboat or the mill.

Now we trust the reader will discover that each one of these globes must be a locomotive machine, and generate its own forces within itself, independently of all the others, and that these forces when so generated, are disposed in a manner that will guide and direct them all in their predestined orbits. Most certainly, there can be no more propriety in supposing extrinsic force is brought to bear in propelling worlds in their orbits, than there is in driving the locomotive across the plains, or the majestic steamer across the ocean. For we must admit that the power and wisdom that could project, and produce worlds and set them in motion, must have been competent to have made an application of the required forces necessary for their propulsion, as easily as the builder of the steamship or locomotive; and further, we discover that these forces, being exhaustive of their own energies, must be generated in a somewhat analogous manner.

We trust the reader will, by a perusal of the preceding pages, be comfirmed in some important principles that seem to occupy a conspicuous place in the natural realms, and which have apparently been overlooked by very many men of scientific attainments.

First. All forces that are brought to bear in the performance of their labors in the various departments of nature, must have been called into requisition, and applied by a power and wisdom entirely sufficient to control and regulate the forces so applied.

Secondly. All forces are either positive or negative, male or female, and they must act in conjunction before they can produce important results, or accomplish the purpose designed, as vapor must be combined with caloric in order to become a power.

Thirdly. All positive, active forces are exhaustive of their own resources when in activity, hence, they must be constantly generated and replenished, or their effects will cease to be produced.

Fourthly. All negative elements are perfectly inactive, and only manifest inertness, unless combined with the positive, so that the fluid particles of electricity, *per se*, are as quiet and harmless as so many particles of oxygen or Indian meal.

Fifthly. The so-called physical forces are but etherealized fluid particles, eliminated from the grosser material, and their power over gross matter, depends upon their degree of fineness or etherealization.

Sixthly. There is no line of demarcation that can be found that divides so-called spiritual essences from gross material, so that we cannot say with propriety, this is matter exclusive of spirit, or that is spirit exclusive of matter.

Seventhly. Each one of the natural forces must act in their own particular department, and they must be commensurate with the magnitude of the duties they are called upon to perform; hence, the most stupendous labors must require the most exalted powers.

It will now be discovered in view of these several conclusions that the different planets must be in possession, independently of the various forces that are requisite in the performance of their several evolutions, and that the forces are so disposed as to be constantly replenished by suitable apparatus, quite analogous to the forces in the animal economy, by which they are enabled to perform their allotted functions.

It will also be plain that where we can find forces upon a planet entirely sufficient to give it the power of locomotion, there will be no trouble in finding those that may produce and regulate the tides, for certainly the periodical ebb and flow of the tides are trifling matters compared with the revolutions of mighty worlds in their orbits, with a velocity that almost bewilders the human mind in its contemplation. We will refer to these subjects again, in another connection.

CHAP. VIII.

THE SUN AND ITS INFLUENCES.

The sun's influences appear to be so intimately connected with much that appertains to our earth, and is withal so conspicuous an object in our planetary system, that it seems almost a duty, to pay our humble respects to this majestic orb of day in something more than a passing notice. By so doing, we may possibly make some discoveries, and obtain a clearer view of the nature of the powers and influences, we are daily receiving from his bounteous store house. There seems to be a direct and intimate relationship existing between this great ruling monarch of light, and very much of the varied phenomena that are found upon the surface of the world we inhabit. It has been thought by many learned men, that the sun was not only the bountiful dispenser of all the light and heat we enjoy upon the earth, but that it also furnishes the motive power by which we are propelled in our great annual revolutions, and it is no marvel that this conspicuous member which seems to occupy so important a position in the planetary family that constitutes our solar system, should have received such marked attention from the learned and the unlearned of the different ages of the world.

When we contemplate the ineffable glory and majesty of this King of day, as he seems to rise upon us from his gilded couch in the eastern horizon, and, as it were, sitting in his resplendent chariot of fire, pursues his continuous journeys through the heavens, dispensing light and life, and innumerable blessings to all who behold his brightness, we can but wonder with increasing astonishment; and we must reverence and adore those powers that have been competent to produce such incomprehensible results.

We can hardly look upon it as sacrilege or idolatry, in the Aztec or Persian, who bowed down in solemn reverence, and offered their most fervent devotions to this luminary as their highest conception of a God. Very many of our predecessors have looked upon his smiling countenance, and endeavored to gain admittance to his audience chamber, and to learn from himself his own story concerning the eternal laws by which he is governed, and the principles and attributes that appertain to his organization. They wish also to learn the means by which he extends this wide spread profusion of blessings, over such a vast domain, giving to each of his dependents a portion in due season, sufficient to supply their necessities, and how and where he can store away such a wondrous treasure of genial magnetic light, and calorific influences that reach out to inconceivable distances, distributing life and animation and vigor throughout the numerous revolving worlds.

If others have prosecuted their inquiries to such an extent, established theories, arrived at conclusions, and published their opinions to the world, why may not we institute some inquiries also; for we are persuaded the harvest of truth has not all been gleaned, concerning that monarch of our solar system, with whom we have been so familiar during our entire lives.

It is more than probable that our philosophers and scientific men are somewhat at fault concerning this whole subject of solar influences, although so many learned essays have been written explanatory of their phenomena; and so much time and attention have been expended by very many eminent persons in its consideration. We are told that the sun is the source of light and heat, and that somehow from this great fountain, those necessary elements come to our earth; and some of the learned men of a rather modern age, have adopted the so-called corpuscular or emanating theory, which teaches that light consists of extremely minute particles of a fluid essence, that are thrown off from all luminous bodies, and which travel the whole distance between such a body and the eye in a very brief space of time. That these particles upon their arrival, may strike or impinge upon the retina of that organ, and produce the sensation of light, just as particles thrown from an odoriferous substance come in contact with the organs of smell. This was the theory, adopted by Newton and most British philosophers. But others have conceived a different idea, and hold the so-called undulating theory, and assume that all of space is filled with an exceedingly subtile imponderable medium, known as ether. So, that a luminous body, millions of miles distant, somehow produces activity in this great mass of ether, causing minute waves or undulations, that pass out into the realms of space, like the surface of a pond rippled by throwing in a stone. These waves, they say, are transmitted with inconceivable rapidity till they reach the eye, strike the sensitive membrane or retina, and produce the phenomenon of vision.

This theory is said to explain many of the phenomena of optics, and is now quite generally received. However, we modestly express an opinion that both these theories are liable to objections, and that in the ages of the future they must be superseded by more harmonious views, that will have a broader scope, and admit of being extended, out into the distant realms of the universe, or at least into the exterior portions of our own solar system. It is much to be feared that, when we undertake to supply the inhabitants of Uranus or Neptune with light and warmth, upon the principles adopted by either of the theories presented, we shall meet with an entire failure, for, it cannot be presumed that either the solar particles, or the undulations of ether can reach those distant planets with sufficient force to produce any beneficial results. As it is a well understood fact, that one of the properties of light, is to diminish its intensity in proportion to the square of the distance from the luminous body.

As Uranus is nineteen times farther from the sun than the earth, and the square of nineteen being three hundred and sixty-one, that planet can only receive about 1-360 part of the solar influence enjoyed by the inhabitants of the earth, and Neptune whose orbit is 3,000,000,000 miles distant from the sun, can only obtain 1-1,000 part of the light and heat from the great fountain in the center, that is vouchsafed to our own planet. Thus, we discover, that although, these theories might answer very well if we had one world only, but like some of the doctrines of the theologians, for instance, the vicarious atonement, they become extremely frivolous and are entirely inadequate, even, if we barely take into consideration the existence of our own solar system. They, by no means, meet the wants, neither can they be applied to the circumstances of the exterior planets that are revolving around our great central luminary in their wide extended orbits. Philosophers and theologians will, doubtless, at some time, learn to take a more enlarged view of the natural realms, and adopt theories that will prove to be of more universal application.

Our little world, though it may seem large and stupendous to us, is but a very diminutive portion of the great macrocosm, and any universal law that controls either matter or spirit upon this comparatively inconsiderable globe, must be applicable to, and in harmony with all laws and principles existing in, and governing every other globe in all portions of the universal domain, where suns and planets, or visual orbs to behold them, can possibly have an existence. Therefore, it is useless, and worse than idle, to devote our time and labor in the elaboration of theories which will not harmonize with principles that are of universal application, and that are adequate to extend out, and contemplate the existence, not only of worlds, but of systems of worlds unnumbered, all moving in their ample rounds, and composing one harmonious whole.

One of the objections to the first named theory, is, that, the process of continuously throwing off fluid particles, would certainly prove exhaustive of the resources of the great fountain of light, for particles are something, and no matter how large the reservoir, this continuous extracting something from its contents, and sending it away not to return, would finally drain the fountain to the very bottom; and the great luminary would disappear, having distributed itself among the different planets and satellites. And they, after receiving all these elements, would be able to furnish from this source, their own light and heat independently. The sun is said to be more than five hundred times as large as all the planets of our solar system, we shall then readily perceive that he need throw off and send to those planets but a very small part of his fluid particles of light, before they would all be supplied with a sufficiency of those elements, to enable them to set up for themselves, and in this respect to do business upon their own account, for, most certainly, such particles, sent out by a luminous body, could not be lost, but must remain somewhere in the broad realms forever. So we are compelled to conclude that these fluid particles cannot be arriving in such extensive quantities from that source.

Again, if those particles are coming to us in that manner, as emanations from the central sun, they would necessarily proceed in all directions from that luminous body, and consequently fill the immensity of space, just as far as the influence of that luminary extends. Hence, to the farthest limits of these fluid particles, or emanations, light would necessarily exist, and there would be no darkness, even in the immediate shadows of the several planets and their satellites; as we perceive in this case, all would be light in the regions of space wherever the emanations of light could penetrate. But, on the contrary, we find all is coldness and darkness beyond the earth's atmosphere, and it is not known that the sun exerts any influence whatever in this respect, beyond the atmospheric envelopes of the several planetary bodies.

It seems to be well understood, that all the light and heat existing in the great universe is found contiguous to the heavenly bodies, and within the boundaries of the atmospheric particles that surround them. So we perceive, that the light we obtain, depends entirely upon conditions attached to our own globe, and unless these conditions are favorable, a thousand luminaries would be of no avail. We perceive clearly, if all of the regions of space around our globe, except the funnel shaped shadow of the earth, were enjoying the full blaze of daylight, then there could be no such thing as darkness within the limits of the shadow, and no such thing as night could prevail at any time. For the overwhelming amount of light existing upon all sides of the umbra or conical shadow, would penetrate its borders at every point, and entirely overcome any considerable influence arising from the absence of the illuminating body. Again, we should at any time be able to look out laterally from the shadow, into the broad light enjoyed beyond. So take what view of this matter we please, we shall discover that light as well as heat, the two elements that are so intimately connected, only exist in appreciable quantities within the limits of the atmosphere of our planet, and any other of those bodies where their benefits are enjoyed. The supply can only extend to those portions of the great universe, where such elements are required. As there would be no more necessity and propriety in manufacturing light sufficient to fill the broad realms of all space, than there would be for the citizens of any single town to procure a supply, sufficient to light an entire state or extended district of country. Men are usually smart enough to understand that it would be time and means thrown away, to manufacture a thousand times more light than would be required for their own use; and, we must conclude that all the light that ever did exist in any portion of the universe, has by some process been manufactured. We need not suppose, therefore, that those powers who are competent to manage the affairs of nature's great laboratory, and produce the light of which we enjoy such a bountiful supply, are any more reckless and improvident, or less shrewd than men dwelling upon the earth, and it would be impossible for any intelligent mind to discover the utility or necessity for lighting up the boundless regions of space. In relation to many features of the undulating theory which is generally received by the philosophers of the present period, we are compelled to notice some serious difficulties, and, perhaps, fatal objections; and we feel almost to regret that we are obliged to deviate so far from the beaten path which has been traveled by men of science. It certainly would be far easier to adopt their ideas and copy their opinions, than to establish theories of our own, and send them out before the world, to run the gauntlet of public investigation, if they should even be deemed worthy of notice.

But we are persuaded that new ideas must be presented, and new theories must arise, in relation to most of the subjects that have received the attention of men, and those that have the temerity to present them, must probably become the targets, against which the shafts of conservatism will be hurled, and, perhaps, we having no well-earned reputation to lose, can stand up against them as well as any of our fellows.

We may notice that this vibratory theory assumes the fact, that there exists out in the realms of space, everywhere, minute particles of fluid ether, that like water, are sufficiently compact to be influenced by waves of motion, and they assume also, that all luminous bodies are in constant agitation, or vibratory activity, and these bodies communicate inconceivably rapid waves of motion to this universal mass of fluid particles they call space ether, and those waves continue constantly to arrive within our atmosphere, and by the excessive rapidity of their motions, penetrate the eye, and impinge upon the retina, thus producing the sensation of light.

We venture to remark in relation to this space ether,

or mass of fluid atoms, sufficiently dense to admit of continuous uninterrupted waves of motion throughout the regions of space, that its existence is a bare assumption unsupported by any substantial evidence. There may be vibratory undulations of light within the limits of our atmosphere, and doubtless, philosophers have arrived at very correct conclusions, by numerous delicate experiments and observations, concerning many of their phenomena; but, that there is a fluid ether existing in all the realms of space, sufficiently dense to serve as a medium for the continuance of these undulations, from the great central luminary to the remote portions of our solar system, is a mere hypothesis, and still remains to be proven. Of course, it cannot be fully established that light comes to us in any such manner, unless the medium upon which it is said to be transmitted, is known to exist. Then both these positions become mere visionary speculations, and we trust we shall find both, upon careful examination, to be as false in fact as they are unsound in philosophy.

Now suppose there may be space ether, existing sufficiently dense to admit of uninterrupted waves of motion, of what could it be composed? most assuredly, of material particles; and they must be in close proximity in order to carry the vibrations, and we should discover that in order to have the vibration come directly from the luminous body, the great mass of fluid material atoms must lie in repose, or in an undisturbed condition. For, were we to cast a stone into a great lake, and should the ripples pass out from that center of activity, they would be liable to be overcome or absorbed in their passage, by any greater disturbance in the waters, as, a steamboat might intercept these retreating waves, and entirely arrest their progress, by absorbing all their undulations into the more violent agitations that would necessarily be caused by its revolving wheels. We think by examining the matter carefully, we shall find that similar disturbances must exist in this vast, universal body of space ether, which our philosophers have imagined, was placed between us and the sun, as well as throughout all space. We see very clearly, that in consequence of the several motions of the heavenly bodies, disturbances would naturally arise, which must effectually destroy all continuous vibratory motion.

For instance, our earth has an axial motion of over one thousand miles per hour, and she carries with her a certain portion of this space ether, while the remaining contiguous portions are stationary; and wherever this moving orb of material particles comes in contact with the concave mass that is stationary, there must be a terrible grinding and clashing; not only that, but a disturbing agitation that would entirely cut off and absorb any wave motions coming from the great luminous body in the center. Thus we see, in this case, there must be an immense globe of this space ether, containing the earth with its atmosphere in the center, presenting an exterior convex surface, which globe is rolling upon its axis in the midst of this great mass of ether, in direct contact with a concave surface.

The reader will now discover, that at the point of contiguity, where these two surfaces must necessarily collide, a most violent agitation would naturally result, entirely sufficient to prevent any continuity of vibratory motion, arriving from a distant planet. Again, there is another still more rapid motion of the earth, said to be 68,000 miles per hour in its orbit, that carries the moon with it, and must embrace all of this ether within, and perhaps for a great distance beyond the moon's orbit. This would give us a globe, of at least 500,000 miles in diameter, rushing through the entire mass of fluid space ether, with such tremendous velocity, tearing asunder those particles, and rendering uninterrupted vibratory movements utterly impossible, at the point of intersection between the moving and stationary fluid.

When we contemplate the fact, that science and philosophy have set in motion such a prodigious ball of space ether, of a density and compactness sufficient to communicate waves of motion from the sun to the earth, and that this immense globe is rushing through an unlimited field of similar fluid particles of the same density, with such a tremendous velocity, the mind is filled with astonishment. And, when we take into consideration the terrible agitation that must ensue throughout that immense region, where the convex surface of this moving body comes in contiguity with the concave surface of the stationary mass, we are still more astounded. But when we learn that scientific men have attempted to bridge this awful chasm of agitated and disturbed fluid particles, and convey the most delicate waves of motion or vibration from the stationary to the moving mass, we can but wonder at their stupidity.

Again, the sun has an axial motion which is said to be over 4,500 miles per hour, and it must carry with it a certain portion of this space ether, and hence, there must be another chasm of disturbed fluid element to bridge over, lying between that moving mass and the great stationary body. It is a very grave question whether nature could stand any such terrible agitations as would necessarily be produced by the incessant grindings and clashings of such vast bodies of fluid ether, moving with a rapidity so prodigious, and making their way through the midst of stationary fluid atoms, of a density sufficient to convey undulating vibrations, for so many millions of miles. However, it must certainly appear conclusive to the most careless observer, that no such undulations can pass any of the lines of intersection, or chasms that occur between the moving and stationary particles, and as a sequence, light can by no means, be communicated from the sun to our earth, or any other planet in accordance with this absurd hypothesis.

It will be distinctly understood that we have no quarrel with the undulatory theory, if confined within the limits of our atmosphere. Our objections lie against the mode of communicating the vibrations from the sun to the limits of the atmosphere. Against the filling up the vast hiatus, with an imaginary space ether as a medium upon which to convey an imaginary motion or vibration, that by no means comes to us all that long distance. There is little difficulty for those who devote their time and attention to the science of optics, to frame an hypothesis which will afford a mechanical explanation of the various phenomena of light, as it exists upon the earth, because more hypotheses than one have been imagined by which most of the phenomena can be explained. Still, notwithstanding all the splendid discoveries that have been made, the true theory of light as regards its connection with the sun, and its communication to the planetary world, no doubt, remains a problem yet to be solved by scientific minds upon the earth.

It is quite evident, that if we adopt a theory, it must be one sufficiently broad in its scope to reach out and embrace all the planetary bodies in the system, for in their different conditions, one might require to be furnished with the needed light in a very different manner from the others. If the planets were all equi-distant from the sun, and all of the same age, and in the same condition of development, then one mode of manufacture and distribution of light and heat, would be all that could possibly be required. But the various planets are scattered throughout an immense region of space, from Mercury whose orbit is only about 37,000,000 to the far distant Neptune who maintains the respectful distance of 3,000,000,000 miles from the great central or apparent source of all light.

We perceive all these different planets must be of various ages and conditions of development, and it follows that there must be various modes of manufacture and distribution of their needed light, to correspond with their very different conditions and distances from the sun. We also very clearly see, that the same plan of distribution which would give the earth just the required amount of light and heat, would furnish Mars too little, and Venus entirely too much; and it would scorch poor Mercury to a cinder, while it would leave the outer planets in the cold embrace of eternal frost, and their icy domains would contain little but sleep and death. Hence, the requisite amount must depend to a very great extent upon the condition of the different planets themselves.

We think the reader will here recognize the great fact, that all worlds must be constructed in perfect accordance with universal laws and principles, and that each one possesses inherent within itself, all powers, and all properties of every other planet, and the grand difference in that respect, is that one is older and more advanced and developed than the other. How came our sun in possession of such a vast amount of light and heat giving influences, and the moon so destitute of both, while our earth in this respect is evidently in a condition between the two? Why should the supreme architect and governor of this solar system permit the exterior planets to travel so far beyond the reach of the sun's warming and lighting influence, unless means were provided to give them what they required, to a very great extent independent of him, and by influences inherent in themselves?

When we fall back upon the development theory, all these difficulties receive a harmonious explanation; and what other theory but that of progressive development, can be introduced into the constitution of worlds and systems of worlds, if that principle exists in all organized living forms that are found upon their surface, and is inherited directly from the physical globe upon which they have their being? There is no species of the vegetable or animal kingdom that is introduced into the world in a state of maturity, but all forms come into existence in an extremely infantile condition, and very gradually attain growth and the development of their inherent powers. It is safe to conclude that these forms of life could not possess such physical attributes, unless they receive them from the earth they inhabit, as that is the great mother from whence they draw physically all that exists within them, and the earth they inhabit could not impart those principles of growth and development to her children, unless she first had them to spare.

Hence, we find that all globes must have commenced their career in a feeble, infantile condition, as regards light and heat, very gradually developing out of that condition to a more advanced state, and hence it is, that all globes or planets in all their several situations are receiving just the amount they need, and no more than will correspond with their several circumstances. Thus, we shall very evidently find that the inherent elements upon the planet Mercury are in a condition to receive just the amount of solar influence required by that body and so of all the others wherever they may happen to be located. It cannot be supposed that all things are burning up that are found upon the surface of Mercury, and yet she is in a position to receive seven times the amount of solar influence that comes to the earth.

Then we must conclude that the development of her inherent powers are such as to modify their solar influences, and consequently afford her the needed amount in her present condition, and so of the moon which revolves around the earth. For certainly, if the moon is in the same condition of the earth, she ought to receive the same amount of solar influence, and instead of presenting the pale, cold, electric appearance upon its face, it would exhibit that more ruddy glow, and those warmer tints that seem attached to more advanced heavenly bodies. We must consider it idle and unphilosophical to suppose, that new influences are arriving upon the earth from the great central orb, soon after he presents his shining face upon each and every morning, either in the shape of emanating fluid particles, or undulating waves of motion; for we can be assured that all of solar influences which we enjoy, have been within the boundaries of our atmosphere, from the earliest period of this mundane existence. This positive power has spread itself over one-half the surface of our globe in one broad mantle, and it has never been withdrawn for a single moment, since the morning stars sang together at its birth, and the sons of God shouted forth their welcome exultations over a new born world.

The magnetic positive life giving powers of the great luminary, have been permeating the more negative electric elements upon the surface of our earth, and the rest of this planetary family, impregnating the fluid particles existing within their several atmospheres with energy and activity, in accordance with their developed capabilities of receiving and appropriating these influences. The great mantle of positive power that envelopes the one-half of the globe, must remain stationary, and only changes its position relatively to the earth, which rolling upon its axis once in twenty-four hours, brings nearly every portion of its superfice directly under the influence of this positive mantle; for about one-half the time, while the other half is turned away, and is consequently in a more negative, inactive condition. All worlds that have axial revolutions, and that are under, and receiving solar influences, must experience an equal amount of the positive and negative forces during each revolution.

Thus we have alternations of day and night, or light

and darkness, or a positive and negative condition of the elements by which the surface of our globe is enveloped, and the positive or active condition of the superficial or more refined elements which are found contiguous to it, are evidently engendered by an Electro-Magnetic battery, the positive pole of which, is formed by the exceedingly magnetic activities existing upon the sun's surface and the negative in the more electrical inactive elements upon the earth.

This highly magnetic and positively spiritualized luminous body which exists in the center of our system, has evidently come up to this largely developed condition, from the lowest negative electrical state, passing through all the intermediate changes like all other suns in the vast firmament, in order that they may take their respective places in the center of their own systems, and dispense to their dependents, the bounteous gifts which all have received in their turn.

We have already noticed that the material of which worlds are composed, in its primeval condition, must necessarily be of the most inactive character; and hence, that all worlds in their early condition, are preponderatingly negative, and more positive extraneous influences, are necessarily brought to bear upon them, to assist in their growth and development, through the intermediate stages from this negative or electric state up to a magnetic positive condition. Our own world has certainly left upon her record, undoubted evidences of having passed through these various stages. It is a well known fact to every geologist, that untold thousands of ages must have passed away upon our earth, before the elements surrounding it, were capable of sustaining any form of organized human beings, and the fossilized remains of the early paleozoic stratifications, show that the forms of life existing in those remote periods, were of the lowest order, possessing little activity, and in a comparatively negative condition.

Living organisms were of the most inactive and sluggish character, and confined to the very lowest species. A few varieties of the Radiata, including the star-fishes coral polyps, sponges, and those creatures known as zoophytes, or half plant and half animal, are all that can be found belonging to those early periods. The animal and vegetable forms of higher, and still higher character, have come into existence gradually as the surrounding elements have developed, until we come up to the more active and positive of the animal race, and finally to man. We discover that the development of the surrounding elements, in which these organized forms of life existed, must have preceded the organizations, for the more positive and active organization could not well exist in the negative elements; neither do the animal organisms that flourished, when all the elements were developed, find a genial dwelling place upon the surface of the earth at the present time, when all the elements are more evolved, and hence, their extinction.

So, the great fact becomes apparent, that man the highest organized form of life, could not exist until the surrounding elements were so elaborated and improved as to be commensurate with his demands, and further that man cannot advance and unfold to any considerable extent, unless all of nature by which he is surrounded, advances and unfolds also. Thus it becomes evident, there must be a very different state of things upon our earth, and in the etherealized fluid particles by which it is surrounded, than could have existed in the earlier ages of animal life; and also before those organizations first made their appearance, and hence, the apparent solar influences must operate in a different manner. All things have changed from a comparatively inactive, negative, to a more relatively active, positive state, and if we should inquire, whether this change had taken place with the sun or upon the earth, we should find that the improvement was principally upon our planet.

We behold an unfolding of those inherent powers that we possess, and always have possessed in a latent condition, that will ultimately render us less dependent upon the great orb of day, because we are developing the same powers that exist in the sun in all their magnificence and glory. And if it is conceded that we have unfolded in any sense of the word, that we have traveled a portion of the journey from the electric condition of the new formed moon, to the resplendent magnetic glory of the full-grown sun, what shall hinder our accomplishing the entire distance, and becoming like the sun entirely dependent upon our own resources for light and heat?

We shall doubtless be compelled to admit, when it is conceded that we are in the enjoyment of a larger amount of positive, active element, than we once had, that we furnish this excess by the unfoldment of our own latent powers, and if so, what shall hinder our entire independence, when we are completely unfolded or developed.

If we institute an inquiry concerning the peculiar elements that exist upon the earth, from which light and heat may be manufactured, we shall be apt to find carbon, oxygen, hydrogen and nitrogen, also fire, caloric, and magnetism with electricity and aura; all these several elements which are acting in their various capacities, seem to be in abundant supply. Somehow men have learned to commingle, and make use of some of these elements, in the production of light and warmth in the absence of solar influences, they manage to light and warm their apartments, or the largest halls and the deepest mines, in the depths of winter as well as in the darkest night, In view of these facts there can be no doubt but the wisdom and power that contrived the machinery of the solar system, can ultimately furnish the means for lighting and warming each one of these planets independently, upon the very same principle that those means and appliances have been furnished to the great central orb.

We modestly express the opinion, that, if we should travel out to the sun, and take a survey of his vast domain, from the boundaries of his atmosphere down to the depths of his darkness, we should find no elements of a higher character than those we have upon our earth. If we have the very same elements, as are contained upon the sun, what should prevent, when their latent powers are sufficiently unfolded, and we have gathered the requisite quantity, using them for the same high purpose, and what shall prevent using them now as far as they answer the purposes.

Now, we think the reader will discover the folly of importing fluid particles of light, or wavy undulations, all the long distance from the sun, in order to dispel the darkness of the preceding night, for all that can possibly be received from the sun, has been with us from the earth's earliest history, and that is this subtle, magnetic, positive influence that wakes into activity the inherent powers belonging to us, that are of the same character precisely, as those with which the sun has been far more bountifully supplied by the interminable processes of elaboration through which that central orb has passed, during its lengthened existence.

To make the matter more clear, we may again state that electricity is but expressive of coldness, inactivity, and darkness, that matter, to remain in an unchanged condition, must necessarily be entirely negative, which means in that condition,we call death, and that magnetism is a synonim of life, heat, and activity. Hence, when the negative element becomes permeated to any extent with the positive, it is immediately subject to change, and becomes progressive; for, the positive and negative being male and female, reproduce themselves or their likeness, and whenever or wherever the two elements come in contact, from that moment change and progress commences. There can be nothing unchangeable in this universe, except it be material in a purely negative condition, absolutely divested of any positive influence, and that would be electricity, entirely distinct from magnetism.

So, if worlds in an infantile condition are almost purely electric and negative, then there can be very little magnetic or positive element within them, with which the great fountain head of these powers, can affinitize, in order to produce those activities and frictionizing processes that result in the light and heat experienced upon the surface of the different planets.

Hence, we perceive that Mercury being younger and less developed, is, of course more electrical and has more of cold, darkness and inactivity, and less positive, active elements to assimilate with those contained in the sun; but she has some advantage in point of distance, and that fact assists in modifying her light and heat to suit her condition, and so of all the planets that are dependent upon solar influence, and experience those alternations of light and darkness.

It will be discovered that both light and warmth being active, positive conditions, are produced by vibrations, or frictionizing activities that continually exist in the fluid essences found upon one-half the earth's surface, caused by coming more immediately under the influence of nature's great Voltaic battery. In order to make this battery effectual in producing the required results, there must be an element existing upon the planet that will assimilate to those where the battery is erected. It is well known, that in telegraphing successfully, the elements at the point of reception must be undisturbed, and in quite a similar condition to those where the battery is erected, which seems to cause the vibration of the electric fluid that transmits the message, as any change or disturbance in the elements entirely prevents the harmonious activities of the instruments, and of course, failure ensues.

We trust then, the reader will learn that the quantity and quality of light, as well as heat depends almost exclusively upon the conditions of the several planets, and the various changes are evidently produced by changes upon them, instead of the sun which acts as the great central Electro-Magnetic battery. Darkness and cold being inactive and negative, or an absence of those violent frictionizing activities that produce the more positive conditions of light and heat, of course, occupy that half of the globe directly opposite the great magnetic mantle, and these two different conditions are continually changing places from east to west, as the earth rolls upon its axis in the other direction.

The fluid elements within the limits of the atmosphere and contiguous to our globe, upon that side which looks toward the sun, and which are enveloped within the great positive covering of light, being evidently excited to a vibratory frictionizing activity productive of illumination and caloric, as a matter of course, assimilate more nearly to the character of the great positive globe in the center. While the same elements upon the other side that look out upon the vast, cold, dark, negative space where inactivity reigns, become torpid or inactive, ceasing to a very great extent, their rapid, frictionizing movements. They become cold and dark, assimilating to the negative conditions that exist in the unlimited regions of space, outside the influences of any planetary bodies.

The reader will doubtless discover that the only reason why darkness occurs upon that side of our earth which is opposite the sun, is simply because the positive, active life and heat dispensing elements of magnetism, aura, and empyria, or primal colors, are not sufficiently unfolded and elaborated, to produce the necessary activities independently; and that in our partially developed condition we still require the energizing influences of the great positive power contained in the sun.

But there cannot be a doubt that when a billion or

more years have passed away, and our orbit is extended beyond the one in which Jupiter now travels, and the annual revolution of the earth shall equal twelve of our years instead of one, the feeble light producing elements upon this globe shall be developed to that condition, in which they will possess the power to furnish the necessary illumination and caloric upon every side, and in all latitudes. We shall become comparatively independent of the central luminous orb, and enjoy a beautiful mellow light adapted to a more advanced condition, which shall be continual, and diffuse itself upon all portions of our globe, in such an equable manner that the torrid heats of the tropical, and the terrible frosts of the polar regions shall be unknown to the inhabitants. When all the great battles between the antagonistic elements of heat and cold, of light and darknes, shall have been fought to the end, and those mighty contests shall result in an agreeable diffusion of those various elements in a manner perfectly adapted to the wants of a harmonious and highly developed race of intelligent beings.

It seems to be conceded upon all hands, that so-called solar influences are produced upon the earth's surface by frictionizing activities, and the grand question is, to ascertain precisely the causes productive of the vibratory motion of the elemental fluids, or the exact method by which light and caloric is manufactured upon the earth and other planetary bodies. Now, if we find that neither emanating particles, or undulatory waves can come from the central orb, and that an Electro-Magnetic battery does produce activities of the kind mentioned, and that our solar system is one grand

Voltaic battery, such as is required to produce those grand and beautiful results, then we may consider that the great mystery has to a certain extent been solved.

It is quite evident that nature contains all the elements from which all the artificial batteries are projected and enabled to operate, and it is no marvel then, if nature has within herself, one grand battery that operates throughout our entire solar system, embracing all the the positive and negative elements within the whole machine. Our limits forbid any extended discussion of a subject that might require volumes to elucidate to its fullest extent, but we feel impressed that the volumes may some day be written elaborating the whole theory in accordance with the few ideas presented.

We think the reader will have discovered that all light and heat being positive elements, must be manufactured, and that being exhaustive of their own resources, they must in some manner be continually generated to supply the demand, and also that there must be in nature a variety of modes by which these elements can be produced.

It can by no means be supposed that the exterior planets are dependent upon solar influences for their change of seasons, and that seed time and harvest, summer and winter, should only alternate in such lengthy periods; for, it would be extremely difficult for us to conceive how a race of living beings could be sustained where the periodical harvests only occur once in twelve of our years, and where the winters must necessarily be prolonged to twelve times the length of our own, as would be the case upon the planet Jupiter. But when we go still farther out, and find that there are planets that could not enjoy these alternations of seasons oftener than once in eighty-four years, as upon Uranus, and one hundred and sixty-four upon the planet Neptune, it then becomes conclusive that some other plan must be introduced, which will provid e for their seed time and harvest, than the one that prevails upon our earth. Consequently, they must occur entirely independent of solar influences, and the active light and heat dispensing elements must have arrived to that positive condition, in those remote and far more ancient orbs, that they regulate their own temperature, and produce any alternations of seasons, and all other phenomena connected with light and heat which they require, entirely independent of all extraneous influences, except that general sympathetic chord that links and binds all worlds together in one harmonious whole.

It will be discovered that light and darkness, as appreciable conditions upon our earth, are rendered so to us, by the peculiar character of the visual lenses through which we behold these different conditions, and if we had no eye we could not discover the difference, so that both are relative, and depend upon the peculiar character of the vision with which we are provided. Most probably if we had the eye of an owl or a bat, we should look upon the whole thing very differently, and prefer the shades of evening to the glare produced by the mid-day sun, and our day would only commence after that luminary had disappeared behind the western hills. We may well suppose that nature provides in her store house ample materials from which lenses could be produced that would render our light extremely dark, and our darkness agreeably light, or that would enable us to see when all the fluid elements by which we are surrounded, are in a state of inactivity and rest, instead of this active vibratory motion which we call light.

So after all, we perceive the necessity of adapting the eye to this peculiar state of things, and without such adaptation, there would be no light; and although light seems to us to be absolute, probably by a careful observation, we shall discover that it is only relative and depends entirely upon the eye or the peculiar vision. Doubtless we could just as easily have been provided with lenses that could have discerned all objects in the absence of the sun as in its presence, or they could have been adapted to a negative condition as easily as to a positive. For we very readily discover that the lenses used in a spiritual condition, one step in advance of our own, must be composed of materials that are entirely independent of all influences that render objects visible to us, and that our darkness to them is resplendent with all the effulgence and glory of an eternal day, simply because their vision is more powerfully intensified, and the thick darkness presents no obstacle to its penetrating glance.

The question which very naturally arises in the mind concerning lighting and warming the interior surface of this spherical shell, we trust has been to a certain extent, answered in the preceding pages. We show not only in this chapter but in other portions of this work as clearly as possible without exceeding our limits, that all the elements exist inherently upon our earth, in a partially unfolded condition, from which to manufacture the needed light and warmth for the exterior surface. We also show by reasoning from the analogies of nature that the interior of this shell is in a more developed condition than the exterior, and that these elements produce their own activities independently, and to an extent entirely sufficient for all the purposes required, and that the aura and empyrial light of the interior world, must necessarily be soft and mellow, and devoid of those oppressive glaring influences which we experience upon the exterior surface.

It is by no means difficult for the ordinary reader to comprehend that light and heat can be as easily manufactured as anything else, if the materials are all provided from which they are produced; and when we learn that our earth contains a certain amount of all those materials, and that the interior contains all that is necessary to supply her entire wants in this respect, then the great mystery is solved and it all becomes plain.

There can be no more trouble in producing light than there is in engendering heat, and every one understands that all animal organizations have the apparatus within them, and are provided with the elements that enable them to generate the requisite amount of animal heat, and that it is done entirely independent of the temperature by which they are surrounded. We very well know also, that the animal organization has no element of any character in its possession, that it did not receive from the great parent, then if the mother had those powers to impart, why not permit her to use them for her own purposes, and generate her own light and heat within herself for the benefit of that beautiful world yet unexplored by mortal man.

CHAP. IX.

THE INHERENT POWERS OF NATURE; OR THE EVOLUTION AND ELABORATION OF WORLDS.

It is quite evident we inherit an entire physical organization from this earth, upon which we live, move and have our being. If so, then the physical globe or the mineral kingdom with its appertainings, must be our great parent, both male and female, our father and our mother also. Philosophers say there are sixty-four primary elements connected with this earth, and that most if not all these several elements enter into the human organization, thus constituting man a microcosm of the whole, or a part and parcel of the entire mass. It would then follow as a sequence, that, if we comprehend the human organization in all its parts and relationships, in all its working processes, and its variously complicated machinery, we may begin to form a tolera bly clear idea of the entire world of which this organzation is a specimen in miniature.

If this intimate relationship exists, and we can properly call the earth our parent, and if all we physically possess, is received from this source, then we must hold these elements, properties and attributes, in common with the parent. If these elements and attributes with which we are endowed, and have received from the parent, have ultimated in this physical constitution which may be properly termed an animal organization of smaller proportions, then why may not the earth be considered, in some sense of the word, an animal organization of vastly larger dimensions. The earth evidently possesses a superabundance of the elements and properties, necessary to produce the animal organizations. She has an entire sufficiency for her own purposes, and enough for all her children; and if the earth does not perform some functions analogous to the animal race, for what purpose does she use all this vast store house of elements and attributes, that she is constantly giving off to her children so bountifully, and of which she has such a superabundance?

How can this parent of ours give to her children, what she does not possess herself? How could she give to the animal race a nervous network, and arterial and venous circulation, if she has nothing in her organization, analogous to all this in the animal? How could she bestow upon the animal race, an apparatus for inhaling and exhaling the atmosphere, and extracting and using those properties necessary for the preservation of life, if she had no organs that were analogous? How could she impart to our physical structures, powers of locomotion, if she had no such powers to impart.

The entire animal race, from the most infinitessimal, up to the largest living beings that walk the earth, swim in the ocean, or float in the atmosphere, are so many locomotives or self-moving machines that possess this ability inherent, and generate the power within themselves, by which they act and perform their proper functions; and they have received this element from the parent. Does she have so much to impart, and shall she not use the same element herself? Philosophers discovered some centuries since, that the earth turns upon its axis, and that the exterior surface moves at the rate of 1,000 miles per hour, and that it has another motion in an orbit, of 68,000 miles per hour, and if so, that must be locomotion, and the machine must generate the forces within itself, that enables it to perform these wonderfully arduous duties. We perceive, we cannot possess any power or material in our physical organisms, we did not receive from this great parent, and we perceive also that our great parent must, if she has a superabundance of these elements and materials to impart to us, use them herself, in a somewhat analogous manner, and that she had evidently attained quite an advanced condition, before she was capable, or sufficiently matured, to give birth to animal or vegetable life.

So, we think it will not be disputed that all these different organized forms of life which exist, were evolved from the materials and elements belonging to the earth, and that we may trace back the parentage clearly and distinctly, and ascertain that they all are a part and parcel of the whole. Therefore, we can possess nothing in our natures, the earth did not possess before us, and this our parent possessed a redundancy of those elements and materials; that is, enough to supply her own wants, and also the wants of all her numerous children, belonging to the vegetable and animal kingdom.

Now, we trust, after a careful and scrutinizing examination of this matter, we shall find a perfect harmony and analogy, existing all through these various organizations, and where we find peculiar organs and functions in the plant, or the animal, or in man, we shall find something somewhat analogous in the great mother the earth; for truly she could not impart anything to her children, she did not possess within herself. Do we find a nervous network, ramifying every portion of the animal organism, upon which the nerve aura is traveling back and forth, giving information and transmitting the orders of the great monarch that sits upon the throne, within the front brain or cerebrum? We also find a corresponding net work of Electro-Magnetic currents, permeating all portions of the earth and atmosphere upon which those elements may travel with equal celerity, performing all their proper functions, imparting vigor and animation, and perhaps generating the proper forces and conditions, that enable our globe to perform her various labors.

Do we find a circulating fluid that is passing and repassing through all portions of the animal structure, in appropriate channels fitted for the purpose? We also find the earth has its blood, and great reservoirs in which it is contained, and a multitude of channels in which it travels, both upon the surface and far below in the depths, and she has also a means of transporting this, her blood, to the highest sources of all the various channels. It would be extremely interesting to notice the various means the earth has adopted, in order to keep in operation a perpetual circulation of the waters that rest in and upon her bosom. The winds are made active agents in agitating the great ocean, and the smaller lakes, sometimes with a force that stirs them almost to the bottom, then, the never ceasing rolling tides are constantly at work, moving the waters with an irresistible force, and again the voluminous oceanic currents are running hither and thither regardless of all other influences, except the one that impels them forward, some from the equatorial to the polar regions, and others in the opposite direction. So, that there is hardly any portion of the great oceans that are not more or less affected by those numerous currents. Then, the amount of water that is dissolved by caloric, and taken up constantly in the form of aqueous vapor, to supply the springs of the highest mountains, and that falls again to the earth in the shape of rain, hail or snow, would in no great length of time, equal all there is upon the globe. Thus, we perceive the earth had this element of circulation to impart to the various forms of organized life she has produced.

We discover that the animal and vegetable races are surrounded and enveloped by atmospheric air; nitrogen and oxygen, and that they require a constant supply of this element in the interior, and that without this continuous supply, they perish; and also, that our earth is surrounded and enveloped in this element. It is said to be forty-five, and may be one hundred miles in depth, and that it weighs fifteen pounds to every square inch of the 200,000,000 square miles of the earth's superficial area. In the animal organization, there are constant currents passing to and from the interior, through the apertures prepared for that purpose, and they have inherited *this* organization from the parent, then, must we not suppose that the parent has some analogous organization. If we cannot subsist without atmospheric air in the interior, how can the parent subsist without a similar condition; then, a supply of the same element in the interior of the earth, must be imperious, and a demand which nature must furnish, if we inherited all physical characteristics, and are composed of material, and moved by forces, drawn from this great parent. Can we have a general organization that the parent does not in some analogous form possess? Then, we begin to see that the earth must also be supplied with those elements, oxygen and nitrogen, in the interior as well as upon the exterior.

We perceive also, that the blood in the animal organism, is very much confined to the interior; the channels run deep and many of them very near the interior surface, and thus we shall find it with the parent also. Our earth has an enormous quantity of oxygen and hydrogen upon the exterior, and as we must conclude, also, upon the interior surface of her spherical shell. Now, why all this great superabundant supply of that element, unless it is required for her own use, in a manner somewhat analogous to that in which it is used by the living organisms she has produced? We shall find as extensive currents, and quite as much circulation and activity in the atmosphere, as we find in the water, and there can be no doubt that the circulation extends to the interior surface, with the same activity, as manifested upon the outside.

The animal kingdom exists upon the surface of this globe, but, it is in the midst, and dependent upon a variety of gasses, essences, or elements and forces for its continuance, and but for these, it could not exist for a single day. All the members of this extensive kingdom must have nutritive elements that come from the earth or mineral kingdom, and they come in the shape of vegetable productions. By this means the earth furnishes with nutrition, all the animal race; they must also be provided with hydrogen, oxygen, and nitrogen in the form of air and water, with carbon, caloric, and a variety of other essences, which are but the spiritual elements of the mineral kingdom, but which are absolutely essential in supplying their wants. Magnetism and electricity are very important in the performance of certain offices within them as well as the aural element to invigorate and give the needed activity, and the higher element we call empyria that impregnates them with the life principle, and which is able to maintain it as long as it would prove a blessing. All such elements and forces we must have, and all these the whole animal race enjoy from day to day, or they would not subsist; and all are received from the great parent the earth.

As the great parent must have existed untold millions of years before it arrived at a condition in which it was possible to produce animal life, and was in possession of all elements, essences and forces, to a certain extent during that long period, therefore, she must have had use for them all the time previous to the existence of living animal organizations, and they must have subserved her own individual purposes. The elements, quite analogous to those that now enter into and constitute the animal organisms, and which are provided for their subsistence, must have been used by the parent for similar purposes,. the whole time of the earth's history antecedent to the existence of the animal organisms, or else those elements possessed by the parent would have been inactive, and without utility for all those lengthy ages, which evidently, could not be the case.

Again, we discover that the earth has a great redundancy of all the elements and forces mentioned, that she has an ample supply for her own private use, and also for the use of all animal organisms. Go down into the fountains of the great deep, and ascertain how much of this aqueous element is required for the use of the animal race; look into the wide extended treasure house that contains all the different fluid essences, and you will find the supply quite as ample and superabundant. One half the globe is oxygen; there is a great and overwhelming sufficiency of the other gasses; caloric and magnetism, and electricity are bountifully distributed everywhere, and managed and applied with the utmost care and discretion, lest these powerful elements might produce disturbances of a fatally injurious character. Now, we trust it must become plain, that this analogy between the great parent self-moving machine, and all the smaller machines that are moving upon the surface, does actually exist to a very great extent; and by a parity of reasoning, we must conclude it holds good through the entire organic arrangement.

If every one of these animal productions are locomotives, and generate the power within themselves by which they perform their movements, then the great parent which is known to be a locomotive also, must generate the necessary power within herself, by which she performs corresponding functions. It is entirely unphilosophical to suppose the earth, if she travels at the speed represented in her orbit, and upon her axis, receives this necessary momentum from any other similar body or planet, for what power have they to spare? Would it not be as well or better to let each one and all attend to their own particular business concerns; and why is it that philosophers have undertaken to make one of these bodies, dependent for their powers of locomotion upon the other, as they have by so doing, only involved themselves in greater difficulties?

It seems to be conceded by the popular school of philosophers who follow Newton, that all the prominent forces in nature, which apparently act so conspicuous a part in giving propulson to the planets in the solar system, were entirely insufficient to produce the required momentum in the outset. Hence, they have been compelled to appeal to the arm of an omnipotent being to start the machine, by applying some peculiar kind of force that is not recognized within the realms of the natural universe. It is this unnatural mixing up of supernatural forces, with those that are within the limits of the universe, that involve men in so much doubt and uncertainty, for if it was necessary to go outside of nature, and call upon an omnipotent power, to set the globe in motion, we might as well have let him run the machine himself.

Most assuredly, if this omnipotent being was so deficient in mechanical ability, that he could not contrive a power with all the forces in nature at his command, which would have started the various planets and set their machinery in operation, it would certainly be somewhat doubtful whether he would be able, unaided, to keep our world in motion, until it can work out all its sublime purposes. So, it would appear quite evident that our philosopers must be somewhat at fault, as no doubt the genius and wisdom that could contrive and keep in operation a perpetual motion, for so many long ages, by natural causes, must have been abundantly competent to have brought to bear forces that would have started the machine, within the range of natural causes also.

If this globe is a locomotive machine, it must be made upon the principle, and endowed with the characteristics of other locomotive machines. We find an abundance of these smaller locomotives every wher , scattered all through the realms of organized animal life, that we can examine at our leisure, all inheriting their peculiar characteristics and organs from the great parent locomotive. And we may ascertain that every one of them, generate their forces in the interior; within the walls of their individual structures, by the use of certain organs therein contained. Must we not then conclude the great locomotive generates the necessary powers in a similar and analogous manner, by the use of certain organs that exist in the interior, and within the outer walls of the great orbicular superstructure?

After grouping together the various facts and phenomena which present themselves to view in relation to this subject we trust, but little if anything is wanting to establish the absolute truth of the position assumed.

First. We have this stupendous locomotive, the earth, which is evidently a mechanical structure of the highest possible order; we have all the elements and forces necessary to supply the power to run this machine.

Secondly. We have a great multitude of smaller

locomotives that are run or kept in motion by use of the same elements and forces, of which the large one has an abundant supply.

Thirdly. The small machines are supplied with interior organs, and by their aid generate the forces, using the same elements, which are carried by suitable avenues to the interior for that purpose. Now, when we consider that the small machines inherit all their organism from the larger, the links to be supplied to make this chain of reasoning complete, would seem to be narrowed down to the smallest possible number.

It must be admitted also, that, if all small locomotives are hollow, and have their organs in the interior, then large ones must be hollow also, and there can be no doubt when we can get access to the interior, we shall become acquainted with this organism, and discover the perfect analogy which exists throughout the entire realms of organized material life, from the largest to the most infinitesimal.

Permit us now, to take from this globe of ours sufficient of the supposed interior contents, to furnish materials for about thirty-five other globes of similar dimensions, we should then have a spherical shell of nearly forty miles in thickness; a beautiful mechanical structure maintaining the principles of the *arch*, the symbol of strength, in every square mile of its two surfaces.

Suppose we furnish a suitable breathing apparatus at the north or positive pole, and from the abundance of oxygen, hydrogen, nitrogen, carbon, and other elements in nature, supply the requisite amount of air and water, and all else that is needed for the interior, as well as the exterior surface. We should then have a world about one thirty-fifth part of the supposed weight of our globe, built in accordance with the highest principles of art; comparatively light and buoyant, and that might be handled with perhaps one-twentieth part of the physical force required, for the clumsy old hulk full of molten lava, which has been erected by the philosophers of a somewhat modern age.

We may now conceive it possible with a properly formed mechanical structure and a superabundance of the required elements, to generate all the necessary forces for the propulsion of such a globe in both its axial and orbital revolutions, without being compelled to go outside of the natural universe to ask for aid, or without even seeking the reciprocal gravitating influences of any other of the heavenly bodies.

There may be found in and upon our own planet, all the propelling forces that can exist in any other portion of the universe; all the positive and negative powers, quite sufficiently elaborated to subserve all such purposes. Then, why go abroad to obtain that of which we have an abundance for our own use, and of which this or no other planet has an excess beyond their own demands. We cannot entertain a shadow of doubt, concerning the skill and ability of those powers that projected, and set in motion the great self-moving mechanical structure that we inhabit. We cannot doubt but they must have understood perfectly well, the principles connected with locomotives, quite as well as the engineers of the present day, who seem to construct and run those of smaller dimensions with such marked success.

Every principle connected with locomotion has been in existence from all eternity, and it can hardly be supposed that such important matters were overlooked in the construction of the various planets. All the forces by which these various machines are successfully operated, have eternally existed also, and we can by no means suppose that a proper application of these forces, would have been neglected in the propulsion of the machinery of a solar system, where they would seem to be of such absolute importance. Indeed, a proper application of the requisite forces, that would render all the planetary bodies, self-moving machines or locomotives, would seem to have been a grand desideratum; an attainment which must have become perfectly indispensable.

It is quite obvious that the forces exist in nature by which the whole machinery of solar systems are successfully operated; it is also obvious that those forces must have been applied by competent intelligence and power, and further, that the requisite forces are applied to each planet distinctively. There can certainly be no more propriety in a reciprocal exchange of motive power between planets in the solar system, than there would be between so many animals, or members of a human family. In every case, each must become an independent, self-moving machine.

It may not be given to us to discover the exact nature of the organs by which this force is generated and brought to bear, but we do show most clearly, the necessity of some such organs, and we open up to view a locality amply sufficient for their most extended operations, and also show that our mother the earth is in possession of all the requisite powers which will enable her, if properly applied, to attend to her most arduous duties, without calling upon any other heavenly body for assistance. If we shall succeed in opening up this vast interior world to the investigation of future generations, we shall be entirely satisfied, without being able to explain, or give an elaborate description of the minutia of all the vast and complicated elemental machinery, it must necessarily contain.

This working machinery of the interior of the shell, evidently constitutes our globe, a great parent locomotive, and enables her to work out in accordance with natural causes, her ultimate destiny, and perform all those various duties that usually devolve upon planetary bodies. We now have a mechanical structure presented to our view, relieved of its enormous load of bungling imperfections, and unnatural incongruities, as well as an overwhelming quantity of material which is worse than useless to this world, and which would be quite sufficient to supply the wants of thirty-five others of equal dimensions. Give us a magnificent world of this character constructed upon those harmonious principles of architectural beauty and strength, in all its vast proportions, and it would then certainly reflect the highest possible credit and honor, upon the supereminent skill, the exalted genius and wisdom, which could project and execute so astonishing a work. We should certainly behold its beauty and increased utility with higher emotions of reverence, than could possibly have possessed the mind, accustomed to think of our old world, filled brimming full with useless rubbish, or terribly heated molten lava. The latter idea is calculated to shock all the finer sensibilities of our nature, and leads the mind to institute a standing inquiry, if it might not have been constructed upon some more philosophic and harmonious principles.

Before leaving this subject, we notice another important analogy existing betweeen the great parent, and the smaller organized locomotives which is founded upon the principle of exhaustion, and continued accumulation of the needed forces; for, it is a well known fact that a constant supply of forces must be generated in order to enable the smallest insect to perform its proper functions. The surrounding elements must be constantly had in requisition. The animal must be supplied with the required amount of nutrition, out of which to manufacture blood, fibrine, and all the constituent materials of the system, in order to supply the waste; and also atmosphere, electricity, magnetism, and all the needed elements, out of which his interior forces are evolved. An unceasing supply must be had to enable it to perform its continuous work; for labor, in all cases, is exhaustive of the forces by which it is performed.

It is no matter whether this labor is accomplished by the industrious ant that piles up its conical domicile, the bee that labors to lay by its luscious hoard, the fleet hound that pursues the frighted deer, the laboring man that delves in the earth to obtain his subsistence, or the vast world that rolls upon its axis, and pursues its rapid course in its mighty orbit around the central luminary. All must in some manner be constantly supplied with the needed forces, and all must generate them for their own purposes; and one globe can no more depend upon another for assistance in generating and thus producing those forces, than one of the animal race, the insect or the man; each must eat its own food, and elaborate the elements that subserve those purposes for himself, by the use of the organs that are inherent in their natures, and thus we see our globe must have analogous powers inherent in her nature also.

When philosophers learn all the facts in relation to this subject, they will ascertain that our mother earth contains, and possesses within herself inherently, all the organic structure, and is capable of elaborating all forces for her own purposes, and is continually exercising her locomotive power, in a manner perfectly analogous to those of her children who have drawn upon her resources for all the power they possess, and by which they are enabled to perform all their varied functions and duties.

Moreover, we shall find all solid bodies to be inactive, inclined to repose, and that solidity is synonymous with inertia, that solid bodies do not move unless extraneous force is brought to bear upon them, and hence, it became necessary for philosophers to call upon some outside force to propel the planets in their various movements, as long as they recognized the solidity of the earth and other heavenly bodies. If the planetary worlds are solid, or contain no machinery by which they may generate their own self-moving powers, they would be so many dead weights suspended in the universe, and require the continuous exertions of all the spiritual forces in existence, to keep them moving.

Even then, we are apprehensive the machinery would drag and finally cease operations in consequence of an exhaustion of power, and we very much doubt if sufficient forces could be found in all the spiritual realms, to propel and sustain our own ponderous globe, if it was solid to the center, or if it had to depend upon such extraneous force.

The most careless reader will discover at a glance, the utility, harmony, and beauty of such a self-propelling arrangement, and will be compelled to admit, that a globe without the needed apparatus for performing its own proper functions, in accordance with universal laws, would be an extremely clumsy and unmechanical affair. It would be a mere botch, and as useless as a steamer or cotton-factory destitute of motive power; and it would necessarily bring its designers and builders into lasting disrepute. So we perceive, in order to construct a world in accordance with the higher principles of the art, and one that may do credit to the projector, by answering all the purposes for which it may be designed, it must be built hollow, or in the form of an orbicular shell.

There would be as much impropriety in building one solid, or in filling the vast interior cavity with an intensely raging fire, as there would, in constructing the steamer or the manufactory upon similar principles; both must be hollow or contain a great internal cavity in which is found the necessary machinery, that utilizes these structures; and both are constructed upon principles that harmonize with those that are inherent in the physical globe. And it must be conceded, that if the powers of locomotion are inherent in this globe, then all other powers that are properly attached to globes in their more advanced condition, must be inherent also. That, its ability to furnish its own light, warmth and life essences, energizing influences, and all other powers and forces that may be required in worlds, during all their stages of unfoldment from their periods of infancy up to the highest condition, must be inherently attached to the individual world itself. Although these powers may exist for interminable ages, in a latent unevolved condition, and although our world is at this time apparently dependent upon the great parent the sun for its reflective influences, in producing the required amount of light and heat. Yet, it is quite evident that it has in a latent c ondition, those powers within itself, that may at some future day be elaborated, so as to subserve all the purposes of this planet, and not only that, it will be able to furnish such beneficial influences, to the satelites by which it may be surrounded.

We might inquire, if this is not the case, where the great luminary of day obtained the unbounded surplus of the light giving and heat dispensing influences with which it seems to be endowed. Can it be supposed that it was created or formed in its present condition, or like all things of which we have any knowledge, did it not once exist in a state of infancy; and develop itself up to its present stupendous proportions, in which it may dispense all these beneficent influences to those planetary worlds which seem to sustain the relationship to him, of younger and less developed children?

Every intelligent individual who, with the means in his possession, takes a survey or makes an examination of the so-called luminary in the center of our system, the earth we inhabit, and the moon that accompanies us in our journeys, must inevitably conclude that these three planetary bodies are in very different conditions of elaboration or unfoldment. They must concede that the sun is more advanced, and is in possession of powers far superior to the earth, and also, that the earth is in a far higher condition than the moon, and, that the age of these several orbs must bear a similar relationship to each other. As, it must be acknowledged that it has required time to elaborate these different planets, and furnish them with the various elemental powers they possess, commensurate with their varied conditions.

The nebulous theory contemplates this vast difference, in the relative ages and development of the heavenly bodies, and recognizes the idea that the younger precedes, or is thrown off from the elder in a very unevolved condition. In fact, there can be no intelligent theory of any kind established, without recognizing some such relationship, and some such principles of unfoldment, for it cannot be supposed that any one with sufficient intelligence to contemplate subjects of this character, can entertain an idea that all the planetary bodies are of equal age, and in the same condition of development.

If the planetary bodies are subject to evolution and advancement in any one particular, then it may well be supposed they are alike subject to evolution and unfoldment in all particulars; and, that all their inherent elements and powers are gradually changing to a higher condition. Hence, we are driven to the conclusion, that those which seem at present in an infantile condition, and manifest only feeble, inactive, negative forces like our moon, will in process of time unfold their latent powers, and shine out with all the positive, magnetic glories of a sun in the firmament. That, they will rise from the feeble dependent conditions in which all their latent inherent powers are inactive, to a gloriously independent condition, in which those elemental forces shall be unfolded, and exhibit themselves in their stupendous proportions.

We observe upon our earth, while we at the present period, are appparently dependent upon solar influences, to impregnate and energize the elements inherently in our possession, in order to produce warmth or caloric, that, those elements are more active upon that portion of the globe contiguous to the equator, and less active as we approach the polar regions. There are, no doubt a superabundance of the positive, active forces in the torrid zone, and an equally large supply of the negative in the frigid or higher latitudes, while the intermediate zone seems to enjoy a sort of happy equilibrium, or an alternation of heat and cold; and is therefore called temperate. All this would seem to depend, and perhaps does, upon the particular manner in which the sun's influences fall upon the different portions of the globe; whether vertically or more obliquely.

However, there are evidences which are undeniable, that climatic phenomena depend upon conditions found upon the earth, still more than upon solar influences; else, how could there be an open Polar Sea with a temperate clime in the extreme north, beyond the frigid belt of perpetual ice?

Again, how could the enormous quantities of fossilized remains of tropical plants and animals, found in the extreme north, have been produced, if, during the mutations of the earth's history, this portion had not at some period enjoyed a tropical clime?

If we could carefully examine the sun which appears

to be the great beneficent fountain of the essential elements that we require, we shall no doubt discover that there can be no difference in regard to temperature, between the equatorial and polar regions, because of the fully developed condition of all the positive magnetic active forces. They have necessarily diffused themselves upon all portions of his surface, and spread around his electric orb an atmosphere of magnetism and aura, so that all there is of negative elements attached to him are deeply enshrouded in this highly unfolded positive covering which seems to reflect itself upon us with such astonishingly resplendent beauty and glory. But, that there is still an opaque negative element within this brilliant magnetic exterior covering, is fully proven by the numerous broad spots that appear upon his surface, with their shadowy, fringed penumbras, with centers, that are filled with opacity and darkness.

It would be impossible to take the most casual survey of this broad universe, which can come to the notice of mortal vision, and behold all the wondrous variety of planetary worlds in their different conditions, and not adopt the conclusion, that the sun has arrived at his gloriously magnetic condition by passing through elaborating processes, that must have required almost an infinitude of succeeding ages. We must admit, that this conspicuous orb has been, for an inconceivable period, unceasingly working out and unfolding the stupendous designs of the supremely wise architect who projected and set in operation the infantile planet which has so long been the central apparent luminary of this magnificent solar system.

It will be observed, then, that latitudinal distinctions or differences of climatic temperature cannot exist upon the sun, for the reason that all its elemental powers must be in a highly elaborated condition, operating harmoniously and uniformly throughout all its various realms from the equator to the poles. No scientific mind will contend that the sun is dependent upon another orb for any of the vast powers which it constantly displays, and which it evidently has in its own possession. It is obvious, then, if the sun has arrived at an independent condition, generating its own elemental forces, without any extrinsic aid, those forces must operate uniformly upon every portion of its superficial area.

We think that few men of independent minds will be inclined to deny the unfoldment, or evolutionary doctrine in respect to worlds, because it is so obviously written upon every accessible portion of the universe. Hence, all planetary bodies must evidently possess every power within themselves in a more or less advanced state; and as a sequence, the period must arrive in the history of all worlds, when their powers become sufficiently unfolded, so that light and warmth must diffuse themselves to all portions of their surfaces equally, the same as upon the sun.

Without doubt, a period must arrive, when they, like the sun, do not receive sufficient of such elements from other sources, or when in their spiral orbits they attain to that immense distance from the parent luminary, that his influences are not equal to the supply of their wants, and when they have developed their own inherent powers sufficiently for their own requirements in those respects. For, it now becomes evident that a planet sufficiently developed to generate its own light and heat, would diffuse those elements upon all portions of the exterior surface, and that there would be a very general equilibrium, and that all portions of such a globe would enjoy an equal supply; so, there could be no torrid, temperate and frigid zones, because all would be alike.

There cannot be a shadow of doubt, but a higher, advanced condition of a world is far superior to a lower, more undeveloped condition; and their projectors and builders must have been capable of carrying out the grand purposes for which worlds are constructed. So, we shall discover, the inhabitants of the exterior planets must be blessed with perpetual day and eternal summer; for there can be no influences we can discover, that would produce the rigors of severe winter, or the scorching heats of a tropical season, where all elements are brought up to that harmonious and elaborated condition of self-dependence that assimilates to the character of the central sun.

Violent extremes of heat and cold are evidently produced by an inharmonious condition of antagonistic or positive and negative elements; and doubtless where those elements are properly evolved and equalized, a happy equilibrium of temperature will prevail. At the present period in our earth's history, we find great diversity of temperatures in consequence of the unelaborated condition of the elements; at times, and in places, we have too large a supply of the magnetic, and of course correspondingly warm weather; on the other hand, wherever and whenever electricity predominates, it necessarily produces cold in excess. But, we entertain an unbounded confidence, that those powers who are able to construct an infant world, and manage its affairs successfully until it attains its majority, gets from under parental influence, becomes independent, and is able to supply its own wants, will be abundantly competent to preserve an equilibrium of the various forces necessary for its continuance, until it accomplishes all its ultimate objects, and to the fullest extent, the original design of the projectors.

Although this portion of the subject is by no means complete, yet we may possibly venture some further reply to the early inquiry that has presented itself to the mind of the reader, when told of a beautiful world in the interior of the spherical shell which we inhabit. A world, too, far more elaborated, and in a more highly finished condition, than this exterior surface which we occupy. The query of course relates to the manner of obtaining illuminating and warming influence, in the absence of the great central magnet of our solar system. We simply remark concerning this matter, that all will become plain, when it is conceded that worlds possess the latent powers within themselves, which enable them to generate those elements, when sufficiently advanced or unfolded.

The interior surface being in a more highly developed condition than the exterior, it has become already capable of generating and producing its own light and warmth, upon the same principle as those planets that are entirely beyond the lighting and warming influences of the sun. The brilliant displays of aural lights that are so frequently beheld emanating from the arctic circle, have thus far baffled all attempts of scientific minds to unfold their mysteries; and these phenomena remain to-day, as they ever have, entirely inexplicable. Although they sometimes light up a great portion of the northern hemisphere with unequaled beauty and grandeur, with their softened mellow scintillations, yet all the causes that produce their glories, are shrouded and concealed from the minds of men, in the darkness of Egyptian night. Very many observations have been made by men of learning, in order to penetrate this mystery, but, as yet, they have resulted in very little that would explain the philosophy of the aurora borealis. They have learned some few facts in connection with those magnificent displays, and there the matter rests, as far as science is concerned.

It will be noticed that they make their appearance almost universally in the night, and very seldom when the sun is shining; as the sun's influences seem to be more powerful upon our earth than the elements that produce the aurora. The aural element, when in activity, displays a softened and mellow light; but still, in the extreme north, even upon the exterior surface of the globe, one that is at times entirely sufficient for practical purposes; and, we hesitate not to say, that an exploration of the grand interior, where this kind of light universally prevails, would give us a lucid explanation of the whole subject of aural phenomena. If the aural light has no connection with the interior world, how strange that it should occur at the poles, the natural center of extreme cold, where the least possible amount of solar influences can be extended, and the only portion of our globe where can possibly be found accessible apertures that would connect the two surfaces; and how singular that such lights should exhibit themselves in their greatest glory in the absence of the sun!

Here we may discover two great facts, which present themselves upon the broad face of universal nature. One is, that by certain inherent powers existing upon our globe, elements may be found that produce a beautiful light, sufficient for all human practical purposes, in the absence of the sun; and another is, that certain of the planetary worlds attached to our solar system, have extended their orbits so far from the grand central luminary, that it is a simple impossibility for them to be lighted and warmed from that source. Hence it becomes absolutely necessary for them to depend upon their individually evolved resources, generating their own illumination, and producing their own general temperature, in a manner that would correspond with the production of the aural lights, and the warm clime of the open polar sea in the extreme north upon this our more undeveloped earth.

We conclude it is not too much to say, and we venture the opinion, based upon analogical reasoning, that the interior surface of our globe is already unfolded to a condition quite as high as the exterior of the outer independent planets. That the beautiful aural and magnetic lights, and genial warmth, are all produced by the more advanced inherent powers existing within this shell, and that the aural polar lights are to a great extent generated by powers and elements that exist in and emanate from the interior world. We hesitate not to assert, if there was no such beautifully unfolded inner world connected with the polar regions, there would be no such grand illuminations in the north, or in the south, to awake the sublimest emotions in the mind of every beholder.

Dalton, no doubt very correctly conceived the idea, that the aural element crossed the electro-magnetic currents at right angles, and thus the fine etherealized fluid particles, frictionizing, might produce the aural lights, and when we consider that the longitudinal currents are continually converging to a center at or near the poles, we may well suppose that illuminating influences might be produced, to a certain extent, in that manner, upon the exterior surface. But we are persuaded that the more brilliant displays are dependent upon interior influences.

We have now discovered very clearly, that all of nature is not dependent upon solar influences for light and heat, but, that those elements may be produced upon other globes that are sufficiently advanced, as well as upon the sun, and that he cannot possibly possess any more advantages over those that are younger, than the fully grown and developed man possesses over the child or mere youth. Another great fact we learn in connection with this subject, is, the existence of solar systems, and, from an examination of this one, in which our earth holds a position, we are impelled to conclude that the whole universe is constructed upon a similar plan; or that we only behold, when we survey the great expanse of the siderial heavens, one vast assemblage of solar systems, or rather the grand centers about which they revolve. If solar systems absolutely prevail through the immensity of the universe, and this is the general plan everywhere adopted in the production and arrangement of worlds, we may well institute some inquiries in regard to their natures, and the method of building and congregating planets together in this orderly manner.

If we take a cursory survey of our solar system, we shall find that most of the primaries have become centers, about which more or less satellites are revolving, in various periods of time, according to their several distances from the respective central foci, about which they revolve. Our little earth already has one, Jupiter four, Saturn eight, Uranus six, and perhaps more, while Neptune is supposed to have two, and for aught astronomers absolutely know, may have a numerous family of attendants. All these look very much like planetary systems in a certain stage of development; and it would evidently be far easier to produce a solar system from one of the planets with his attendant satellites, than to manufacture one from entire new materials, or in any other manner that the human mind can contemplate.

In fact, are they not all solar systems, in the proper sense of the term, already? They certainly look, to an observer, very much like such, and seem to contain within themselves all the inherent properties and qualities of the parent system, to which they are attached. They evidently resemble the parent quite as nearly as the child can the more fully grown man, and all they seem to require is age and further elaboration; and, there cannot be a doubt, if we give them sufficient time, they will equal the parent in every sense of the word. The exterior satellite of Saturn is now said to be nearly two and a half millions of miles from the planet, and supposed to be about the size of Mars, while the size of those interior diminish as they approach the planet.

Now, it would not be very surprising if at some time in the ages of the future, at no very distant period, the larger moons of Saturn and Uranus should be attended by satellites also. It will be noticed that Neptune, the most exterior orb known in our system, is purely a telescopic planet, and hence it is so extremely difficult, even by the aid of powerful lenses, to become very well informed in relation to its moons. It has taxed all the energies of a Herschell, to form an acquaintance with the moons of Uranus, and distance is no doubt the grand reason why our astronomers are not better acquainted with the operations of the outside planets, and the systems of worlds revolving around them.

The planet Neptune is said to be 1,200,000,000 miles beyond the orbit of Uranus, and still beyond the orbit of the former, may be found within the limits of our own solar system, ample room for numerous other heavenly bodies, without interfering with any of the systems that exist in the vast sidereal heavens. This inconceivable space is no doubt occupied, to a certain extent, by other planets, surrounded with their retinues of satellites, all of which, have as yet escaped the notice of astronomers, and are probably beyond the reach of the most powerful lenses yet manufactured by men. Now, if these partially elaborated solar systems exist, as we have shown, contiguous to, and within the purlieus of this larger one, then we may well suppose that the central orbs of the less finished or smaller systems, have become independent of the great parent sun.

Now, it cannot, upon any principle of sound reasoning, be supposed that the sun, the great central luminary, possesses one attribute, or displays one power, or quality, that does not exist, in a latent condition, in the earth or in the moon, and in all other planets and satellites of our solar system. All were brought into existence, and elaborated in accordance with the same universal law, by use of the same character of forces, and the same kind of material, but all are evidently of different ages, and in different conditions of development, and hence it is, they present such very different conditions and varied manifestations. The sun has an orbital and axial revolution, and it cannot be supposed that it receives the power to perform those revolutions from any outside influence, but we must believe it generates its own forces. It also has a sufficient supply of light and warmth for its own purposes, and it apparently possesses very much to impart to those who seem to be dependent upon him for those elements so necessary to existence.

No person who gives the subject a moment's reflection can entertain the idea that the sun is dependent upon any other orb in the sidereal heavens, for his large supply of the necessary elements, light and heat, but that he produces them by powers inherent in himself. If so, we must conclude that the sun has arrived to this super-eminent positive condition, like all other things in the natural universe, by processes of development; that, he has passed from the lower or negative condition, where he was a recipient of such favors, to the higher positive state, where he may be a bountiful dispenser of these precious gifts. Then, we may well inquire in relation to the condition of those planets in the exterior orbits of our solar system, in respect to their dependence upon the sun for light and warmth.

The quantity of illumination received from the sun upon Uranus, is three hundred and sixty times less than that upon the earth, and yet, Dr. Dick, after making this statement, offers many frivolous arguments to show that such an amount might be sufficient to supply the wants of the inhabitants, and answer all the purposes of that far distant planet. If he had at the time of these remarks, possessed any knowledge of the existence of Neptune, which is revolving in an orbit so many hundred million miles beyond Uranus, he would doubtless have brought to bear the same arguments, although the sun would appear to its inhabitants but as a twinkling star in the far-off universe.

But, can a reasoning mind suppose, that 1-360th part of the illuminating power we receive from the sun, would produce any perceptible influence, in giving light and warmth to a world? All the arguments that could be brought to bear, by the ablest men that have lived, would still leave a planet dependent upon such resources, for its necessary warmth and illumination, in the coldness and darkness of eternal death. So, that the exterior planets must be either deficient of those warming, illuminating, and positive influences, or else they must have possessed such powers latent, within themselves, ready to be developed when circumstances required.

We then discover, it is an absolute necessity at the present time, and has been for innumerable ages in the past, that the exterior planets in our solar system, should furnish their own light and warmth, not only for themselves but for the use and benefit of the secondaries that surround them, and that they must have passed on from a negative, electric condition of darkness, and cold, to a magnetic, positive condition of illumination and warmth. And evidently they must ultimately assume the same position in the midst of their satellites, as our sun has assumed in the center of his planetary system. Consequently all orbits of all planets and satellites, must be spiral, and tend outwards from the center, and we must conclude that there must have been a time in the infinite ages of the past when our sun was young and preponderatingly negative, electric and cold, and dependent upon some central orb, for its light and warmth, and when it made its orbital revolution, about its central parent in a few months, or perhaps a few days. Evidently its period of revolution has very gradually enlarged, until it has attained to the incomprehensible dimensions that are almost beyond human conception, and that tax the utmost energies of the mind, in their computation. So that through all these interminable ages, it has been developing and unfolding those powers that it possessed in a latent condition from its earliest existence.

Astronomers are now well satisfied that the sun revolves in an orbit, carrying with it all our solar system, at the rate of 28,000 miles per hour, and that it would require 18,200,000 years to make a single revolution, and that it has only traveled 1-3000th part of its orbit, since the bible history of earth's creation. With this wonderful fact in view, we may consider the sun as one vast luminous planet, sustaining the same relationship to some central orb, as the primary planets sustain to him, and as the secondaries sustain to their primaries. And if this relationship, which is recognized by astronomers, is a living fact, can they suppose it was attained regardless of the eternal principles of evolvement and growth, or has it been arrived at and produced by the same great law of progressive advancement that ultimates in such relationships, among all things that exist in every portion of this universe?

Can we suppose that our moon or the moons of Jupiter or Saturn, some of which revolve around their central orb in a very few days, and at comparatively short distances, commenced their existence coeval with, or that they are of an age equal to the sun who requires such interminable ages to perform a single journey? We think the candid reflecting reader will arrive at the conclusion that the sun must have passed through all the intermediate conditions, that are possible between the present state of those moons and its own; that from a secondary it became a primary, with a family of satellites about him, and from that condition, it gradually became the great central luminous body we behold, after our system had in its spiral revolutions, traveled beyond the influence of the older central orb, to which our sun with his satellites was originally attached.

Now, upon this theory, we may suppose, which is no doubt the fact, that Neptune has her full quota of six to eight moons, which, though entirely beyond the reach of the best arranged telescope, are revolving around this planet in orbits at various distances. It has, as we have discovered, become an independent orb, generating and furnishing, not only her own magnetism, but also sufficient to dispense to her family of moons, for, if this is not the case then they are destitute of light and warmth, as it is very evident the amount they can receive from the sun, must be an infinitesimal quantity, and entirely insufficient to produce any beneficial result.

The planet Neptune being at a distance of 1,200,000,000 miles beyond the orbit of Uranus, it will be seen, that there is room for a solar system, of 1,200,000,000 miles in diameter, and that her outermost satellite might revolve in an orbit 210,000,000 miles larger in diameter than that of Jupiter, without interfering with any of the neighboring systems. All this might be done, even if the orbits of the different bodies in those systems were upon the same plane; and that might be considered a very respectable amount of territory for a young planetary system to occupy. But, if the planes of the orbits of Neptune's satellites should diverge from those of Uranus, which of course they do, then they could stretch out in their spiral journeys to an indefinite extent, without interfering in any manner with other systems; thus extending their limits through all the eternities of the future, as other systems have through the eternities of the past.

Objections may be made against the idea of spiral and constantly increasing orbits of the heavenly bodies, from the fact that it is not known that our solar year has increased in length so much as a minute in all time. Neither can it be proven that it has not increased, for no accurate observations could have been made previous to the introduction of the Copernican theory, which was presented to the world only 360 years since, and it will be impossible to establish the fact, that in 400 revolutions, the earth has not receded from the center sufficient to make our year one minute longer. One minute in 400 years is a very small amount of time, but give us that minute, and we shall establish our theory beyond the possibility of contradiction; and we assume in accordance with the analogies existing in nature, that our annual revolution has not only increased in point of time, but that the earth with all the planets is gradually receding from the central orb, just the same as the sun has receded from its grand center until it requires over 18,000,000 years to perform a single revolution.

There is no living astronomer, who can prove that our earth has not passed spirally outward from the sun one or even five million miles, since the Bible history of creation, or within the past 6,000 years. Neither is there any person who can show, that our lunar attendant has not gradually receded in her orbit, more than half her distance from the earth, since her first formation. We claim that all the heavenly bodies in the broad universe, no matter what their present condition may be, have once been infantile satellites or moons, and that they have been constructed or built mostly from materials taken from the central planet about which they revolve. We claim further, that all have commenced their career in an orbit not over 100,000 miles from the parent planet; and, that they have very slowly moved outwards in spiral orbits, as they have developed their own latent powers.

Thus we find the interior satellite of Saturn but 120,000 miles distant from that planet at the present, and there are doubtless some others invisible to human eyes much nearer than that to their parent orbs. Now, for purposes of computation we may suppose that the orbit of our earth increases so that 400 revolutions might add one minute to our year; and we may make this calculation, keeping in view the great law that seems to hold good as far as our solar system extends, that the larger the orbit the less the velocity. We should find, if our orbit enlarged and our year increased in length at the rate above mentioned, that in less than half a million years, our annual revolution would be one day of twenty-four hours longer than at the present time. We might also find that in something over a billion years the orbit of the earth would be extended to 500,000,000 miles from the sun, or beyond that in which Jupiter now performs his lengthy journeys; and, that our annual revolutions will require twelve of our years in their performance.

When we take into consideration the movements and revolutions of worlds and planetary systems, what is a billion or ten billion years? Nature, or those powers who manipulate its forces, have never been niggardly of time; when they require it, to accomplish their purposes, they draw upon the inexhaustible fountain, and the vast eternities always furnish the amount demanded, whether it may be millions or billions of ages. If the mind should revert back through the eternities of the past, to any conceivable, or computable number of centuries or millions of centuries, it would bring us no nearer the commencement than we are to-day; neither would such an interminable period in the future approximate any nearer the end.

So we perceive, that length of time required in order to carry out the great purposes of the divine architects, who construct and exert an influence over the powers that move worlds in their orbits, is a matter of no consideration, and whether it takes innumerable thousands, or millions, or billions of years, to perfect their plans, it is all one to the spirit intelligences who know no beginning of days, or end of time, but who are ever in the morning of their existence, though cycles of eternities may have passed away.

It must then appear very evident to the mind that gives this subject a thought, that our sun was once but an ordinary planet surrounded by its secondaries precisely the same as Jupiter, Saturn, or Uranus, for astronomers now pronounce it a vast luminous planet, pursuing its journey in its own appointed orbit, in the same manner with the primaries, only its orbit is vastly larger. We cannot possibly suppose that the sun has been governed by any different laws, or composed of any different materials, or that any very different processes were introduced in its construction, but that it commenced its career by the same general mode of procedure, upon the part of those who engaged in its production. Neither can we suppose the exalted intelligences who superintend the construction of planetary bodies during a comparatively more modern period are any less competent than those who projected and set in motion this great parent of our system, together with all the innumerable hosts of glistening orbs that shine forth in the sidereal heavens.

A very cursory glance at our solar system will show that all the more recent formations of this character have been produced in the shape of moons revolving around the various planets in small orbits, and performing their revolutions in a very brief space of time. It can by no means be supposed that these youthful orbs are to remain moons to all eternity, and be confined to their comparatively narrow limits, but on the contrary, without doubt there is not a moon in our solar system, but may go on and progress through the different changes, and arrive at the most exalted conditions during some period in the eternal ages of the future.

Reason, common sense and all the analogies in the natural universe, conspire to support and establish the theory, and, we hesitate not to say, that it is the most natural and harmonious view of this subject, that has ever been presented for the consideration of the human mind. The old fossilized idea that an infinite personal intelligence spoke all things into existence from nothing, by the word of his power, and set the whole machinery of the universe at work by his fiat, in a single week, has become too absurd to be received by enlightened minds of the present day, unless they are still bound by the triple chains of an old and decaying theology.

The Laplace or nebulous theory, is clumsy, unnatural, and open to a great number of grave and fatal objections, and must eventually fall to the ground, by its own cumbrous weight; notwithstanding, it has received the endorsement of so many eminent men, since it was presented to the world of mind. This theory recognizes the rational idea that our solar system sustains the relations of one grand planetary family; that the sun is the great parent of all; and, that all this numerous family of children have proceeded, or been born of this parent; but they have come to the birth in a most singular manner. The peculiar method adopted by this positive or male parent of our solar system, by which his planetary children are brought to the birth in accordance with this theory, is perfectly unique, and evidently at war with all the analogies found in the universe of nature.

It presupposes that the sun was one huge mass of nebulous matter as large in diameter as the entire solar system, somewhat lens-shaped, and, that by some inexplicable cause it acquired or received an axial motion. They say, the great activities of the exterior and equatorial portions of this immense mass of gaseous material, naturally produced condensation of particles, and when this took place the more condensed exterior could not possibly cling to, and be held by the more rarefied interior mass. Hence the vast parent orb in its earlier etherealized condition was subject to these periodical peelings, and in this manner, from time to time, gave birth to new planets, which formed themselves into such, by rolling or coiling up somewhat in the manner of a broad ribbon.

The coiling operation was of course imparted by the axial motion of the original mass, and this movement was continued until the new planet was formed into a globe, and received the requisite impetus to move onwards in its vast journeys, as well as to revolve upon its own axis. We discover, upon this hypothesis, that the new planet or young world, being in a more condensed condition than the parent, of course must be more evolved and consequently further advanced in point of development than the older one from which it proceeded. For very evidently condensation was a part of this process of evolution which all worlds must have passed through in order to arrive at the condition of solidity and materialization we find upon our earth, and which must necessarily exist upon all planetary bodies.

Now, the young planet which was thrown or peeled off from the original gaseous body, being more condensed than the parent, it might become difficult to subject this offshoot to the same peeling process, and hence the production of moons becomes quite problematical, and a doubt arises whether they could possibly be produced by any process recognized in connection with this theory. It might, however, be contended by its advocates, that matter was thrown off for the formation of the young planets in an extremely rarefied condition. But we remark, if material for the new worlds was detached into rings in this very evanescent and gaseous condition, it is quite strange how the planet Uranus came to be located 1,200,000,000 miles within the orbit of Neptune, or that the great parent mass should have receded all that long distance, before it was prepared to throw off or give birth to another infant world.

The very fact of any recession would prove conclusively, that condensation was one of the necessary conditions that must be attained by the great nebulous orb, before it could give birth to new or infantile planets; and, as a sequence, the infants must be in a condition far superior to the parent from whom they proceeded. For the parent must, during all this lengthy period, have been throwing off that portion of itself which was most advanced and unfolded, while the more rarefied or unelaborated portion remained; and while the exterior planets might have been developing up to a high state of unfoldment, the great central body must have remained in a static condition. Or, in other words, no heavenly body could possibly have passed through any processes of unfoldment, while they were giving off material for the production of dependents or satellites; and hence, the sun could not, according to this theory, have commenced its own unfoldment, until it gave birth to Mercury, or until the last primary shall be thrown off, and it has completed this portion of its duties.

Admitting this hypothesis to be correct, then all the primary planets must have remained in this gaseous condition until all the moons in our solar system were thrown off or came to the birth, and, of course, if any other moons should be constructed hereafter, they must accompany such planets as are in this rarefied condition. It follows then, that the earth can have no more moons, because the materials of which it is composed, are already quite too much solidified, and, as far as our globe is concerned, the business of world building has come to a final close. It will also be perceived, that the grand and majestic Jupiter must either still remain in a gaseous, rarefied, undeveloped condition, or else this monster specimen of planetary architecture, must be content with a much smaller number of moons than have been vouchsafed to those that are quite inferior in point of size and importance.

We think, however, that the absurdity of the nebulous or igneous theory will become obvious to the reader, not only from its unnaturalness, and inharmony, but from the utter impossibility of carrying out its clumsy details. Its incongruous method of bringing the infant worlds to the birth, is only exceeded in extravagance by filling them to the brim with incandescent molten lava after they are born and have attained maturity. We could wish that we had more time and space to devote to this very attractive and interesting subject of the development of worlds, from the lower negative conditions, to the higher magnetic state of those orbs that present themselves to the eye of the beholder, throughout the vast canopy of the sun-studded heavens. As, in all this vast array of stellar glory, among all this inconceivable twinkling display of revolving worlds, not one secondary or primary planet can be discovered by the unaided eye, if even with the most powerful lenses. For, all such are too small and in too crude and undeveloped a condition, to come within the reach of the most piercing human vision; so, all that are beheld, except our few planetary neighbors, must have arrived to the exalted condition of our own luminous orb which is the great central magnet of this solar system. All are elaborated to the condition of suns, and doubtless many are the grand centers about which systems of fully unfolded suns are wheeling in their vast and incomprehensible revolutions.

How superlatively glorious and exhilarating the contemplation of even the small portion of the universe which we can grasp within the narrow range of our conception! To behold such an infinite number of worlds and systems of worlds, all moving forward in harmonious order to a higher and still higher destiny, all working out their own advancement by forces and elements inherent within themselves, all elaborating and unfolding to the most exalted condition, is sufficient to overwhelm the reflective mind with astonishment and reverential awe. But, how much more glorious and ennobling must be the contemplations of those minds, who entertain a firm conviction that all this innumerable host of worlds and systems have been produced by finite intelligent beings, who have passed through similar experiences with ourselves! Cheering and elevating indeed must be the thought, that we too, who are now groping our way in comparative darkness through the mazes of this life, may yet arrive at the high position of those who have projected and launched forth worlds, that are now shining in all their regal splendor and magnificence. If the principles of eternal progress are admitted, this is no vague chimera, but an absolute living fact, that must necessarily take place in the order of universal nature.

It is to be hoped, that at some future day, some mind that has ability, education and time, will seize upon the few ideas we have written upon this subject, and elaborate them in a systematic manner, eliminating the great facts and principles in nature's laboratory, that would support and establish a theory of the construction of worlds and systems, that would commend itself to the highest order of intelligent thinkers. Quite certain it is at the present, we have no theory which maintains in all its different phases, a harmonious interblending of all the great principles and analogies of nature. All those which have been presented by the philosophers of the past ages are, to a certain extent, vague and unsatisfactory, and leave the mind clouded by doubts and uncertainties. And we modestly venture an opinion that the view we have so briefly presented is less cumbered with objectionable features than any which has yet come to the notice of the thinking world.

CHAPTER X.

WHO ARE THE WORLD BUILDERS?

We met a fisherman one day, who, apparently, had recently wakened to the fact that there was much in this world to be learned, and manifesting a desire to commence near the beginning, he directly inquired, "Who made God?" and we were compelled to confess our ignorance and entire inability to give him any information upon that interesting subject. However much men may have talked of such a being, and told us concerning his divine attributes and characteristics, it may be very much doubted whether the wisest of them really know anything in regard to this infinite intelligence, about whom they are so constantly and familiarly prating. They tell us what he likes, and what he dislikes, what we must do in order to gratify and please him, and also what will be very offensive, and excite his anger and great displeasure.

We are told he is self-existent, and the creator of all things, and hence there must have been a time, when nothing except him, had an existence; when he was all alone, a unit, in this vast universe. We are persuaded, however, not one of the wise men, who know, or pretend to know, so much of this being, could have given an intelligent reply to our fisherman; and we are also persuaded that, if these wise men should compare notes, they would find that each one had a somewhat different view of this being, with whom they seem to be so familiar.

The various sects evidently have diversified opinions in regard to his likes and dislikes, and his peculiar notions and preferences, as the forms and ceremonies introduced in their worship would indicate. Surely the Catholic cannot entertain the same idea of his characteristics as the Presbyterian, for, if so, their worship would be the same. Neither can the Quaker, with his plain dress and simplicity in worship, hold the same views with his neighbor the Baptist, who practices the hydropathic method of gaining his favor. We trust if we could carefully examine the mentalities of all the people who claim so much knowledge concerning this being, we should be led to conclude, there existed a profound ignorance upon the whole subject; and that each individual possessed a God of his own creation, in accordance with his own conceptions of greatness.

If such a being could have existed as a unit, at a time previous to all other existences, either spiritual or material, and before a single world had been created, then that being must certainly have been devoid of all experience in regard to the creation of worlds, and the undertaking, to say the least, must have been an untried experiment, and the first world that was produced, must have been created without any previous experience in world building. We can very easily discover how an intelligent being, alone in the universe, could have been possessed of infinite wisdom and power, because, he would have had all the wisdom and power there was in the whole, if the whole contained nothing but himself. But at the present time, when we find great multitudes of individuals in possession of given quantities of wisdom and power, it is extremely difficult to understand how one being can be so constituted as to possess it all.

If the universal worlds are filled with individualized intelligences, and each one has in possession more or less wisdom and consequent power, and they have this belonging to themselves as identities, then how can it be said, that one single personal identity can possess all the wisdom and power which can possibly exist in all these universal realms? If it is acknowledged that globes or worlds are mechanical structures, and that it requires wisdom and power to produce them, and there are almost infinite hosts of intelligent beings who possess a certain amount of the requisite qualifications, what then, the necessity or propriety of calling upon a single individual, however wise and powerful, to perform all the labor of building all the worlds in the vast universe? For, if worlds are mechanical structures, and built from gross materials, there must be a great amount of intelligent labor to be performed by some living beings, in managing and directing the forces that may result in the orderly arrangement of all the materials of which a world is composed.

"What can we reason, but from what we know?" But men have commenced at the other end, at what they did not know, or could not possibly comprehend, and reasoned from infinity downwards, and have found themselves in confusion, darkness and uncertainty. They have been compelled to assume that infinity exists in a single personality, and then reason from the infinite identity, of which they could know nothing, backwards to those things of which they may form some rational conception by actual contact of the senses. And thus, they assume the existence of an eternal infinite being, whom they choose to call God, who, they say, by his omnipotent fiat, produced all things from nothing, and they are then out in the depths of an unknown sea, enveloped in obscurity. For, there is not an intelligent living being upon the earth, or above the earth, who possesses the least substantial knowledge of that personality, who, they say, is the author and creator of all worlds with their various appurtenances.

In this manner, they mix up natural forces with special powers, cause and effect with supernatural interference, universal law with a God outside the universe, who controls law to suit his own purposes, or in answer to the earnest petitions of some of his special favorites. Thus all is confusion and bewilderment, because we cannot know where the natural leaves off, and the supernatural commences, and neither can we know how far nature extends, and when we shall get outside her boundaries, nor where or what we shall be, when we arrive at such a destination.

Hence, in this condition, and with this view, it becomes necessary for faith to take precedence of reason and knowledge, as all things have commenced, they now exist, and must ultimate, where reason and knowledge cannot extend. Thus faiths and beliefs came into requisition, as they can extend into all possible conditions, and they can be enjoyed largely, by the most ignorant, far more easily than by the learned. We are doubtless to a very great extent, indebted to the various faiths and beliefs, for the bondage and darkness, that have overshadowed humanity in the past, and the same result must follow in the future, until substantial, progressive knowledge takes precedence of blind and unsubstantial beliefs.

The human mind is entirely incapable of conceiving how any living sentient being can obtain wisdom without experience and observation, or unless he obtains it by the same processes, which all intelligent beings who have acquired knowledge, have necessarily passed through. A certain kind of knowledge, possessed by the highest spiritual intelligence of which we can entertain an idea, must be identically the same when understood by an ordinary mortal. The only difference there can possibly be in the two cases, is that, the one possesses a larger fund of knowledge to draw from than the other, and consequently has become a superior being.

A mathematical problem understood by a child, can be nothing more than such a problem, although it may be part of the wisdom of a spiritual intelligent being, far beyond any conceptions we are able to entertain concerning a God; and it must be admitted, that the power which can grasp and comprehend this problem, is of a similar character in both individuals. Then, we must conclude that the most exalted intelligent being must at some period in his history, have acquired the ability to understand the problem, in the same manner as the child; by the exercise of the mental powers. If a knowledge of any given subject, is the same in all portions of the universe, and all knowledge may be found in one great treasure-house, then it follows, that mentality, or the power of grasping and comprehending knowledge, must be of the same character also, whether found in the school-boy, or the highest individualized spiritual existence. What can we say then, of the exalted living intelligence who has acquired the knowledge and consequent power to plan and superintend the construction of a World? We must necessarily conclude that he arrived at the position, and acquired all he knows, in precisely the same manner as the one who can only construct a watch; by experience and observation.

Paul found at Athens an altar inscribed to the "un known God;" and claimed that he could illuminate their minds concerning the invisible being whom they ignorantly worshiped. But did he do so? He simply told them what their own poets had told them before, that in him we live, move and have our being, and that we are also his offspring. Thus he left the matter shrouded in the same darkness as he found it, and with all that his successors have ever written or said, it still remains inscribed upon the altar of every intelligent mind, "The unknown God."

No higher idea of a God has ever been expressed in modern times by the most intellectual Christian, than was taught by a Grecian heathen. Parmenides, who lived before Plato, said, "Since, therefore, it was not generated, it is, and always was, and will be, and it is infinite, for it has neither beginning nor end." This was a part of his conception concerning the unknown being of which he knew quite as much as Paul, or Spurgeon, or Beecher.

The human intelligence in its investigations can have

little to do with that which is entirely beyond any conceptions it can entertain. It being entirely impossible for us then, to entertain any rational conception of what existed previous to the commencement of the eternities of the past, it would be worse than foolish to base any conclusions upon what we might possibly conjecture did exist. Any such conclusions would of course be utterly without foundation, and must ultimately fall of their own dead weight.

We may expand our thought particles to their furthest tension, into the eternities of the past, yet we shall be quite unable to fathom or conceive of a beginning; much less, a period previous to the beginning of all things. But, on the contrary, we shall only be able to contemplate a universe in active operation, with hosts of planetary bodies in the material realms, peopled with rudimental beings, and incalculable numbers of spirit individualities, actively engaged in their several duties; some assisting in the completion of worlds, and others pursuing enterprises of perhaps less importance.

Suppose now, we come back nearer home, and base our conclusions upon foundations composed of those materials of which we may acquire some definite knowledge. Perhaps, we may discover some method by which the exalted intelligent beings who are competent to plan and construct worlds, may be produced, in harmony with laws that exist within the realms of the natural universe. We may discover the great fact, that it would not absolutely require an infinite being to project and set in motion a world like ours. We think we are quite safe in the conclusion that spiritual entities exist, who have had a portion of their early discipline and education upon globes no larger or better than the one we occupy, and who have become entirely accomplished in the stupendous art of world building, and possess the ability to project and execute an undertaking of that character most successfully.

It is quite evident also, they may possess all the requisite qualifications without laying claims to infinite attributes, in any proper sense of the term; for, as we have said, a being who is infinite must possess all the attributes and characteristics of all the beings which exist. They must live within him, and if they are finitely bad, then he must be infinitely bad as well as good; because, all that is bad is contained within him, as well as what is good. He must be the infinite whole, hence, nothing can exist beside him, and all vile and abominable things must be a part and parcel of his infinite personality, as nothing but his personality can exist, if that is infinite.

If all finite beings proceeded from, or are the children of an infinite personal father, then they must have inherited all their characteristics and personal attributes from the father, and they of course can be nothing finitely, except he is the same in an infinite degree. Consequently, if a large portion of the inhabitants of the earth are heathen, barbarous, and savage, then he must be an infinite heathen, barbarian and savage, as well as infinitely good, powerful and wise. He must be infinitely antagonistic, as well as harmonious, and all wars and conflicts proceed from him, as well as all of peace and quietness, for all exist in him. In fact we find this infinite personal being rather more than most devout people have bargained for.

Now, if we cannot discover some means, by which such an infinite personality might be formed, we should have very good reason to doubt, whether he has an existence; for, the human mind is incapable of entertaining any very rational idea of a being, unless he can first form some conception of a manner in which such a being might be produced, in accordance with laws and principles of which he has some knowledge. The time has come in the history of human research, when blind faith will hardly answer the purpose of thinking minds, when beliefs and tacit assents do not suffice. Considerate persons very properly ask a reason, and most assuredly it is quite time for all who would improve, to keep within the bounds of their own reasoning conceptions; for they can certainly gain nothing by going outside. Our mentalities can in no way be benefited or improved by going beyond our rational conceptions, taking things for granted, and adopting a blind faith unsupported by evidence.

Doubtless all will admit men exist as intelligent beings, and that all they have in their organization, either of a physical or mental character, they must possess inherently within themselves, and all of this must have been aggregated or gathered from some source within the spiritual and material realms. It must be admitted also, that all beings possessed of spiritual organizations, must be similar in their natures and properties, whether the spirit is clothed with gross material, or that which is finer. As a sequence, then, if one spiritual being, capable of comprehending ideas, has existed from all eternity, all spirits endowed with such capabilities must be eternal also. For we discover, the one who comprehends a larger fund of ideas, is only more progressed and exalted, and has had more experience under favorable conditions; give the others similar opportunities under similar conditions, and they may arrive at the same point of exaltation.

There is evidently no intelligent being who is able to inform us of the method by which something may be made from nothing, because the human mind cannot possibly entertain any such conception. We are forced then, to conclude that every particle of matter which is now sufficiently gross in its character to be visible to us, had an eternal existence. If so, spiritual substances which are so much higher and finer must be eternal also; and, an eternal existence, as we have said, involves an eternal history, with an experience of the same duration.

We find the spirits that exist in man, and are brought up to a state of development commensurate with such existence, are intimately connected with material organizations, and do not leave such organizations, until a dissolution of material particles commences, and many times not before much of the organism is wasted away. May not the same spirit have been connected with some material organism, during all its previous history, and passed out in a similar manner? Physically man seems to be a microcosm of the whole, and has in his organism a part of all organisms below him, that is, the material of his physical has been prepared for him by coming up through all the forms that are below; so that he is the grand culmination of all those inferior animal organizations, and depends entirely upon the lower forms of organic life for his existence, as well as continued sustenance.

Suppose by the use of food, we incorporate into the physical structure the peculiar elements contained in the vegetable and animal kingdoms; and most people are in the habit of using more or less of this kind of food. In doing so, they swallow so much of the positive and negative elements which existed in the mineral kingdom or in the earth, and which have been extracted for the use of vegetables and animals they have eaten, as well as for themselves. The vegetables and animals were composed of carbon, oxygen, hydrogen and nitrogen, together with all other elements needed to build up the human structure, and sustain life. If they eat an egg they obtain very nearly the same essences, served in a little different form. Give an individual the nice wheaten loaf and well-made butter, and life may be sustained by adding the needed amount of fluids. If so, those articles must contain the very elements that compose the human physical system. We should find in the wheat, silicon, carbonate of lime, magnesia, allumina, oxide of iron and manganese; in the butter, carbon, oxygen and hydrogen, and if you add cheese, much the same elements. Those are precisely the essences or spiritual substances which exist in the earth in such profusion, and they are precisely what we require to sustain life.

Yet we would not care to sit down to a repast of silicon, carbonate of lime, nitrogen, etc., unless served up to us under their various disguises, to make them palatable and attractive. We would not desire, either, to sit down to a dish of insects and worms, however nicely they might be prepared, but we do sit down and relish with great gusto the broiled chicken or bird that has subsisted entirely upon worms and insects, and has incorporated them into the very flesh we are eating with so much satisfaction. We turn with disgust and loathing from the snake that crawls upon the earth, and the garbage that is thrown into the street, yet the pig seems to delight in them, and devours them with no seeming repugnance, and we do not hesitate to eat the flesh that is partially composed of such materials. We convert the contents of our barn yards and privies into the vegetables produced in the fields and gardens, and partake of the very elements in this form that were so disgusting in the other; and we may eat or drink what we please, we find we are only gathering some element that originally belonged to our great parent the earth. But, all the elements are purified and refined by passing through the various forms of organized life, and thus prepared to enter into, and form the component parts of this highest physical organism.

It is a well-established fact that man has arrived at his present physical condition, upon the principle of reproduction; then it follows, that he must have originated in the very lowest organism capable of performing that particular function. His origin, then, could not have been in the earliest vertebrate or the exceedingly diminished living animalculæ, but must have been with the most infinitesimal atom, and during the inconceivable millions of ages or eternities, he has come up to his present condition by natural processes, subject to the law of eternal progress. For, if some miraculous power has been connected with his experience or history, if some supernatural forces have intervened, when could the miracle have come in? at what period in the history of the race, was this remarkable supernatural interposition of miraculous power introduced? If such power was necessary in the production of man, then why not in the production of all other forms of organic life, and all aggregations of atomic particles? So in that case, natural forces would have been entirely unnecessary.

If the law of reproduction brings into existence animal and human organisms to-day, and it is an eternal law, which all must admit, then, we ask, when did the law of reproduction commence its operations? Being like all other material or spiritual laws in its character, it could have had no beginning, but has been continually operative wherever and whenever atomic particles have existed. And they have eternally existed, positive and negative, male and female; and wherever two atoms have been united, this great law has been there to produce its result. Is there any difficulty, when you have the law, the elements, and the material, to produce all the forms of organic life, from the lowest to the highest, without any miraculous interposition in the one case more than in another? But this subject has been treated upon extensively by numerous authors, and it is unnecessary for us to reproduce their views, that prove most clearly, we came into our present condition in accordance with universal law, and inherit all our being, or physical organism, from the earth our parent.

And now comes in the more difficult question of the spirit entity that is attached to the physical, and during life is inseparable. We notice that all aggregations and particles of matter possess inherent properties, attributes, and constituent elements, as well as form, size, affinities, etc., and what are these but the spirit of the particles and aggregations? All atoms are either positive or negative, male or female, and hence they may affinitize; all atoms also being possessed of form, size, extension, and other attributes, we claim all these several characteristics to be connected with the spirit of the atoms, and this spirit having an existence, must continue forever; for whatever has an existence in the realms of nature, must continue, as you can no more return something to nothing, than create something from nothing.

If you pass the so-called inorganic atomic substances, and come up to the realms of organized living forms, as the animalculæ and infusoria, you will find entities with still more apparent attributes and characteristics, they have life and locomotion, and are sensuous; they taste, see, hear, feel and smell, have desires, and fears, with combativeness and destructiveness, and are to all intents individualized living entities, and are evidently preparing for a higher condition, and what should hinder their occupying this higher condition, in accordance with the immutable law of progress? If there had been no spirit in the animalcule, it would not have been a living organized being, with all the attributes we have found it to possess, and there can be no doubt but the spirit must have been developed, in the inorganic atom, and prepared to unite with the living organism, and in this condition is preparing for still further advancement and growth. When we learn that the spirit entities are the real existences, that are clothed with organic forms, we shall find a key that will unlock much that has been dark and mysterious in regard to the origin and multitudinous changes that have taken place in the lower forms of organic life.

Darwin has labored through a volume, to show that so-called different species have been produced through all their variations, by natural selection and change of condition. But, had he discovered that each organized being had a spiritual entity, that was susceptible of change and growth, and that the spirit had power to modify the form of the living materialized being, he could have explained the phenomena of the origin and various transformations of the different species much more easily, and given a clearer explanation of the whole subject; because, upon this hypothesis we readily discover how changes of visible forms must and will necessarily take place. The spirit in its upward progress necessarily demands a higher and better form for its residence, than it had previous, and nature provides means to satisfy that demand, in a superior being of the same species, or else it must advance to some form in a higher species. All spiritual entities being eternally progressive, there being no stand-still in the universe, must progress to a certain extent during their residence in any and every form of organic life they inhabit; hence, a form precisely the same as the one occupied previously, would not answer their purpose. We have noticed that spirit, being sublimated and finer, exerts power over grosser material; so, it must have a controlling influence in modifying and changing the materialized forms into which it enters, to adapt them to its improved condition.

In defining our position more clearly, we remark that we shall be forced to admit, that all material atoms must be attended by corresponding spirit entities, or, in fact, the atom is a spirit entity which may have gathered a materialized form around it; and further, it is an uncreated eternal existence. We know atoms exist, and we cannot conceive, that they were produced from nothing, by any power or principality above or outside of nature, and we can entertain no conception of any law within the natural realms, by which that result might be attained. We learn also, that certain aggregations of material atoms are endowed or accompanied by corresponding spirit entities, which fact is very generally admitted; because the activities and attributes of the spirit individualities in the human form, are too palpable to be denied. The human spirit, if it is able to contemplate eternal entities, can much more easily comprehend the idea, that there might have been, from the eternal ages of the past, an infinite number of simple and homogeneous existences, than to grasp the thought, that there sprang into being, or that there was one single complex heterogeneous infinite self-existent personality. It is far easier to conceive the idea, because it is more in harmony with natural principles, to conclude the lesser existed first, and ultimated in the greater, than that the greater existed previously, and produced the lesser from nothing by his infinite power. The first conception is comparatively simple and natural, while the latter is marvelous and inexplicable, and its contemplation leaves the mind in a state of utter confusion and darkness.

We do not wish to assert that there is not such a

being, somewhere in existence, who exercises universal control, and who is capable of supervising all the universal worlds; but we must think, it would be a hardship to place all those vast burdens upon his shoulders. A general supervision of all the machinery of all worlds would certainly require his constant and unremitting attention and care, while there must be infinite hosts of spiritual intelligences, who have come up through all the lower forms and conditions, and having had untold billions of ages of experience and observation in the realms of progressive knowledge, in which to acquire ability, ought to be abundantly competent to act in a thousand different capacities in the administration of the affairs of worlds and systems of worlds, and they all seem to be existing in a state of listless idleness.

I hope we shall not be charged with irreverence, if we should express the opinion, that it would not require infinite intelligence and power, to construct and take the entire supervision of the affairs of the world we inhabit, because comparatively it is a small world, and evidently very inferior, in some respects, to others in our solar system. It has not the belts of Jupiter, or the rings of Saturn, or the light and heat dispensing power of the sun; hence, we may conclude, that it would require a more extended knowledge to produce worlds with those several appurtenances; still we should be compelled to entertain the highest reverence and admiration for a being who was able to produce one like this, and supervise its affairs successfully; although we might conclude there were other heavenly bodies, very many thousand times larger, that would require still greater knowledge and experience to construct and manage.

Moses and Joshua, David, Daniel and Paul talk very familiarly of the God of Gods and Lord of Lords, and if they mean anything, they must mean, that the one God is higher, and exercises authority over the others; the same of the Lord, as the term is used indiscriminately to represent the same idea. The God referred to and spoken of by Moses so constantly, must be far from an infinite being, as the history is conclusive upon this point, and shows him to be deficient in very many respects. He made great blunders, and then, vain and unsuccessful attempts to remedy his mistakes. He done many things for which he manifested great sorrow and regret at a subsequent period, and he partially destroyed the results of his own labors. He could not have been the author and parent of the whole human race, for if so, he would have manifested the same parental care and solicitude towards the whole, and treated all his children in a similar kind and fatherly manner, as any good, just and honorable father would be pleased to do. But we learn, this Hebrew God chose one people as his especial favorites and rejected the balance, treating them with great unkindness and severity. He made use of his own chosen people to drive the rejected nations from their homes, destroy their property, deprive them of their liberties and lives; and, in some instances, totally annihilate all except the virgins, who were spared for the use of the soldiery.

We perceive it would be impossible, taking all this history into consideration, to entertain a very exalted respect for the God who is represented in its pages. So far from being infinite and entirely beyond a desire for earthly honors and earthly enjoyments, he prescribed minutely the forms of worship he preferred, and the numbers of beeves, and sheep, and birds with which he would like to regale his senses, and we must rise from the perusal of that history, with the conviction, that if there is an exalted being in this universe, all of whose attributes and perfections are infinite, then Moses and the fathers have not described him, neither could they have had any rational conception of such a spiritual personality.

We notice, that we find certain material organisms we call human, possessed of spiritual entities, with peculiar and very numerous attributes, which we discover might exist independent of this particular form through which they now manifest themselves, and that such spirit entities only use their present forms, as a medium of manifestation and preparation for a more advanced condition of existence. One prominent reason why we say they are endowed with what is called immortality, is that they possess properties and attributes entirely distinct, and not at all dependent upon the gross material particles composing their organisms; attributes that may as well exist in some other and higher condition. We clearly perceive that joy and sorrow, love and hatred, hope and fear, an ability to grasp thought, ideas and principles, and to discriminate between truth and error, are attributes of spiritual entities, and not of gross material forms, and we cannot doubt the continued existence of those spirit individualities who have in possession, characteristics and endowments of so sublime a nature.

We should look upon the author of our existence as extremely unjust and cruel, who could place within us, fondly cherished aspirations and lofty hopes, and then cut us off in the morning of our history, without any realization of those bright visions, that he had brought so prominently to our view; and as no such injustice and cruelty can exist, then the spirit personality must live. It must also live because the numerous attributes it has in possession, of which the spirit is composed, are eternal and cannot die; and also, because it can cope with, grasp, and comprehend, and make its own, ever-living principles, and solve problems that have existed from all eternity, and will so continue. It will live because it is a living entity, a something, and cannot be put outside of the realms of nature, and changed into nothing.

If we look along down through the lower forms of organized life, we shall find some living entities who can safely lay claim to a portion of the same characteristics that exist in the human organism. We have learned, that a marked feature in the spirit individuality of the human, was the possession of attributes which distinguish it from the grosser material, that may dissolve and fall into decay. The query now arises, with regard to the number of those attributes and endowments that might be required, to constitute a living spirit entity in the proper sense of the term. We shall find some human beings who possess vastly more endowments and attributes, than some others; but, it will be admitted that the weakest men or women possess within themselves undying spirits. Then we find, that the imperishability of spirits, does not depend upon the number of their endowments, but upon the fact that they are spirits, or individualized living entities with certain attributes, they hold in common with the human race, however small may be the number of those attributes. If the number is small to-day, time, and the unchanging law of progress will necessarily carry all these spiritual entities to higher conditions.

We think, if we carefully examine the natural history of the dog, his habits, customs, peculiarities, endowments and qualifications, we shall be compelled to admit, there is much in him perfectly analogous to the human. Does he not manifest strong affection for his friends, remarkable fidelity, and care, patience and watchfulness, concern for his master's interests, and wonderful sagacity? Has he not combativeness, destructiveness, inhabitiveness, cautiousness, and an organized brain stored with various faculties, all ready to be called into activity, as occasion may require? Volumes might be filled with remarkable and very interesting incidents of canine sagacity, and faithfulness, and all these traits of character, they hold in common with man, and many of them are classed among the higher virtues, when exhibited in the human race. Some of these animals appear so noble, that we form very strong attachments for them, and are almost inclined to bow with respect when they enter our presence, and there can be no doubt very many of them possess spirits entirely too large and expanded for the forms they inhabit, that are only waiting to go forward upon their journeys.

We call those same endowments immortal when they exist in man, and if so, why not in this lower organized being? We must conclude that the dog is possessed of mental or spiritual qualities and attributes. If so, he must become an individualized spiritual entity. Such being the case, how can we say, this entity has not been prepared to enter this condition by passing through all forms and organizations below him. If we are driven to the conclusion, that the dog has within him, a living spirit entity because we see in him qualities and characteristics, distinct from his material form, and perfectly analogous to those in man, then we shall be forced to admit the same of all forms and organizations below the dog, both in the organic and inorganic realms. Suppose we examine a grain of sand, we find about one-half silicon, the other oxygen. It has form, extension, and qualities that are independent of the material, and though it has fewer attributes, it has sufficient to make it a spiritual entity, as well as a material form, as we see the silicon is the visible materialized portion, while the oxygen is a part of the invisible spiritual entity that exists in this particle of matter, and which has become an individualized entity, and must remain so when the silicon is dissolved. This spiritualized entity may change its form and progress, but it can by no means be expelled from the universe or changed to nothing.

If we admit that there must be spirit entities in any form of organic life below man, because we find them possessing a sensuous nature, with organs, faculties, and all attributes the same as man, then where shall we find the line that marks the boundaries, or the line of division upon which we may stand, and say, upon this side all forms have living spirit entities, upon that side they are destitute of such properties or attributes. Eternal progress must be an unmeaning term, else we shall be driven, without the least possibility of escape, to admit that the infinitesimal atom is possessed of a spirit entity that cannot die, but must rise through all the gradations and successions of aggregations and organic forms, unfolding and taking on at each step in its journey, until it ascends through the entire scale, to the highest condition of which the human mind can entertain a conception. We must adopt this idea, or abandon all idea of progressivve existence, for, if we have progressed up to a given point, where could that progression have commenced, unless at the lowest? and, if we are to progress in the future, where can we terminate, but at the highest? if we can have any proper conception of the highest, or the ultimate of all progression.

Then, what can be required in order to produce worlds in accordance with eternal laws and principles existing within the boundaries of nature's realms? We answer, that we must have progressed, intelligent beings, who are able to bring to bear and manipulate the requisite forces, by which the atoms and corresponding spirit entities may be moulded into their million different forms, with sufficient time for the necessary evolutions. With these conditions, there can be no need of introducing a single miraculous interposition during the entire process, but, all may be accomplished, from their inception to their comparative maturity, in strict conformity with universal laws. But, we are asked, how all these things could have existed without being preceded by an infinite God? and we ask in return, how the supreme infinite God could have existed unless preceded by all those lesser things? and it is quite proper to inquire which theory concerning this matter is best sustained by universal facts and philosophy?

Now, what fact is there that clearly proves that a personality does now or ever did exist, who holds in his individual possession, all wisdom and all power? Not one; for we clearly perceive that those attributes are subdivided among untold millions of intelligences, and it follows that one single being cannot possess all that is so extensively divided. We are told that it would require infinite intelligence to produce all worlds. That might be so, but there is no proof, and far from any probability, that one being did produce all worlds; there was certainly no necessity, for, there must have existed plenty of intelligences who knew how to build worlds from as remote a period, as can be conceived of by the human mind. Should we look all over the broad universe for a fact which would sustain the hypothesis, that such an infinite being sprang into existence, possessing all knowledge and power, without previous experience, who framed and enacted all the multitudinous laws by which nature is governed, in its various departments, who produced from nothing the atomic particles, out of which the globes are composed, we shall find no such fact, and surely all the analogies in the natural universe are in direct opposition to any such idea.

We do not wish by any means to deprive our friends, who stand in need of such a being, of their long-cherished idea of an infinite personal God, whom they have been honestly endeavoring to adore and worship with becoming reverence. But we say, without fear of successful contradiction, that if they ever really find the being whom they have vainly imagined, they must find him outside the realms of universal nature, in some imaginary domain which they will scarcely reach during all the eternities of the future, because nature embraces all there is, or ever will be in the material or spiritual worlds. Infinity means all of all things in the broadest sense of the term; so, it is absolutely impossible for one personality, whether it may be in unity or trinity, to possess and comprehend all, while other individual entities possess anything. If they have power to move a hand, that power belongs to them, together with all other forces inherent in their individualities.

When Jesus said to his disciples (if he said it), that "all power was given him, in heaven and upon the earth," it was a terrible exaggeration, or else a simple mistake; for, take the literal history of this person in its broadest sense, and there is not a particle of evidence to prove the fact, that he was in possession of all power, either before or after his death. The history establishes conclusively, that he possessed but a limited amount of power, or that he, like others, was subjected to the control of law administered by higher powers. He certainly did not possess the power of the Jewish Sanhedrim, or the authority that Pilate received from the government at Rome. If he had, he certainly would not have perished upon the cross an unwilling victim of Jewish hatred and prejudice. He surely would not have erected a cross for himself, and nailed his hands and feet to its timbers, or provided any other means for such a death; for, then he would have been a suicide. He died, then, by a power and authority over which he exercised no control; and he evidently did not acquiesce in the arrangement, for if so, why was he agitated in such a manner as to sweat so profusely, "like great drops of blood running down to the earth?" Why did he pray so earnestly, saying, "If possible, let this cup pass from me, nevertheless, not as I will, but as thou wilt?" showing conclusively it was not his will to die, and that he only manifested that resignation, which thousands of others, both before and after, have evinced in their trying moments. He, like the others, submitted to a fate which could not be averted by any power they could bring to bear.

All of his doings that are any way marvelous, are said to have been performed independent of, or in opposition to, natural laws; but what wonderful thing did he do, or could he have done, inside of the domain of nature? So far from having all power, he had not the least power or influence in any one of the civil governments then in existence. Does any one pretend that he possessed wisdom or power sufficient to superintend the construction of worlds, or that he could have supervised the building of a moon upon correct mechanical principles? We doubt much whether the most ardent Trinitarian ever conceived any such idea, or that he could even now, with all his additional experience, be competent to act in any such capacity, or perform any labor of that character. We are quite sure he never said he could, and he never during his earth history, accomplished anything which would indicate that he possessed powers and abilities sufficient to have contrived and built a solar system, with all its complicated machinery; and that, would have been but a trifle compared to the whole. The power required to project and set in motion all the untold number of solar systems in the broad universal domain, would stretch infinitely beyond what would be required to produce the single system attached to our central sun.

Then how senseless and ridiculous has it been, through all the long ages, to deify this simple, unpretentious individual, and endow *him* with infinite wisdom and power, who never manifested sufficient ability to construct, and give life to the least insect, or animal organization, and who never made any pretensions to any knowledge of the original universal laws and principles which must be so prominent a portion of the wisdom of a God!

If infinity means all, it comprehends all there is of matter and spirit, of laws and forces, of space and time, of positives and negatives, of male and female, of life and death, and individual and collective forms, and if there is such a personality who embraces all these things, then all are absorbed and swallowed up in this infinite being, and the idea of infinite hosts of personal individualities, is a myth and a delusion, and not to be entertained. Again, if there is an infinitely omnipresent personality, who fills alike the immensity of space, then there can be nothing in space but that omnipresent person, else space, would be more than filled, which cannot be, and if this infinite being possesses all the knowledge in the vast universe, and all other infinite perfections, and has so possessed them from all eternity, then he is evidently devoid of some attributes and qualities of an essential character, enjoyed by lower spirit personalities. Because, with him there could be no change, and consequently he has no enlivening hopes or bright aspirations which may reach into the future, and the eternities of that future must roll on with him, in one dull, monotonous round eternally, destitute of the cheering expectations that animate the souls of all intelligences throughout the earthly and spiritual spheres. There can be no such thing as an unchangeable being, no matter how exalted he may be. Every day's experience must produce some change. The great universe moves onward in its ample rounds. It is not to-day precisely as it was yesterday, and something will be added to-morrow. Unchangeability is death, because it is a cessation of activity; where there is life there must be change, and when any positive living entity is prepared to live without change, he becomes negative, goes down into *Belisma*, and there rests till he is ready to rise and go forward in the ever-changing history of all living intelligences, high or low.

Then let us come back within nature's domain, where we shall find all the materials and forces requisite to produce the mechanics who can construct all the worlds that are necessary to be built, without miracle or supernatural or unnatural means. Why are men so willing to go outside for power to produce what they behold, when they are so unacquainted with the thousand laws and forces inside of nature's realms? Evidently, because it has been much more easy to imagine a miracle, than to open and peruse understandingly nature's great volume; again, the so-called sacred writings, which talk so freely about miracles, and seem to ignore philosophical and natural deductions, have been thrust upon the masses as the only true guide to eternal truth. But, however much our great mother may have been ignored, she has existed, and has been, with her silent processes, working all the time that men have been disregarding her teachings, and she has provided infinite atoms, and spirit entities, that are working and toiling their way upwards, as we have already shown, and the requisite laws have eternally existed, by which they may rise from the lowest possible condition up to the highest, constantly ascending by the means provided.

Mark, now, we do not say man has been an ape, or a dog, or the moss upon the rock, but we do say that our spirit entities have progressed from a lower condition, and if so, in that lower condition they might have been well adapted to occupy the physical form of the ape. But then, it was not man; it was a part of the same living entity less developed, and of course not then in a condition to exist in man, so that man could not have been a chimpanzee or anything lower, although the living spirit within him might have traveled upwards through that common highway; it might during its progressive history, have passed through those conditions.

The fact seems pretty well established, that we have some forty different faculties of mind, and about the same number of organs, and that we possess many of them in common with the lower forms of organic beings. Some of the faculties or organs may evidently come up to us well developed or fully rounded out, from their experience and expansion in the lower organisms; for instance, combativeness and destructiveness surely find quite as favorable a field for their active exercise and development in many of the animal species as they do in the human, and we must admit, they are identical in both. We look out upon the face of human society, and find multitudes of people who have evidently brought very much of the animal with them, for they exhibit traits of character that are far below, rather than above some of the animal race, and prove too clearly from whence they came, and what is their inheritance.

Doubtless if we were the immediate offspring of a perfect being, we should inherit all the characteristics of that good and perfect being, and that we should be comparatively good and amiable, just and upright, and we could have no bad propensities, no combativeness, no destructiveness, nor any evil passions; because we could not possibly have inherent in our natures anything we did not receive from the parent, as all our component elements would have come from him, and consequently we should be like him, good, just and holy. As we discover we are full of all manner of so-called uncleanness, evil passions and propensities, we must conclude we came from the other direction, and are gradually unfolding to a higher state and condition; and as we *are* very evidently progressing, there need be no apprehensions, but sufficient experience will bring us to that more advanced and improved condition, that is entirely commensurate, with our highest aspirations.

Yet the affairs of our world, from its earliest history, must have been under the supervision of intelligence. But, we must conclude, it was an intelligence which was acquired in accordance with the general law governing such matters; that it was obtained by experience and observation, the supervisors having passed through all conditions below. Hence they had become qualified to understand all those conditions, and all laws appertaining to all the organizations through which they have passed, from the most diminutive atom up to their exalted and gloriously supernal heights, and depths, and lengths, and breadths of knowledge and power, that enabled them to undertake and successfully accomplish the wonderful project of constructing and managing the affairs of a world.

Suppose now, it becomes necessary and proper, that our earth should be accompanied in her long and tedious journeys, with a second moon; where do we expect to find intelligent beings that would be competent to undertake its construction? Is there a doubt but we have within the limits of the spiritual spheres, immediately attached to our world, hosts of living spirits, who have made this matter their especial study, and who are abundantly able to take a world in pieces, and re-adjust it again, in all its parts, with the utmost precision and correctness. Or even, if our world's spirit spheres do not produce those that have sufficient age and experience, there are plenty of other worlds, and other spheres, that must have existed immense cycles of ages longer than our own. We cannot apprehend any serious trouble in obtaining the necessary skill and wisdom to superintend such a structure, among the untold millions of spiritual spheres. However, there can be little doubt but all the needed ability may be found at home.

Suppose we reduce the world to the age of the Mosaic history, and allow an intelligent person five thousand years in which to obtain a knowledge of the forces and materials found in nature's realms, and the multiplicity of laws governing the various departments. That would be equal to 500 collegiate terms of ten years each, and taking into consideration the superior advantages that spirit intelligences must possess over feeble mortals, as they can see, and handle, and thus become familiar with those spiritual essences and sublimated materials of which we can only learn from a careful observation of their effects. Even that length of time, or a far shorter period, would be amply sufficient in which to acquire all the knowledge and experience necessary to render an intelligent person competent to superintend the construction of a satellite or moon, which some time might ultimate in a planet, or even a sun. He might have spent the first 2,000 years in obtaining a theoretical knowledge of all the sciences requisite to be understood, and then the other 3,000 in a practical application of this acquired knowledge as an assisstant in the mechanical department of any of the numerous worlds, that are constantly being constructed in every portion of the great universe. For, upon no principle of philosophy or common sense, can we suppose, that all this immense and inconceivable host of planetary bodies were constructed simultaneously, but, on the contrary, that they have been produced at various intervals, from the remotest eternities of the past, and that the business of world building will continue, as long as there is space to occupy, and materials and forces that can be brought to bear, and all these must be as endless and inexhaustible, as the eternities of the future.

Dr. Dick remarked, that "80,000,000 of heavenly bodies had been discovered with the telescopes then in use, and that each one of them represented a solar system, and were, consequently, suns around which planets and satellites revolved." Supposing each system might have thirty planets and satellites, it would be 2,400,000,000 planetary worlds within the reach of telescopic vision at that age. Since Dr. Dick wrote the above, one planet with her moons, and many asteroids have been discovered in our system, and some astronomers swell the number of worlds within the reach of telescopic vision, to 20,000,000,000. From the fact, that, as lenses of greater power are produced and applied, they serve to reveal new glories and wonders, and increasing numbers of worlds, we must suppose, that the immensity of space has by no means been discovered, in all its amplitude, by any instruments of man's invention, and that, let us extend to the farthest stretch of our limits, it would be but a drop to the vast ocean of planetary existence. All this infinite number of worlds must have been constructed by skilled workmen, during the eternal ages of the past, and still the work goes on, and must, during the eternities of the future, else there will be no farther use for certain elements that exist in our spiritual nature, and for want of the needed activity, those elements would die.

Can we suppose constructiveness, a prominent attribute in man's organization, is only to be used during his material residence upon the earth, in this rudimental and preparatory condition? This organ has evidently been developing to a remarkable extent in the lower animal races; the bee builds its cells with curious mechanical precision, and they are most admirably adapted to the purpose designed. The beaver erects his dam with wonderful engineering skill, and makes a barrier across the stream capable of resisting the influences of the largest flood. The birds construct their nests in a great variety of ways, and in exact accordance with their several necessities. Shall the development of this important faculty cease with man's material existence, or is it being disciplined for higher and nobler purposes in the spiritual realms? If so, then we may find an ample field for its exercise, upon a broader and grander scale than most minds have contemplated, or could possibly conceive, under the old teachings; for under them, no such high and majestic exercise of our faculties awaited us in the interminable ages of the future. The Doctor referred to, says that, "arithmetic, mathematics, geometry, astronomy and chemistry, and all the long catalogue of known and unknown sciences, will be interesting subjects of study in the future realms, because they will enable us to better understand the beauties and glories of creation, and necessarily inspire us with a higher reverence for the almighty Creator." He evidently saw that such like scientific acquirements must be a part of the knowledge of an infinite God, and, that it would be necessary for us to acquire knowledge of the same character also, before we should be able to come to an understanding and appreciation of such a being. But, we discover now, a higher object in view, a more practical purpose, and nobler ends to be attained, by the acquisition of scientific attainments in the spiritual state of existence; and one of those ends is, that we may aid in promoting and carrying forward the great business of building up and adorning, as well as adding planetary bodies to the great universe.

For we clearly see, if the universe is composed of planetary bodies, so inconceivable in numbers, and also in variety, and they have all been constructed upon mechanical principles, it must have required, during the eternities of the past, infinite hosts of mechanics, to have performed all this overwhelmingly vast amount of labor. There is not shadow of doubt but the moon, which is a constant attendant upon the annual journeys of the earth in its orbit, was formed long since the earth. The nebulous theory contemplates the same idea, and all astronomical discoveries would support the uninhabitable and comparatively crude condition of all things upon that orb. Then it doubtless must have been projected and formed as an appendage to our world, after the globe had become sufficiently advanced to require the services of such a satellite. It certainly did not build itself, and it would not have been built if some intelligent being had not concluded it was necessary and important.

Who, then, could have been so much interested in that matter, as those living within our spirit spheres? Those living within the spheres of Jupiter, have built four of their own, and those attached to Saturn have constructed eight, besides the two rings. They have certainly had sufficient to attend to, in managing their own affairs, and Uranus, with its six or eight satellites, must have given sufficient employment to the spiritual mechanics that have found an existence there, without coming to do our labors. Our moon evidently would not have been built, unless for a purpose, and doubtless it was constructed by mechanics, in accordance with a preconceived plan, or form that must have had a multiplicity of details, which were to be adhered to and carried out in all the processes of building, from its commencement until it was so far completed that it would require less attention; for, it is very doubtful if the human mind is capable of contemplating the entire completion of any of the heavenly bodies.

Like all other events in history, there must have been a time in the history of universal world building, when it became necessary that our globe should be provided with a lunar companion, or we may say offspring; and there must have been great abundance of intelligent beings who were competent to understand that fact, as there was a time arrived when it was necessary that a steamship line should be established between San Francisco and China. When that occurred, there were great numbers who understood the necessity, and some were found who had the ability to construct or procure the vessels suitable to place upon the line, and although it was a project involving vast expense, enterprise and knowledge, we were not compelled to call upon the gods, or even go outside of America, to obtain the men, the means and requisite skill. So, when it is found that any of our planets need attendants, it will probably not be necessary to import from any distant orb, the ability requisite to construct them in accordance with correct principles, and to manage them successfully after they are so constructed.

It was, no doubt, well understood, previous to the glacial or drift period, that when all that vast amount of ice and water, which had accumulated upon our globe, had subserved their purposes, it would be necessary to remove the ice fields, and large quantities of water, so that fruitful fields and cheerful homes, and a busy population might exist where once was nothing but widespread desolation. They also understood that by the formation of a satellite, they could withdraw a large portion of our surplus electricity for the use of the infant orb, and thus start a young world and benefit the old one by the operation. Hence an immense extent of territory that was cold and frozen, has been filled with the busy haunts of life. The new or young world required negative elements in its formation, and we, having a superabundance, required a place for their disposal, and thus a satellite of our earth has been constructed to subserve our present purposes, which in the ages to come may ultimate also, as the parent of a numerous retinue.

The time has no doubt arrived in the present epoch of the history of the universe, when our globe has accumulated a redundancy of the electric elements in the shape of glacial formations and extensive ice fields, which exert a chilling influence upon the atmosphere of the arctic regions, and to a great distance from those icy zones, and the increasing population of the world requires that those elements should be gradually removed, and give place to a greater extension of habitable territory. So the intelligences of the spheres that have a perfect understanding of this matter, are engaged at the present time, in constructing another lunar world to bear us company in our future. This will add one more to the number of heavenly bodies in our solar system, and one to that infinite number that is comprehended in the vast universal realms.

It is said with much assurance, that unless all the planetary bodies had been contrived and formed by one architect, there would have necessarily been a clashing, and general disturbances in the various parts of creation. But, we might say, with equal propriety, unless all the steamships had been constructed by one master mechanic, there would be clashing and disturbances; the cases are perfectly analogous, there is quite as much room for each separate world to navigate within their respective solar systems, as there is for the different steamers to navigate our largest oceans. It is well understood, in the construction of steamships, that certain laws must be complied with, if they expect to run them successfully, and those laws are universal, and when understood and kept in view, there is no difficulty in constructing the boat, if the necessary forces and materials can be brought to bear. So, in the construction of satellites or planets, there are also universal laws to be complied with, and these, necessarily, must be understood and applied, in all their details, and then, there can be no difficulty, and unless they are built in conformity with universal laws, they must be failures, the same as would be the steamships. But, where there is a necessity for producing a world, and a sufficient amount of knowledge to control the required forces, and plenty of materials, with the requisite number of workmen, what is there to hinder building a world, as well as a steamship, or any other mechanical structure? What hinders the accomplishment of this grand object, by a great diversity of intelligent beings; providing, they have sufficient knowledge and power?

Why the great anxiety upon the part of so many good and eminent men, that one personal, individualized intelligence, they call God, should build all the worlds, and retain the entire control and management of them to all eternity? Is it a special mark of goodness, virtue, morality, or integrity, to hold this idea? which is but a bare assumption, and cannot be supported by a single fact or any of the analogies in nature. We are fully of the opinion, if the great truth of progressive intelligence should dawn upon our world to-day, and the masses should come to view this matter with illuminated visions, and discover that all intelligences had come from the lowest, and were upon their progressive journey to the highest condition; and that all would at some day be prepared with wisdom and power to engage in the most exalted enterprises of which the human mind can form any conception, virtue and morality would by no means suffer.

On the contrary, the higher attributes of man's nature would be brought more prominently to view, and human society would be greatly improved, by divesting the mind of those cringing, servile, and abject ideas, connected with the teachings of the past. How elevating and inspiring the contemplation, that at some period in the future we may rise to the most super-eminent condition, and notwithstanding our ignorance and feebleness at the present, we have that within our own individualities, which by expansion and growth may enable us to engage in the most exalted occupations; even those we have been wont to think, required the wisdom and power of a God to accomplish. We are apprehensive that a firm conviction of this rational idea, deeply impressed upon the minds of the lowly and uncultivated would do more to raise their aspirations from debasing and groveling objects, than all the various gospels that have been thundered in their ears from the earliest period of man's history. But our purpose is not to present the moral view of this subject, we only desire to find the truth, the moral aspect will take care of itself.

Our astronomers have been troubled, during all their past researches, to find the motive power which impels the various globes in their orbits, and upon their several axes, and, says Dr. Dick, "It would be easy to show, that unless an immaterial power continually re-excited motion in the material universe, all motion would stop in a very short time, perhaps in less than an hour, except, the planets themselves would run out in right-lined directions, and then nothing would ensue but confusion, darkness and chaos; then, a presiding divinity is continually exerting his attributes, impressing every part of the universe to which he gave existence." Now we see, if he expresses the general view upon the subject, and no doubt he does, that in addition to the immense labor of constructing all these worlds from time to time, as they were required in all the various portions of the universal domain, this power must be compelled to turn all the cranks, or apply continuously the momentum that sends all the untold billions of planetary bodies with such tremendous velocity through the regions of space; also, attend to all the diurnal revolutions, and all other phenomena that takes place upon the separate orbs. It is little wonder that, with all these arduous and unremitting labors, he became wearied and exhausted, and needed rest after the six days' work required to complete the little world we inhabit.

There are several difficulties about this theory which our philosophers have not seemed to discover. One is, they have subjected to unremitting labor and care, without a moment's cessation, from eternity to eternity, the very being, of all others, upon whom they should confer tranquility and repose. They have appointed him to perform the very arduous and continuous duties, that might just as well have been done by some finite entities; while they have left the lower intelligences in eternal repose, and without employment. Another more serious difficulty is, they have overlooked the great fact, that any skilled mechanic is abundantly qualified to contrive motive power and place it within those structures which are to perform journeys; they are also able to construct an apparatus that will generate forces productive of the required momentum, not only for its own propulsion, but which is able to perform an immense amount of additional labor. Then, if the globe we inhabit, and the others we behold, are moving bodies, we cannot certainly entertain a very exalted opinion of the intelligent being, who would construct them without the motive power. If our world is designed to travel through space with such velocity, why did he not arrange the machine so that it would generate its own forces, and not be compelled to "re-excite motion," or run the thing by hand to all eternity, lest it go off the track and run into "confusion, darkness and chaos."

How can they suppose for a moment, that an infinitely wise being would subject himself to such inconvenience and uninterrupted toil, while there are plenty of finite and even earthly beings, who do so much better, by making very complicated machines and placing the required power within them, that will do the necessary labor. If they cannot conceive of an infinite intelligence who can turn off a better job, it would be far preferable to trust this world building to finite beings who have served an apprenticeship, who have come up through all, from the lowest atom, and consequently had an experience that would prepare them for such an enterprise. They would doubtless construct globes with the motive power which furnishes the needed propulsion, inherently attached in its proper position. They would also provide the necessary safeguards which would entirely prevent any possibility of running off the tracks on which the globes are running, independent of gravity or centrifugal forces.

The materialist must admit, that, if globes are mechanical structures, and built by the use of forces and materials, there must be some intelligent control of the forces that exert an influence over the materials of which the globes are composed. If there is an intelligent control of forces, that intelligence must exist in individualized beings, and they of course must occupy a position in the spiritual realms, for no gross material being can possibly engage in any such enterprise. One planet cannot be built upon another, and launched like a ship into the depths of space, but they must be constructed out in mid ether, and as material beings cannot well get there to assist, the mechanism must be performed by those who can travel in the ethereal regions, and perform their labors out in the spacious firmament. Therefore, they who commence and carry out so grand a project must be spiritual in their nature. We have never heard of an intelligence clothed in a gross physical garb, not excepting Jesus, who could make so much as a mosquito or the most diminutive insect, for how could they see the fine material from which their various organs must be produced?

The contestants who have heretofore engaged in the long-existing warfare between old theology and modern science have been very anxious to decide whether an infinite God, entirely outside the domain of nature, who was self-existent and supernatural, with self-constituted infinite powers, had spoken all things into existence from nothing, and had taken the supervision and management of all things in some supernatural manner, or whether unchangeable law has ultimated in the production of all visible objects, and in the control of those objects after they are so produced and brought into existence. Both parties have equally ignored the idea that finite spirit intelligences could have anything to do in the production or the management of either inorganic or animated nature, or that they could possibly exert their powers and faculties to advantage in any constructive department of the universe.

Theology inaugurated a general fight with science, until it was found that science carried too many guns, and that her batteries could by no means be silenced, as her armament was constantly being strengthened by new and valuable discoveries. A portion of the belligerents seemed to enter into a kind of involuntary truce, resulting in a tacit stipulation, that theology should retire to its own domain in the supernatural, where they suppose dwells revelation, spirituality, doctrines, devotions, moral virtues, and all that does not exist in the natural realms. While science might revel in the material to his heart's content, and extend his surveys into the vast expanse of nature, as long as he did not infringe upon the province of the spiritual or the supernatural; and thus the matter seems to stand with the parties at the present. Still the great difficulty remains, for each party to define their ground, and decide exactly how far the natural universe extends, and precisely where the realms of the supernatural commences. To tell which part of the great universe has been produced by the almighty power; which part of all the numerous objects that come within the range of our vision, were brought into existence by the infinite fiat, and which was produced by natural immutable laws; which part is governed and controlled by special providences, emanating from that infinite father, in answer to the multiplied petitions of his favorites, and which is governed by established laws, that seem to pervade the entire universe.

These vexed questions are by no means settled, nor will they be fully disposed of until humanity recognizes the fact that spiritual intelligences not only exist, but, that they are actively engaged in the performance of their several labors and duties, in accordance with their capacities, their experience and their knowledge. Until men shall have discovered that neither an infinite, almighty being, they are pleased to call God, watches over and attends personally to the minutiæ of all the particular affairs in the endless diversified compartments of all worlds, and on the other hand, that they are not governed solely by natural forces, uncontrolled by intelligence; but, that infinite millions of spiritual beings who have lived upon our earth, and who bear a sort of natural relationship to the things of the earth, are everywhere delegated to give attention to all the details and minutiæ, both in the material and spiritual realms. That, there must of necessity be all grades of ability and knowledge, and no lack of labor and duties for all these different capacities, from the one that sits upon the eternal throne, to the very lowest that has an existence in their spirit abodes. And, it must be admitted that there is something vastly more sensible, natural and democratic, about this idea of the division of labor in the spheres, than in the idea of placing all upon the shoulders of one individual being; for, labor is labor, whether performed by spirits or men. It requires thought, time, care and attention, both to produce and to manage the productions, after they are brought into existence. The time cannot be far distant, when large masses of individuals shall have discovered the fact that all human intelligent beings have progressed upwards, through all the various forms of inorganic and organic existence, to their present condition. And further, that they may properly indulge the exalted hope of passing through the multitudinous changes incident to the spirit spheres, until they may arrive at the loftiest condition of supernal glory, far beyond that of which our minds can take cognizance, or even entertain a conception. They may learn other facts connected with that existence, and discover that an eternity cannot be loitered away in droning out praises and adoration to any high personality whatever; but, that it must be occupied in those more active and important enterprises becoming superior intellectual beings. Those who have had broad experiences and discipline in the lower schools, are prepared to enter upon the broadest possible field in the spiritual realms, where they may engage in the proper exercise of all their spiritually intensified faculties and powers.

The intelligent reader has doubtless long since discovered, that there can be no mistakes or casualties connected with any portion of the great business of world building, because the projectors must necessarily have an accurate knowledge of the whole matter before they can engage in such an important undertaking. There must, in every instance, be a perfect adaptation of means to the ends they desire to accomplish; also, a strict compliance with the universal and eternally existing laws in every particular and minutiæ, else the whole undertaking would prove a failure, and the world could not be built any more successfully than a smaller, less complicated machine. When we get a clear idea of the grand purpose for which worlds are built, then we may form a very correct conclusion in regard to the form in which they must appear. If the grand object for which they are constructed is carried out, principally upon the surface, then the more surface the more extensively this object can be carried out. There can be no doubt that all intelligent beings will, in their progressive history, become as familiar with world building, as they now are with the erection of their own residences or those of their neighbors.

CHAPTER XI.

DISSOLUTION AND RECONSTRUCTION.

For the purpose of getting a clearer and more perspicuous idea of the constituent elements and machinery attached to our globe, and the various processes by which the component materials are operated upon by such machinery, perhaps, it might be as well to contrive some means by which the beautiful fabric may be taken to pieces, and resolved into its original elements, so we may have an opportunity of examining its separate wheels and springs more minutely and carefully, that we may better form a correct idea of their several uses. If you would learn the young apprentice how to construct a watch or a clock, or any other intricate piece of machinery, you would pursue much the same course; allow him to take one apart, and carefully examine all the separate details, and then re-construct the same again, placing the several parts in their proper position.

If you would obtain an accurate idea of the workings of the human structure, and acquire a competent knowledge of the processes by which it performs its varied functions, and learn all the secret operations and uses of the different portions of the complicated machinery that lies hidden within the human organization, doubtless, the best method would be, to take a few of them apart, to dissect and anatomize them, thus obtaining a view of the whole superstructure. May it not be possible, then, for finite spiritual beings to become possessed of sufficient wisdom and power to bring a world into the laboratory, resolve it into its original elements, and examine carefully all the separate portions of the huge structure? May they not in this manner gain a more accurate knowledge of the secret springs and wheel work which produce the varied activities and effects that we behold in such profusion, in this our world, evidently working out such stupendous purposes, and tending directly towards an inconceivably glorious consummation?

The reader has doubtless become well persuaded that worlds can be easily constructed by the powers and principalities who are competent to undertake such grand schemes, and that beings who possess sufficient ability, and consequent power, can as naturally manufacture and construct worlds, under the proper conditions, as our mechanics can build steamships, or any other structures requiring skill and materials. And in order to accomplish so vast a work, similar conditions would be requisite.

Firstly. Either party must of necessity have a design or plan of what they would build, and also the required knowledge that would enable them to follow the design in all its details. Secondly. A sufficiency of materials from which the superstructure may be erected. Thirdly. The necessary forces to collect and place the materials where they will be most needed, or in their appropriate positions. And Fourthly. The requisite amount of time in which the mechanics may perform the necessary labor, which will result in the consummation of the work they have in view, whether great or comparatively small. It will be noticed, that whether we build worlds, or ships, or edifices, or any other mechanical structures, all these requisitions must receive proper attention.

We cannot open our eyes upon the objects by which we are surrounded everywhere, but we discover that materials have been aggregated by certain forces, evidently controlled and managed by superior intelligences, and that there is such a thing as a world; which, as a mechanical structure, must have been produced by a steady succession of causes that are still in operation. Hence, we are compelled to conclude, they have been in activity through all the various changes and modifications the world has passed, from its inception to the present; when, we seem to behold the general superstructure in such an advanced and elevated condition.

It will be noticed, that when individuals have acquired the ability to construct, by the use of forces and materials, any given work in a manner that will subserve the purposes designed, they must necessarily have learned the additional art of taking such structure in pieces. For, if they know how it goes together, they must of course know how it will come apart, or how a dissolution of the parts can be effected, and we readily conclude that it is somewhat easier to resolve materials into their primeval elements, than it was to take them in that condition, and mould and fashion them into a mechanical structure; it is easier to destroy than to construct.

Men have acquired almost supreme control over many of the elemental forces found in nature; they can employ them to suit their own purposes, whether in building or in destroying and disintegrating that which has been already built, and they probably have learned but little in relation to this matter, that may be learned during their future history, in the home of the spirit. Yet they can use and handle that exceedingly powerful element steam, as a child would handle and find amusement from a toy; they make it perform an inconceivable amount of labor, both by sea and land. Men have also acquired no inconsiderable knowledge concerning that more sublimated element, electricity; they control and use, to a certain extent, this great etherealized force for numerous purposes; they call upon this subtle fluid, and in obedience to their will, it travels across the continent, and under the depths of the ocean, and by its aid they transmit intelligence from country to country, with the celerity of thought, and in conjunction with the great positive element, magnetism, they may find a motive power sufficient to perform all the necessary labor of the world.

They have also acquired a knowledge of chemical analysis that is nearly bewildering to the uninitiated; they can resolve almost any object in nature to its original elements; they can bring to bear, forces that will rend asunder and tear in pieces, those forms and substances that have been erected and finished in a very elaborate manner; and, perhaps, in all the universal kingdom, there is no substance so refractory that may not be decomposed by forces that are under the control of the accomplished chemist. And now, if man has, during his transient and extremely limited existence, under a variety of unfavorable circumstances here upon the earth, acquired all this vast fund of knowledge and experience, what may not the same individuals, with increased spiritualized capacities, attain after having been ages in the higher realms. It is by no means too much to suppose, that it would be within the bounds of their possibilities, and that they might possess knowledge equal to the task, and solvents of sufficient power, to subject this huge globe of ours to a kind of analysis that would decompose its every particle, and reduce them to their primeval condition; and why not? It is a living, absolute truth, that the globe exists as a mechanical structure, and there can be no less knowledge in the universe at the present, than when this structure first commenced its existence, in its more incomplete outlines.

It will doubtless be conceded by all parties, that globes or planets must necessarily be constructed by spiritual agency, whether that agency is confined to a single personality or otherwise; whether they are produced by one being, or millions. If, then, the builders are spiritual, the material used must be spiritual also; it must bear the same relationship to the material worlds as spiritual beings bear to those who dwell upon those worlds, and exist in the most rarefied or etherealized condition; for, we may be assured that those beings can do nothing, unless there is a law by which it may be done. They no more exist and perform their labors independent of natural laws, than ourselves, and whatever they do, must be done in accordance with the imperious behests of eternal law.

The nebulous theory contemplates all world material as existing in the most gaseous and rarefied condition, and that it gradually changed to a more condensed and materialized state, by certain natural processes. It becomes quite evident, then, if there are processes in nature which will change matter from a gaseous to a solidified condition, there must be processes also, which will reduce it back to its original state. We are indebted to this great power in nature, by which material substances may be changed into ethereal, and then materialized again in some other form, more beautiful and complex, for all we behold that is grand and attractive, for all the interesting objects in nature, which are calculated to inspire the mind with pleasurable emotions.

The solidified portions of the majestic oak, were attracted from the earth in the most rarefied condition through the minute spongioles attached to the numerous rootlets, and the materialization has taken place in accordance with nature's invisible processes within the tree. The bony concretions of the whole animal race have been produced in a similar manner from elemental substances existing in the food, perfectly inappreciable and invisible to those who eat. Were there no such changes and modifications of material substances, all nature would remain at a perfect stand-still, progress would cease, and universal death would reign supreme. Had there been no law in nature by which matter could be etherealized, then all would have remained in the materialized condition; and we should not have been provided with those elements so essential in the production and continuance of the vegetable and animal kingdoms.

We then discover, that, with a solvent of sufficient power, applied in a proper manner, a dissolution of the atomic particles of a globe might be a result; the lofty mountain might melt and flee away, and the solid crust of the earth be consumed, or reduced to infinitesimal atoms far beyond the reach of human vision. Doubtless the very processes are even now in gradual operation, that may ultimate, at some far distant period, in such a beautiful and sublime result. Sublime and glorious indeed would be such a consummation. The contemplation that all gross matter is gradually, nevertheless surely, passing through those spiritualizing processes that may, during some of the ages of an unappreciable future, render our earth and its surroundings the happy abode of inconceivable billions of spirit entities, now existing in the lowest materialized forms, is certainly one of intense interest.

Our earth was certainly once less spiritual, or more gross, than to-day; it did not produce or sustain as elevated a race of beings as it now does. Just as surely as it has progressed in this direction, just so surely will it keep on, until all that is now material shall progress, by various modifications, to a more etherealized and elevated condition. The surrounding elements must keep even pace with the progressive advancement of the human race. The highly cultivated, refined man or woman require surroundings entirely different from the gorilla or Hottentot; they are evidently produced from more refined materials. It is by no means visionary to suppose that the inhabitants of our earth, ten thousand, or even one thousand years hence, will be vastly superior to those who live to-day; they will evidently become more spiritualized, and will require more refined elements in which to exist. If we carry out this reasoning we can easily discover the grand culmination.

It must be admitted that power and wisdom exist to-day, quite equal to that which moulded and fashioned our world into its present form; and doubtless, wisdom and power of that character would be quite competent to resolve the fabric to its primeval elements. If we may base our reasoning upon any principle of progressive development, we cannot successfully contradict the fact, that untold billions of intelligent beings must have arrived at as high a condition of knowledge, as the original projectors and fabricators of our earth, since that eventful period when it was set in motion. For, we have already become quite well assured, it did not require infinite ability to perform such a task.

It was said by one whose words have been quoted for many centuries by the most intelligent of earth's inhabitants, as the oracles of divine truth, that "the elements shall melt with fervent heat." If this is correct, the author must have found a solvent of sufficient power to melt the institution, if not to produce an entire dissolution of its atomic particles. If we consult the oracles of science, we shall find the earth composed of comparatively few primary or simple substances; and that over one-half of the ponderable matter is by no means solidified, but exists in a fluid invisible condition. Much of the solids are to a certain extent combustible, and all are subject to changes by the direct action of heat of no great temperature. It may not be supposed that chemists have as yet become acquainted with any degree of heat that will entirely dissolve every element in the original granite, neither can it be supposed that chemists have explored any further in that direction, than they have in others, or that they have arrived at the end of their researches in any given direction. It is by no means probable that the last discovery has been made in this branch of human science; but that it may yet reveal to the world very much that is of rare value, of which the most skillful among them now know nothing. However, they have found degrees of heat that approximate very closely to the decomposition of the most refractory elements in nature. It is only necessary to find increasing powers of generating heat of greater and still greater intensity, until a power is obtained, sufficient to dissolve all the various substances found in the original granite, and the great work of dissolution may be accomplished.

There can be no doubt but magnetism, the concentrated essential element of heat, might be so manipulated by those who have the power, as to utterly annihilate, as far as human vision is concerned, all substances of a negative materialized character. But magnetism, even then, notwithstanding it might become a power sufficient to dissolve and destroy all, being a positive element, would necessarily exhaust its own resources, and hence could not remain, for any length of time, master of the situation. As all positive elements, in the performance of their labors, expend their own forces and exhaust themselves, they of course must become negative. We behold a fire raging to-day with terrible fury; it is positive to all the combustible and all else within its influence, but it has eventually consumed everything within its reach, destroyed itself by its own terrible energies, and to-morrow its strength is gone, it has become negative, cold and dead, and no more to be feared.

So we discover, even if we should find an element of sufficient positive power to dissolve all natural things, that element would finally become negative, because there could be no re-supply of the exhausted positive forces. Hence the concentrated element of heat which is magnetism, after being thus exhausted, would resolve itself into the opposite element of cold, which is electricity, and this power would be all and in all; queen of the wild scene of desolation where naught could be found but darkness, inactivity and death.

If such a catastrophe could possibly occur, as the sudden dissolution of the atomic particles composing a world, we discover at once, that those particles must be returned to their original or primeval condition, and that condition must have been one of absolute negativeness or inactivity. For, wherever we find positive elements, there is a state of activity and consequent change, and hence progress at once takes place, and matter subjected to such influences, can by no means remain in a quiescent, primeval condition. Electricity, being the highest negative element, must then absorb all that has lost its positive character, and, as a sequence, must be the Alpha and Omega, the beginning and end of all things, and holds supreme control throughout the universal realms of space, where positive activities have not been introduced, or where they have ceased their operations.

We may look out into the vast expanse of our own solar system, without wandering off into the distant sidereal universe, and find ample room for the swiftest comets to travel away for centuries, to and from the extreme aphelion of their eccentric orbits, before making a return to the central sun. We shall find also, that only a small portion of this immense space is occupied by planetary bodies or their attendant satellites. Then, if we ascertain the positive active elements are confined to the materialized heavenly bodies, we may learn that almost the whole of this inconceivable amount of space, is in an entirely negative, inactive condition.

But little can be found in all the inconceivable realms of space which are outside the influence of the various planetary orbs, except darkness, coldness, inactivity and death; it is all electrical. The magnetic, living, active, positive forces are confined to the orbs where such forces are needed, as they are entirely unnecessary out in the realms of space. Hence we perceive that life exists in the midst of death. Life has proceeded from death, but in no case does death proceed from life. Life and light, heat, and all positive, active elements have been produced in the midst of this overwhelming region of death, or negative properties, by wisdom and power competent to undertake and accomplish such mighty achievements. Then, we discover the great fact, that all outside the orbs is death, and that the orbs themselves are but a commingling of the two great antagonistic elements, the living and the dead, the positive and the negative. If you wish to destroy an animal, you kill, or take its life. If we destroy a world, we must do the same thing, deprive it of life, and both will resolve themselves back to their original condition.

The solidified portions of our globe have evidently been materialized by active life elements, the same as the animal; deprive them again of those elements, and they both die and return to their primeval atoms. Deprive them of all positive, and they both become negative in the broadest sense of that term; and that term includes dissolution to the farthest possible extent. We can conceive of no solvent that would produce this result more readily than intensified heat, and we apprehend that a thousandth part of the quantity our modern savans have placed within the crust of the globe, would accomplish the grand feat most successfully. It must appear obvious to the reader, either learned or unlearned, that an intelligence endowed with power sufficient to use elemental forces in building worlds, could also bring to bear forces that might ultimate in their destruction.

It will also appear obvious, that in the boundless realms of space, beyond the farthest limits of planetary systems, or outside the existence of all worlds, there may be found unoccupied territory so inconceivably vast in its limits, as to defy all attempts at mathematical computation. There must be incomprehensible realms of inactivity and frozen death, where the great negative elements hold high carnival and enjoy their triumphal reign, where no spirit of life and activity have yet appeared to illuminate their darkness, and introduce living principles and essences, which might cheer their eternal gloom.

We cannot doubt but in the cycles of eternities in the future, portions, larger and still larger, of the unoccupied space shall be built up and smile with beauty and all the harmonies of nature; that where, now, nothing but coldness and darkness exist, at some future period the principalities and powers of new-formed worlds and systems shall peal forth their happy symphonies of joy and gladness. Symphonies which may resound through the arched domes of universal spheres, from centre to circumference, everywhere meeting with a cheering response, and calling forth loud anthems of exultation in honor of the wisdom and power that may accomplish such wonderful purposes. Have "the morning stars sang together," and all the "sons of God shouted for joy," when new-born worlds were ushered into existence, then the "stars" may have frequent occasion to repeat their songs, and the "sons of God" may as often reiterate their reverberating shouts.

There can be no more doubt but the waste places in the universal realms shall be built up, and the illimitable deserts in the vast wilderness of space, shall bud and blossom as the rose, than there is that the barren deserts of our own earth will at some time become fertile and productive, smile with beauty and plenty, and be scattered with the habitations of an intelligent people.

We cannot, upon any principle of analogical reasoning, suppose that the worlds are all finished, or that they are all commenced; but on the contrary, we must conclude, as world building must have occupied the attention of advanced intelligences in all the eternities of the past, such must be the case during all the eternal cycles of the future. New and unoccupied territory must then be explored, and improvements of this exalted character must be made in the spheres which are only bounded by unlimited universal space; precisely the same as the unoccupied territory of our own earth shall ultimately be subdued and cultivated by earth's inhabitants. Thus we learn that this element which impels men to seek distant countries, and which seems to be such a prominent organ in some natures, need by no means die for want of the needed activities in the spiritual realms, for there must be ample fields in which this organ can find active exercise.

We have ascertained, and the reader will bear in mind, that, when we deprive any active living organism of all positive, active forces, death ensues; a dissolution follows, and the whole organization becomes negative, and returns to its primeval, homogeneous element, which is electricity. Then it follows, that whether the eternally existing negative atoms have been once acted upon by positive forces or not, they are in the same relative or negative condition when entirely disconnected with any positive living elements. So, if we find that electricity is the great mother, and may swallow up and contain all in her capacious womb, then we must necessarily conclude that all things have proceeded from this universal mother. That, in the primeval condition, if there could have been such a condition, this element was the grand reservoir of all materials and forces, and that out of this abysmal death came all there is of life, and out of this darkness came light, and beauty, and glory. Out of this eternal repose came all the activities of nature, and this negative condition of atomic particles is, and was, a necessary precedent to all that is positive, and that has become so replete with the living, active organism, which inspires the mind with so much wonder and astonishment; all that is grand and beautiful and calculated to adorn the various worlds, rendering them suitable habitations for intelligent beings, have proceeded from this universal source, by a skillful application of positive forces in the hands of highly endowed spiritual beings.

Suppose we permit the exalted spiritual intelligences

to which we have referred, to enter this vast realm of darkness and chaotic death, and ascertain what may be done in regard to the erection of a world, and we may give them six days, or six indefinite periods, of time of untold billions of ages each, in which to accomplish their work. It is a conceded point that mind exercises control over matter, and it may well be conceded that exalted spiritual mentalities may exercise authority over matter in an etherealized atomic form; in its negative inactive condition, in its unevolved primeval state; so rarefied as not to be discerned by the most powerful lenses yet constructed. This is the kind of etherealized substances that can only be discerned by the penetrating vision of spiritual beings, and handled by their highly refined touch, and controlled by their intensified powers, which is all ready to be converted to use when necessity demands. And this unevolved material must exist in its atomic condition superabundantly in that portion of the vast universal realms which are now unoccupied by planetary orbs in their various stages of completion or progression.

When intelligent beings in the upper spheres discover that a demand exists for the construction and development of new worlds, when emigration in those realms seeks to occupy new territory, or when the mechanical genius of advancing, ever-progressing spirit intelligences require new fields in which to exercise their vast skill and ability, then it is, that this electrical, invisible space ether may be subjected to the control of positive forces, and both the atomic material and the forces are called upon to perform their part in the stupendous drama that brings worlds and systems of worlds upon the stage of the universe. The great work of world building is but partially accomplished, and must go on in all its sublimity and grandeur, through the endless eternities. The individual that has been the successful builder of an edifice like St. Paul's, or of a gallant steamship, or of a pyramid, cannot be contented to rest there. He will, no doubt, in the progress of ages, when he has accomplished everything of a lesser nature, be strongly inclined to try his hand at an asteroid, a comet, or a moon, where he will find abundant opportunity and room for the exercise of his continually increasing wisdom and powers, of comprehending mechanical appliances.

No one can doubt but there must be inconceivable hosts of intelligent beings, who are ready and willing to engage in such a work, and to render their aid in the different details and minutiæ, not only for the purpose of assisting in the construction, but for the higher purpose of gaining knowledge in all the particulars, and in all the complicated processes that are introduced in such an elaborate structure, from its inception until the entire fabric is completed. Now, we may inquire if there are not forces and laws, principles, attributes, and phenomena, to be introduced in the construction of a world or system of worlds, of sufficient magnitude and interest, to engage the attention of the loftiest spiritual intelligent being of which the mind can have any possible conception. If human intelligences are to improve in knowledge from day to day, through the cycles of eternal ages to come, what more interesting field of research can be found, than an inquiry into the most approved modes, in all their particulars of constructing and elaborating a world like this, with all its varied inhabitants?

You, gentle reader, have doubtless had much experience. You perhaps have obtained a knowledge of some of the sciences; you may know something of astronomy, of the higher mathematics, of chemistry, and geology, and perhaps very much of other departments that usually come to the notice of inquiring and educated minds. But ask yourself—how much comparatively do I know to-day, concerning the great macrocosm of which I am a part and parcel? and how am I to become acquainted with the entire lesson appertaining to myself, and concerning the whole, unless I pursue a regular course of instruction?

How very natural, in this earth-life, for persons to engage as apprentices or students in that profession or occupation they would successfully master, and how natural for the self-same individuals, in a higher life, and in a more advanced condition, pursuing further researches and investigations in the great fields of nature, to engage as apprentices or workmen in the construction of those organizations they would thoroughly understand. How else, we ask, can they arrive at that knowledge which they require to give them a clear comprehension of themselves, in all their relationships to the great whole, unless they engage as fellow workmen in the construction of the different complex pieces of machinery that are necessarily introduced in order to complete the whole?

Do not think, then, that you shall pass from this scene of earthly activity, and sit down forever under a bower of overhanging roses, and delight yourself eternally with sipping nectar and tasting ambrosia prepared by angel hands, or by singing long-drawn-out anthems in some diminutive heaven, prepared for a chosen few. By no means. The universe around you is not half finished; work is to be done by brave hearts and willing hands; labor of a thousand different kinds is to be performed, and duties of a pressing nature, that shall lead you in every possible direction, are to receive your attention. New and unbroken territory, that has remained in the regions of *Belisma* from all eternity, is to be encroached upon, subdued, and prepared for new worlds and systems of worlds. Forces, powers, and principalities, are to be brought into subservience, materials are to be aggregated and disposed of in a proper and orderly manner, in obedience to laws and the direction of the great master minds who control and superintend, and there must be every variety of labor to perform, every occupation to pursue, and every position to fill, that can possibly occur upon this our earth; for all things have existed in the spiritual, before they could possibly be materialized and come to us.

All planetary worlds must evidently be governed by general laws which are universal in their operations and influence. Yet there seems to be untold varieties of shapes, dimensions, forms and conditions of the worlds that have already been constructed, and hence it will be absolutely necessary that the great master mind, the superintending architect, should understand precisely the kind of world he designs to build, in its every minutiæ and particular, and exactly for what purpose it is to be constructed. It would be necessary also to inquire in respect to the motions of the world you propose to erect, the rapidity of the movements, and their relationship to the other heavenly bodies in the system, if it has an axial revolution, how rapidly shall it turn, if orbital, in what time shall it revolve around its grand center, as there are no two planets or satellites in our solar system, that perform those revolutions in the same length of time, differing from a few days to 164 years. When these important preliminary matters, and very many others we cannot reach with our limited comprehensions, are settled, we may begin to look around, if possible, where all is apparently void, and where darkness sits upon the face of the mighty deep, and ascertain what may be done towards building a world.

The Hebrew God said under similar circumstances, "Let there be light, and there was light," and if he said it, and light was produced in accordance with the saying, then he must of necessity have had the knowledge and power adequate to its production, and light must have made its appearance in accordance with universal law, and by virtue of certain means that were used for its generation. Similar means would be necessary today, in any place where all is darkness, or at any other time when the circumstances require that light should be produced. If an intelligent being should go out into the darkness in order to perform some labor that would require light by which he could perform it properly, he would most likely go provided with the means, and would probably well understand how he could procure the necessary light, and he might with propriety use the same language, "Let there be light."

If we should penetrate the deep recesses of an icy cave, where all around nothing but darkness, gloom, silence, and death, could be found, where no ray of light has penetrated, where no heat has ever exerted its cheering influence, and no trace of positive element exists, but that we carry with us, we might say with propriety, "Let there be light," for we might carry with us that by which it could be produced. We might use a steel and flint and other requisites, or a lucifer match, and apply a little friction, and behold there would be light. Can we suppose that we possess more wisdom in relation to such matters, than those intelligences who have had untold ages of experience, and opportunities so inceivably superior for obtaining a knowledge of all laws in the material and spiritual realms? Certainly not; for the entire of our knowledge proceeded from them; if we have learned how to produce light out of darkness, they have taught us the lesson. We are indebted to them for the information, and we have learned simply this, that friction will produce caloric and magnetism, and without magnetism there is no light in the broad uiverse; for this element is the father and progenitor of all light, and but for magnetism it cannot possibly exist.

We have already ascertained that electricity had swallowed up all that there was, because all had originally proceeded from this great negative mother, this universal essential element of cold, and darkness, and death, which is the first and the last, the Alpha and Omega, the beginning and the end, of all things, the "all and in all," which sits in silent, undisturbed grandeur, and exercises undisputed authority over all the inconceivably vast unoccupied regions of space, and will there hold universal sway, until those territories are encroached upon by intelligences, who enter the dark solitudes for the high purpose of constructing planetary abodes, and developing other spiritual beings, that are waiting the proper time to rise from their eternal sleep. When the great master minds enter those dark, icy regions of coldness and death, what should they do but say, "Let there be light," and use the requisite means to produce this element by motion or friction, as motion produces friction, and that generates magnetism, and now we have a positive element that brings the sleeping negative powers of electricity into activity, and light and life commence their grand career from that moment; and the powers and principalities that take this matter in hand, are prepared for the great work of constructing new heavens and a new earth.

It is probable that most persons as children have engaged in the agreeable pastime of blowing soap bubbles, and have watched with childish interest the dainty evanescent miniature globes float away upon the atmosphere, ready to vanish into seeming nothing upon the least disturbance of this element. Perhaps older persons, who are wandering far outside of nature's realms in pursuit of knowledge and possible enjoyment, might find profound lessons of instruction in the little airy bubbles that are blown for the amusement of children, for as they dance away upon their brief journey, they exhibit some of the sublimest phenomena in nature. They show precisely the principles upon which worlds may be commenced and established; they represent in miniature just the kind of superstructure we require to insure the greatest amount of strength compatible with the smallest amount of material; and it cannot be supposed that those two great mechanical principles, can be lost to view in the construction of a world, or that any mechanical principle can be introduced into any structure by the inhabitants of a globe, that was not understood by the original builder, and is not incorporated as a part of the globe itself.

It will be perceived that all the elements of soap bubbles, or of globes made of glass or any other material, existed in this dark electrical condition, and that those minds who had sufficient ability, could have expanded that etherealized substance into a globe as easily as the child blows the bubble, or the glass-blower fashions one from the vitreous matter that he takes from the furnace, in its melted condition. Evidently the size of this globe, so formed from spiritualized materials, must depend upon the amount of force brought to bear, and the quantity of matter employed, and the expansion to which it attains, would depend upon all those several conditions. This is certainly a very simple method of producing a globe, nevertheless, we find it to be most effectual, and we may reasonably suppose that the great spiritual mechanics might resort to some similar process.

The materials made use of in the early stages of the formation of a world, are doubtless quite as flexible and easily managed as those from which the child forms his miniature globe; and being entirely negative, and in the midst of inactivity, there can be no disturbances to displace the etherealized atoms, until they may become materialized. Although this method may appear quite simple at first view, yet its simplicity is its chief commendation, and in this lies its great beauty; for all mechanical and scientific principles are extremely simple when properly understood. We now defy all the mechanical or philosophical ingenuity in the wide world, to arrive at any plan or devise any method that would accomplish this object so successfully and completely. In order to produce a world, formed upon any mechanical principle, we require a spherical shell containing the requisite amount of materials, to insure the needed strength, and no more; we need all the superficial area that can be introduced into the structure; as, the grand purposes for which worlds are constructed, must be carried out upon the surface; and all this is to be accomplished from sublimated atomic particles, by spiritual beings, if it is admitted that intelligence has anything to do with the matter. Now, we may inquire in all sincerity — what other plan can possibly be introduced but the expansion of the etherealized elements into a hollow sphere, that would so completely and practically mold those elements into the globular form, and carry out the purposes of the spiritual builders upon scientific and harmonious principles.

If we may conceive it possible for those master minds to produce a globe in such a manner from the ethereal elements, then we may conceive it quite as possible to make the necessary additions of similar elements, until the foundations of an inner and outer world are fully established. Thus in process of time, a stupendous superstructure may be reared and finally materialized, capable of giving birth and sustenance to innumerable billions of human intelligent beings who may in future ages shout forth glad *pæans* in honor of those mighty architects who were competent to furnish them so grand a dwelling place.

It will be noticed, that this foundation or back-bone of a terrestrial spherical globe must be composed of the most negative, inactive and death-like elements which can be found in nature; or rather, that means may not be used, which will render them positive and active, lest disturbances be introduced where all must remain but the materialized symbol of eternal death. For it is hardly necessary to say that disturbing elements in the interior portions of the shell, might be attended with disastrous if not fatal consequences; and that the destruction of the entire fabric might ensue. And those materials must now be added, that affinitize as nearly as possible both upon the outer and inner surface, that no disturbing forces may be introduced into the deep, silent recesses of this shell or sphere, which, in the process of ages is to accumulate continuous accretions of material substances, until it swells out to the proudest dimensions of a stupendous world, furnished with all its attributes and clothed in all its glory.

All new-formed globes seem to be built as dependents or satellites for some other worlds already in existence, which are so far advanced that they stand in need of such secondaries; for assuredly, worlds will not be erected unless they are really needed. We cannot suppose that labor will be expended, and materials squandered in a useless manner; and unless there is a necessity for so doing, and it is done for some high purpose, worlds will not be built. We perceive also, that the secondary must to a certain extent partake of the movement of the primary, and if the parent revolves around a great central orb, the younger one must go also. The reader will readily discover the importance and necessity of placing the most inactive elements in the central portions of this sphere, and building the foundations of our hollow globe from that kind of material that affinitizes as nearly as possible to death and eternal quiet. We think an intelligent architect, who proposed to erect an important edifice, that was designed to be permanent and enduring, would use the same precaution, and make a foundation of those materials least subject to disturbing influences, and that would be most likely to remain in a condition of inactive repose for the longest possible period of time.

But strange to say, the advocates of the very popular igneous theory, have placed within the bowels of our earth an inconceivable mass of the most active, uneasy, explosive, ragingly destructive materials, surrounding it by a frail and feeble crust, entirely inadequate to resist the least disturbance that might occur. They flatter themselves that under such perilous circumstances all things are secure; and no doubt they are, because there is not a particle of truth in the theory—and the real foundations of the globe, upon which the whole fabric rests with so much security and permanency, are composed of the most inactive and enduring materials, that are eternally sleeping in the frozen embrace of death.

It would be strange indeed if the architects who went out to superintend the building of a world, did not have the common sense of the man who would build a dwelling or a church. The igneous or Laplace theory contemplates that worlds constructed themselves, after some unknown power established the motion which revolved the huge mass of nebulous material upon its axis; and, if they built themselves without any intelligent superintendence, then it would be no marvel if they should make use of the most active, disturbing and explosive elements, as a foundation upon which to rear the fabric. But, if we admit the rational idea, that these wondrous, mechanical, self-moving worlds, which display such inconceivable wisdom in their designs, and in all their varied evolutions, were projected under the guidance and direction of super-eminently qualified intelligences, then we may conclude, that the foundations are composed of those materials that are permanent and secure, and that they will remain without producing disturbance until all the purposes for which a globe could be constructed are entirely consummated—until the last act in the great drama of a world's existence is fully performed.

We have little now to do, but aggregate the materials and bring our superstructure to the requisite dimensions, or build upon both the exterior and interior of this spherical shell until we have attained the needed strength, or a sufficiency of ethereal atoms that will give the required strength when materialized. We should do precisely the same thing if we had ability to build a huge animal, or a tree, or any other object that nature has seemed to form by her silent processes. In order to accomplish this great object, it is quite plain, that all the materials must be extremely negative and inactive, in order to be handled and controlled by spiritual beings; and of course, to bring them out of that condition, and elaborate all the latent powers they contain, the great positive force, magnetism, must be applied and brought into conjunction with this mass of electric matter.

It has become necessary, in the materialization of this negative accumulation, to work a radical change to a more positive condition, in which the primary elements existing in nature may become more apparent. So in the progress of the ever-rolling ages, by a judicious application of this positive power, a vast portion of the negative particles lying contiguous to the outer and inner surfaces of this shell, are elaborated and gradually changed to that substance familiarly termed granite rock, which in itself is known to contain all the primal elements that are found to exist in the mineral kingdom. It will be discovered by the student of nature, that this power which, by an excessive application, is able to dissolve all substances, may also be called into requisition, for the purpose of evolution and formation. If magnetism, this prince of positive agents, has combined with electricity in the negative materials composing the globe, in the production of the granite rock, it is no marvel that our geologists and other savans discover indications of the action of such great heat, as to lead them to the conclusion that this rock had been formed by cooling from a molten mass, instead of having been produced from the coldest possible elemental substances.

It is said by modern geologists, that two active agents have been introduced, in the early formation of the various rocks, and that they have exerted their activities and influences in bringing the earth to its present conditions. Fire and water, they say, have produced all the wonders we behold; those two elements have exerted their powers in modifying all material substances, from the gaseous or nebulous condition up to the present, when the earth is clothed with a beauty and magnificence that astonishes the mind of the beholder. Fire and water are evidently not primal causes, but rather, effects that have been produced, and depend upon certain conditions for their existence. Fire is a positive element, and always when in activity exhausts its own resources, and would soon destroy itself if not supplied with combustible material upon which it may exist.

We defy the combined ingenuity of all the scientific men who live, to devise any means by which fire can be kept in activity for any length of time, without the needed fuel; and, if the existence of fire is dependent upon conditions, then there must have been some power or agent by which those conditions were produced, that made it possible for fire to exist; hence, we learn that fire is but a subordinate element, and could not have been one of the primal agents that produced the various modifications. Again, if fire cannot be kept in activity without a continual supply of combustible food, who has furnished the required amount, during all the millions of ages, necessary to modify the etherealized or gaseous substance of which our earth is composed, and pass it through its various changes?

Water is but a combination of hydrogen and oxygen, and like fire has been produced by some antecedent cause, and of course, as a power it occupies the same subordinate position as fire. Those two important elements in nature doubtless have exerted their influences, but it is quite evident that forces far superior to them have been required to act upon rarefied substances such as are brought into requisition in the construction of worlds, in order to transform those substances into a more materialized condition. There seem to be strong indications in the granite rocks, that lead geologists to suppose they have been acted upon by fire; indeed the evidences are so plainly impressed, that they have been unhesitatingly termed the igneous rocks; and this fact has seemed to strengthen the idea that they are produced by the cooling and solidifying of an interior mass of molten lava. It is also supposed by some learned geologists, that large quantities of this molten lava are from time to time being erupted through the various craters, which they say are but chimneys that communicate with the great mass within the crust. The inquiry, then, arises—why this molten lava does not become granite rock, after having been thrown from the various volcanoes; as it is a well-known fact, that all the different varieties of solidified lava differ as widely from granite, as limestone, slate, sandstone, or any other of the sedimentary rocks. Why would not this homogeneous mass form the same substance when cooled upon the outside, as when cooled inside the crust?

Where is the propriety of calling upon that gross element fire, to accomplish that which can be done so much more easily by the sublimated and concentrated spiritual essence of the grosser fluid called fire? We think the day is not distant when our philosophers will call upon powers that are able to perform the labor they discover has been accomplished, and not wake up a puling infant to do that which taxes all the energies of a full-grown giant. Fire is very good in its place, and has certain very important duties to perform, and a wide sphere in which it exerts its powers and influence, but when you wish to get up a severe thunder-storm, or an earthquake, or manufacture or decompose granite rock, you need not call upon fire to accomplish those feats; they are entirely out of its province. It will be found that we require the great positive and negative forces, and with their judicious application, all such effects may be produced with much ease, because they lie within the jurisdiction of those powers.

If, then, we have found powers of this character that have been in a state of activity since the accumulation of this material that composes our globe, we shall find a comparatively easy and natural solution of many of the apparent phenomena that have evidently existed during that lengthy period. If those great powers were brought to bear in effecting changes from a negative to a more positive condition, then it would appear evident, that during all the changes, this globe was continually becoming more positive and magnetic. Such being the case, during the myriad ages of this transformation period, from the negative to the more positive and materialized condition of granite rock, there could be nothing that would hinder excessive accumulations of this positive magnetic element upon the surface of our globe, and that ultimately it might become a power that would prove, to a certain extent, destructive of the very work it had been so long engaged in producing. We think, upon examination we shall find that such was an absolute necessity; for if this granite had not been subjected to the action of powerful antagonistic elements, it would evidently have remained in that condition to all eternity, and naught but one wide-spread scene of desolation would ever have existed. Thus we see the importance of a power that can destroy, as well as produce, and we discover that materialization and dissolution has been the great business of those positive and negative forces, since they were introduced into our world, and from all eternity.

If the granite rock contains all elements that exist upon the earth, in a latent condition, we very clearly see that there must have been a period when none of the elements could have been outside the granite, and hence the necessity of bringing a solvent that would disintegrate and dissolve its particles in order that the spiritual essences might escape. So we perceive that out of this death came forth life, or by a dissolution of the particles of granite, oxygen, hydrogen, nitrogen and carbon, and other spiritual essences, that had been confined, were eliminated and set free. Hence there could have been no atmosphere or water upon this or any other globe, until the original granite was dissolved in sufficient quantities to allow the escape of those elements; and the small amount of air and water that existed in the early periods of this dissolving process must have been, not only very much heated in consequence of activities sufficiently powerful to rend in pieces and dissolve such large quantities of solid granite, but highly charged with sulphurets, phosphates and chlorine, that, render them powerful agents in the performance of the great work of dissolution. We have little trouble, now, in solving the difficult problem of the metamorphic rocks, that present such strong evidences of having been subjected to the action of hot water; neither is there any difficulty in conceiving the impossibility of vegetable or animal life at this terrible period, when all nature was subjected to disintegration by those all-powerful solvents.

The electro-magnetic fluids were evidently in full destructive operation, and this terrific work must have proceeded through almost interminable periods of time, until their own devastations ultimately were productive of causes which would hold them in check. It will be noticed, that the quantity of gasses productive of atmosphere and water, must have been constantly accumulating, and water being a great receptacle of electricity, this negative element was continually increasing in power upon the surface of the earth. Consequently, nature would again begin to approximate towards an equipoise, and we ascertain that the intense heat of the most terribly active magnetic period began to some extent to abate previous to the earlier ages of the silurian formations, so as to admit of the lower forms of organic life in the shape of polyps, radiata, etc.

It was doubtless during this lengthy period, when all nature was convulsed by the terrific throes of those all-powerful clashing elements, to a great distance below the surface, that the numerous mountain ranges and various protuberances that are found upon the globe were upheaved. It was thus that the granite which upon the plains is usually so deeply covered by the sedimentary deposits, may so frequently be found exposed upon the tops of the highest mountains. We remark upon this subject, that nature has no powers in her vast laboratory, sufficient to produce convulsions that will ultimate in such tremendous upheavals, except the great positive and negative elements, electro-magnetism. It is a somewhat singular fact, that most of the mountain ranges of any considerable length, are longitudinal, from north to south.

Although we have but little space to devote to this part of our subject, the careful geological student will be able to trace the gradual changes that have taken place during that inconceivably lengthened period of time, that must have transpired, from the cambrian or lower silurian up through the various stratifications, until we come to the drift or glacial period. He will discover that it was one series of transitions of the slowest and most gradual character, from a very highly magnetic and positive condition, that was dissolving as rapidly as possible the solid granite, and producing the accumulating sedimentary formations, also continually increasing those elements, hydrogen and oxygen, the very home of electricity, until they should finally, in the form of water, envelope nearly every portion of the entire globe. There is little difficulty in discovering why the globe should cool gradually as the waters increased, until it should finally culminate in those vast glacial formations, that are so well known to have existed at a certain period upon so large a portion of the surface of the earth, and which might have existed until the present day, had the same quantity of water remained upon our globe.

But, we discover that when it becomes necessary that this globular shell should continuously pass through changes and modifications that will adapt it to the various conditions and requirements which are to be carried out during its history, nature provides the powers that will produce those several changes and transitions, in accordance with her own peculiar methods. She has never turned to the right or left for the accommodation of the most eminent philosopher or theologian, although they may seem to be clothed with great authority and power.

We find a record inscribed upon the tablets of nature's great volume, which declares emphatically, that there must have been a period of intense heat, succeeded by a gradual cooling process, until water and ice predominated upon a large portion of the world's surface, and this condition has again been succeeded by an abatement of the waters and ice, until a large portion of the same surface has become temperate and habitable. When we find records of such a character, we may be assured that causes have existed fully competent to produce all the grand results which are so plainly recorded. This subject will receive further attention in the chapter that treats upon our moon.

We may notice here briefly, that curious phenomenon which has attracted so much attention, and called forth so many misguided speculations from the learned, in relation to the huge fire within the thin crust of the globe. The well-established fact of the increasing temperature as we penetrate the crust of the earth, has been considered proof positive, that a raging fire existed within, and it was only necessary to go deep enough, to find it in all its terrible activities. We shall now discover that the simple cause of this increasing temperature may be found in the electro-magnetic activities; the solution of this difficult problem is found in the frictionizing processes of those currents as they pass through the different stratifications contiguous to the surface. They are the vital fluids of the earth, continually circulating in accordance with well-established laws, and in fixed channels or currents, the same as vital fluids are producing activities in the animal or human structures. It is very plain, that the more blankets or covering one uses, the more this vital heat or caloric is retained in the system. So of the earth,—the deeper the covering of non-conducting materials over the portion where the heat is generated, the more it is retained, until we pass the region of electro-magnetic activities, where the temperature falls again, and continues to fall until the extreme of coldness and inactivity are found in the deeper midway portions of the spherical shell.

If we ascertain that effects have been produced which entirely baffle our keenest research for an adequate cause, we must study more closely the relationship that exists between causes and effects, and always look for those which are entirely competent to produce the results we have discovered. We must remember that feeble children can never perform the labor of full-grown athletic men, neither does nature employ in her workshop, the grosser elements to accomplish those high purposes that require all the powers of the sublimated essential forces. Hence, when philosophers have called upon gravitation, fire, and water, to take such a conspicuous and important position, in the construction of our world, they have made an unwise blunder, and one that will excite the laughter and ridicule of those same persons when they discover their mistake.

CHAPTER XII.

THE MOON.

It becomes almost a necessity, in connection with this general subject, to pay some passing respect to our nearest neighbor, or that comparatively youthful orb that may be properly considered the first-born child of our own planet, and who has been a faithful companion to this our mother, through all her various vicissitudes, during very many long ages of the past. The unwritten records, however, fail to communicate to us the exact period when its career was commenced, although the first author who wrote upon this matter has unhesitatingly asserted that it was created the same day, and, that it is quite as old as the great parent the sun. He says that this little satellite, whose youthful face bears no marks of extreme planetary antiquity, is quite as old as any of the large magnetic orbs that shine out with such inconceivable lustre in the distant sidereal heavens. But, whatever her age may be, there is evidently a very close relationship existing between this young planet and our own earth, and most of us have been accustomed to look out with great interest and admiration upon her pale, silver countenance, a portion of every month during our lives, and it has become one of the most familiar objects that has attended us thus far in our journey, and that first impressed itself upon our childish brain.

It is very evident, that the moon, like all other things we behold in this great universe, must have been constructed for very important purposes; as it must have received the direct attention of minds sufficiently advanced in knowledge and power to project and organize the forces and materials that have brought this structure up to its present condition. We cannot conceive that minds possessing abilities of such a character, can bring their power to bear, unless some great purpose is to be attained; and we learn at least, that building moons would quite likely result in building worlds, for a moon certainly appears very much like a world, although it may be somewhat diminutive in size. We think, however, almost any practical mechanic would conclude, that it would be much easier to increase the size of a moon, than to build an entire new world of larger proportions, and perhaps at some future time we shall be permitted to know the exact manner in which such worlds may be enlarged. Very much that we said in the preceding chapter, in relation to reconstruction, will of course apply equally well in this, for we must naturally conclude that one general plan is pursued in the construction of all worlds, whether great or small.

We have remarked, in a former part of this work, that undoubted evidence exists of a so-called glacial period; that, during the various transformations and changes which have occurred in the earth's eventful history, there must have been a lengthened period when a large portion of its surface was covered with ice and water. Those who are able to search out and peruse carefully the unwritten history of our earth, discover very clearly, that there has been upon its surface at a comparatively modern geologic period, and for a great length of time, a huge reservoir of cold, electric elements. They also discover that during the processes of further development, this negative element has to a large extent disappeared, and given place to a larger amount of magnetic or positive forces.

The overwhelming amount of sedimentary deposits, or secondary rocks, prove conclusively that water once existed in far greater quantities than at the present, and that it must either have retired to deeper recesses in the earth's surface, or, what is more probable, have been withdrawn for the supply of our secondary or lunar attendant, and perhaps we may here gather some light concerning that great unsolved mystery, the glacial or drift period, when such vast bodies of ice occupied a very large portion of both hemispheres. It will be entirely unnecessary for us to enter into any lengthy description of this period, for such has been done already in the most graphic manner, by a great number of eminent authors, and the reader may learn much upon this subject, even in many elementary works. Suffice it to say, that indubitable evidences exist, both in the northern and southern hemispheres, that a large portion of our globe, during a certain period, was locked, for incalculable ages, in the cold embrace of vast coverings of superincumbent ice, as well as water, and that, subsequently, it has gradually disappeared, leaving but a limited extent, or somewhat narrow belts of those glacial formations, in the higher latitudes, and upon the lofty mountain ranges.

Where the ice fields have gone, and the cause of their disappearance, are questions that have often been propounded, but still remain unanswered; still locked up in the deepest shadows of mystery and darkness. However, we may perceive that the time did arrive, when in the processes of our earth's development, it became necessary to part with those vast accumulations of cold, inactive elements, and, we conclude, our younger sister was prepared to receive this great surplus, that had subserved all their purposes upon the earth, and were ready to be transported to a place where they were more needed. It is quite as important that we should be able to read correctly this page of the earth's history as any other that has been recorded upon her tablets. Here are presented two prominent facts, perfectly palpable to most men who have extended their researches in this direction: one is, that the water at a particular period covered a large portion of the temperate zone sufficiently deep to float immense icebergs; another is, that the water and the icebergs have both subsided. Where has this extensive accumulation of elements gone? It is quite evident that it must have left the earth altogether, for we can find no room, in any of the deep recesses of the ocean beds, for such a vast surplus as must have existed at that time. It was certainly not needed upon the earth, because we have a very large superabundance of those elements at the present. Then, what a beautiful arrangement, if it could have been thus taken to supply the wants of a younger satellite.

What a blessing to our earth, to be able to divest itself, and send away all this vast accumulation of ice and water that had exerted this chilling influence upon the temperate zones for so many ages in the past; for, while it remained, coldness and inactivity held universal sway. There are few forms of organic life that could have resisted the frigid influences of this wide-spread scene of desolation, and while it remained, as a matter of course the habitable, or that portion of the globe that could have produced vegetable or animal organized forms of life, must have been confined to a very narrow zone. It was absolutely necessary, in the progressive development of our world, that all the vast ice fields should be vaporized and disappear; that the active magnetic elements might become more extensively diffused, and a wider and still wider extent of territory become prepared to furnish life and sustenance for an advancing and increasing animated population. We are not permitted to know the precise length of time that has transpired since the glacial period has passed away, neither does any one upon the earth know exactly the age of our moon. We have no data that will enable us to compute the time by centuries, so as to ascertain the number that have existed since the moon was projected, or since the vast icebergs floated over many of the northern states, freighted with their immense cargoes of detached bowlders and drift, which they have scattered broadcast over such extensive tracts of country. But we seem to discover very strong evidences from the records that are imprinted upon nature's tablets, by her own chirography, that these two great events, that form a part of our planetary history, were nearly coeval, and that they must have been connected by an intimate relationship. An extensive array of facts, gathered from different portions of our planetary system, and tend to prove that our moon is comparatively a modern institution, and another set gathered by observations made upon our own globe, would prove conclusively, that the drift period belongs to a comparatively modern age in the world's geologic history.

The glacial, or the drift period, seems to have existed after all the extensive accumulations of sedimentary deposit had been made; only below the alluvial deposits that form the very surface of this globular shell. No intelligent person who examines this matter, can doubt the palpable, tell-tale indices which prove most conclusively, that a very extended portion of the temperate zones were, for an incalculable length of time, covered by terrible accumulations of ice, and thus the frost-king held universal sway, where now are to be found innumerable cheerful homes and fruitful fields, populous towns and cities, with all their business and varied activities, and the ten thousand concomitants of prosperity and plenty. And if we take a cursory survey of our own planetary system, we shall find that most of the exterior planets are attended by more than one of these lunar bodies, and that they seem to revolve around the parents, in orbits at various distances, in accordance with their different ages and growth.

Some of the moons connected with the exterior and older planets in our solar system, corresponding very nearly in size and diameter of orbit with our own, are doubtless very near the same age; while others, revolving in far larger orbits, and very much superior in size, must be correspondingly older. The exterior moon of Saturn is supposed to be nearly the size of Mars, and revolves in an orbit nearly two and a half million miles distant from that planet, and doubtless, if we could become fully acquainted with all the planets and satellites in our solar system, we might discover moons larger than our own earth, with attendant satellites revolving around them. It has been extremely difficult, even with the best telescopes in use, to form correct ideas concerning the moons of Uranus, and almost impossible to make any discovery concerning the moons of Neptune, which are so far beyond. Then we may naturally conclude, that in the vast unexplored fields lying within the limits of our own solar system, still beyond Neptune, may be a number of far older planets that are surrounded by families of moons, in a highly developed condition, that may for centuries to come remain entirely beyond the view of the most powerful lenses that will be produced by the inventive genius of men.

We think, now, the reader has no doubt discovered, by attention to the preceding pages, a few important points, which he may group together, and arrive at a tolerably safe conclusion concerning our own satellite. First. That all worlds are projected as moons or satellites, and that they are usually composed of negative or electric materials. Secondly. That our moon has a general appearance of planetary youthfulness. Thirdly. That our earth presents the strongest indications, that, at a comparatively modern period, there had collected upon its surface, a superabundance of the most electric material in the form of water and ice. Fourthly. That this negative material, the very article that was required in the construction of a new planet, has, for some inexplicable reason, passed entirely from the earth, where it formerly existed, and the climate has become more temperate and genial; and, Fifthly. There are evidently now existing powerful reciprocal influences between our earth and the moon, and consequently there must be strong sympathetic cords in the shape of electric currents that bind the two together, as well as all other planets and satellites in our solar system. We think it will become plain to the most careless observer, that there could have been no kind of difficulty in transporting the surplus ice and water, in the form of vapor or electricity, upon those currents to the new-born planet that was ever to be an attendant in all our protracted journeys through the immensity of space.

It would seem that, although nature, in her great laboratory, must contain an equilibrium of elemental forces, yet not unfrequently either the positive or negative may appear to gain the entire preponderance in working out her grand purposes, and apparently carry things to great extremes. Thus, during that very extended period when the solid granite was breaking up and being dissolved under powerful electro-magnetic, disintegrating influences, the process seemed to continue to an unnecessarily lengthened duration. This labor evidently went forward until it had released a sufficient quantity of negative materials to operate as a check upon its future progress; and, although the dissolving process seemed to be carrying matters to a wonderful extent, yet, when we discover the objects had in view, we can but admire the beauty and harmony of the arrangement. It would be extremely difficult for us to devise any other mode by which the necessary elements could have been engendered, with which the new-born world might be supplied with sufficient materials to make a start in life. Thus we may partially discover how seeming evils destroy their own power and influence, and finally ultimate in positive good. Had not such excessive and powerful positive influences been brought to bear in the dissolution of inconceivably vast quantities of the granitic surface of the globe, until it passed through all the changes from very great heat to the excessive cold of the glacial period, and until nearly the whole surface was covered by one vast expanse of water, then we should have had no proper material to have furnished an infant planet, and most probably, we should have had no attendant moon to cheer and enliven the gloom of night, and render tolerable that portion of earthly existence; for this new planet could not have commenced its career of glory among the heavenly bodies.

We are apprehensive, that this view of the subject will illuminate many very dark pages in the geologic history of our own globe, which have puzzled the brains of the ardent student of nature, for it is not only extremely difficult, but absolutely impossible, to account, upon any other hypothesis that has ever been established, for the various transitions from heat to cold, and then to a more genial climate again in the northern temperate zone, and also the great climatic changes that have taken place in the arctic regions, which sometimes give rise to the foolish idea that the polar axis of the globe, as well as the polar circles, have changed periodically from one position to another. There can scarcely be a doubt, judging from the influence now exerted by the frozen belt that still exists at the north upon the climate of a vast region lying contiguous, that the great glacial period of the past must have extended its influences to the equatorial regions, and caused an almost entire destruction of all but those animals that endure the rigors of winter, and that, if tropical animals existed at all during that period, they must have been confined to a very narrow zone.

Thus, we perceive, there must have been extended ages when the sun exerted very little influence upon a great portion of the temperate zones, because the electrical elements again preponderated, and the condition of things was such within the atmosphere, as to render the sun's positive influences negative; or, rather, there were not in our surroundings sufficient positive elements to affinitize and be wakened into activity by any influences of this great luminous body. Hence we discover, that our climate depends upon the character and condition of our own inherent powers, much more than upon any influences that are coming directly to us from the great luminous body in the centre.

Now, if it was, in the ages of the past, in order to aid in the unfoldment of our planet, necessary to take away a large amount of the accumulations of negative or cold element in the form of ice and water, then it will doubtless be necessary, in view of the future development of our world, to devise means for carrying off very large surplus quantities of the cold elements that still remain; and that continue, by their chilling influence, to render comparatively worthless very large portions of the territory of both the northern and southern hemispheres. Any person, by glancing at the map of the world, can ascertain the fact, that nearly one-half the continent of North America, and vast portions of northern Europe and Asia, are rendered almost useless and uninhabitable, by the cold and inhospitable climate that prevails, while perhaps the soil and other advantages may be fully equal, and in many instances superior, to the more favored and temperate climes. It would appear evident that those vast tracts of country cannot be destined for all time, by the supreme powers that seem to control matters appertaining to our world, to produce little except bears and foxes and a dwarfed growth of fir trees. We have sufficient of this territory in North America to supply the necessities of hundreds of millions of human beings, if but the climate could be ameliorated. Can we suppose it is to remain in this same forbidding and frozen condition for all time? or are those vast uninhabitable fields to be opened, and made to bud and blossom as the rose, and the waste places to be built up—to be blessed with a genial and pleasant climate, and furnish happy homes for untold millions of the human race, with their flocks and herds, and all the appurtenances of an advanced civilization?

We can easily perceive, if we look over the face of our globe, that we have negative element left, sufficient to supply the wants of at least two or three more moons, and the sooner a portion of this surplus electricity is removed, the better for the globe. We have not only the large and extended glacial formations actually existing at the higher north and south latitudes, and upon our mountain ranges, but we have yet a very great surplus of water. When we consider that nearly three-fourths of the earth's surface is covered with this element, we may readily discover that we have no possible use for this excessive quantity, and that we only hold it in reserve for the use of those satellites that are to be produced in the ages of the future. It may prove disastrous to private interests to take away a thousand feet from the surface of the oceans. It might change the conditions of our maritime cities by extending the shore lines of the continents perhaps far out to sea, but it would necessarily enlarge the continents, and the islands also, and doubtless connect many of them together, thus producing new continents where now are but a few scattered isles in the midst of the ocean. Taking this view of the subject, we cannot entertain a doubt but such a disposal of a large portion of the negative elements now existing upon the earth would promote the general interest, and be of vast service to the human race, as it would ultimately change a very large extent of this wide waste of waters to fruitful fields, and most effectually reclaim all the low, marshy deltas in the world, and perhaps add one-fourth to the superficial area of the habitable globe.

Now, we may ask, with some degree of propriety, how this necessary improvement can be made and this step taken in the development of our world, unless by some means this excess of electric material is transferred to some new-made globe or satellite; for, what else can be done with the large amount of water and ice, which appear entirely unnecessary, even at the present time, upon this our planet. This cold element very evidently is retarding instead of advancing our progressive unfoldment as a world. Wherever and whenever extreme cold prevails, all things are effectually locked. in its frozen embrace. No move can be made in the direction of improvement and progress until the cold, electric influences are removed, and conditions are rendered more magnetic and active. Hence, we very plainly discover, that before our planet can arrive at any high condition of development, the climate must be equalized from pole to pole, and hence the preponderating amount of arctic and antarctic electricity must be removed, as well as the great excess of watery element, that now covers so very large a portion of the superficial area of the globe. The reader may not be surprised, if we should modestly announce the fact, that this matter has long since received the attention of the inhabitants of the higher spheres, and that they have already provided a receptacle for a certain portion of the excess of electric material, and that a new lunar attendant for our earth has already been established, whose orbit is about 100,000 miles distant from our planet, or about 20,000 nearer than the youngest and interior moon of the planet Saturn. Our young moon of course is not sufficiently materialized to be discovered by unaided vision, however, before a single century passes away, we dare predict it will be generally known that our earth has another satellite to accompany her in all her wanderings, and to render still more cheerful the evenings of all the future generations, until our great mother shall so far unfold her inherent powers, as to be entirely independent of outside influences for the light her children require.

It is supposed that the new-born satellite which is now in process of formation, will absorb the great amount of cold element now existing in the arctic regions, and a portion of that in the south or antarctic; that it will also absorb a very large quantity of the waters of the ocean, and thus extend all coast lines more or less, and bring to view a large area of land now covered by water; and that by dissipating the cold of the northern polar regions, it will again partially restore that climate once enjoyed there, when it produced and sustained tropical animal and vegetable life.

We have scrupulously avoided advancing any idea, or adopting any theory as authoritative, solely because the invisible spirit intelligences have taught such ideas or theories; we have invariably presented them because they also seemed to our minds best supported by evidences that are absolutely found in the great store-house of nature. We present this theory concerning the formation of our moon, and all other moons that may exist in the solar system to which we are attached, then, simply because we conceive it to be the most rational view of the subject ever given to the world. We claim that the worlds are not all yet built, because we plainly discover that the present era must be right in the midst of the great cycles of time, that there must be just as much time in the future as there has been in the past, and that all the laws and powers which have been so productive of worlds in the past, are in full activity in the present, and must so continue in the future. Hence, the future must be quite as productive in this branch of mechanism as the past, and new worlds must be continually brought into existence.

We claim, and we need not stop to repeat a single argument upon that portion of the subject, that all worlds are mechanical in their movements, and in the appropriate disposition of the materials from which they are composed; and hence, they must have required a vast amount of mechanical skill and ability in their construction. It is extremely difficult for us to discover how an intelligent mind can conceive the idea, that so complex a piece of machinery as a world like ours could have arranged itself during all its various modifications and differentiations, entirely unaided by an intelligent management of the forces which have evidently been used in the accomplishment of the grand result. None but the positive school will attempt to sustain such a view of the matter. But we doubt not, the Christian world will howl forth their usual anathemas and derision at any suggestion of this character. The faintest thought that their infinite Jehovah is to be released to any extent from the infinite labor of projecting and constructing all the globes, will doubtless bring down showers of indignation and wrath upon the unhappy mortal who could have had the temerity to advance an idea so fraught with danger to the thinking world. Yet the simple question and the only issue will be, have all the worlds been constructed by a single infinite intelligent personality, or by infinite numbers of finite intelligent beings? We conceive this to be an issue of vast importance, and cannot doubt but in man's progressive history, public opinion will be wonderfully modified in relation to this subject.

We take occasion to remark, before leaving this subject, that one of the most awkward and clumsy scientific conclusions that ever gained universal credence, has an intimate relationship with this young planet. We mean our present widely accepted theory concerning the oceanic tidal phenomena, to which we have made some allusion in a previous chapter. The oceanic tides are supposed to be governed entirely by the power of reciprocal gravitation, which power is communicated from one planet to another. Thus, the gravitating force attached to the sun and the moon reach out the strong arms of their power, exert an influence over the waters of the ocean, and attract them to a limited extent towards themselves. It will be discovered, in order to do this successfully, it is necessary that this foreign attraction should altogether overcome that which naturally belongs to the planet, where the tidal wave occurs. Again, it is obvious that this so-called attraction must operate in a most singular manner, for when it is high tide at any given point upon the globe, it is also high tide at a point exactly opposite. Hence we learn, that this attraction draws with equal force contiuually in both directions. But science accounts for this strange anomaly by claiming that the moon attracts the water from the earth, upon the side towards herself, and that she attracts the earth from the waters that are situated upon the opposite hemisphere.

We very much doubt whether any philosopher or teacher of this theory concerning the tidal phenomena, has ever been fully satisfied of its real truthfulness. One thing is very clear; very many men of learning have expressed their want of confidence, and entire dissent, but none thus far have seemed to elaborate a theory that is able to take precedence, and it is not our purpose to do so either, in the brief allusion we can make to this difficult subject. We barely suggest that, if it is possible to find a motive power sufficeint to move the world, it would not seem difficult to find one quite adequate to perform the trifling task, of causing the tidal waves to pass in their order around the globe.

Newton conceived a similar idea, and saw quite

clearly that the power that could propel a world in its orbit could readily perform this much smaller task. But, as we think, having made an error in the application of dynamic forces in the one case, he made the same error in the other. Had he found the great moving power that could have given momentum to the globe, without the aid of a God to introduce the initial movement, he would doubtless have been able to have applied the same force more successfully in the production of the tides. We doubt not, that when we come fully to understand the operations and influences of the electro-magnetic forces, this tidal phenomena will become quite plain, and the difficult problem will be very easily solved. We may barely suggest, and in fact we feel quite strongly impressed with the idea, that the action of the waters of the ocean, causing the ebb and flow of the tides, is produced by two separate electro-magnetic batteries; the one formed by our connection with the sun, and the other by our connection with the moon. The two batteries are doubtless entirely distinct and separate in their operations and influences, the lunar battery operating far more powerfully upon the waters of the ocean than the solar battery. We may discover, if we accept this hypothesis, the important fact that the solar battery operates more powerfully upon the positive elements attached to our earth, while the lunar battery exerts the more powerful influence upon the negative elements. Thus we perceive that the earth's reciprocal influence in connection with these two batteries would be to produce the larger tides upon the sun, and the lesser upon the moon.

If the tides were absolutely produced by gravitating

force, we discover at once, that the sun's tides would necessarily be overwhelmingly larger than those of the moon; as the sun is five hundred times larger than all the planets of the solar system, and is said to exert a gravitating influence that controls the whole machine from centre to circumference. How then could those learned men induce the great central controlling orb to exert so little gravitating powers upon the waters of the oceans attached to this globe? The easy, natural reply to this question lies in the fact that the waters of the ocean are indebted to quite different powers for their tidal activities, and we trust that there may now be some prospect that this extremely difficult problem may find a satisfactory solution. If we adopt the hypothesis that electromagnetic force is brought to bear in producing the various movements of the heavenly bodies, then we shall very naturally conclude that the same forces are brought to bear in the movement of the waters in this respect, but we shall leave each party to make the application of the forces in his own manner. We think, however, no one who gives this subject a thought, will experience any difficulty in finding all the necessary elements in nature's great storehouse, from which batteries may be erected, fully competent to perform all this labor in a most satisfactory manner.

We shall now be compelled to leave this portion of our subject, and doubtless very many readers will feel disappointment because we have not given, during our treatise upon the physical structure of the globe, a more graphic description of that interior world which we claim has an existence. We can simply say it would not have been very instructive if we had, even if we could have given by clairvoyant vision, or spirit teaching, an accurate description of an interior world, such as would be found truthful when explored, it would be found of little profit to the reader. The object of this work thus far has been to show that nothing can be found upon our globe that is incompatible with the idea of an inner as well as an outer world,—to show that the earth must necessarily be constructed in the form of a spherical shell, with an inner as well as an outer surface. We have endeavored to prove that no law exists in nature that would be in the least antagonistic to this idea, and that all the analogies in the universe conspire to support this grand theory. We leave the reader to judge how well we have accomplished our purpose. We acknowledge ourselves indebted entirely, for the reasoning in the preceding pages, to the spiritual directors who suggested the writing of the work.

CHAPTER XIII.

VISION.

THE eye being the most delicate and sensitive portion of the physical organization, must necessarily be composed of the finest and most sublimated materials. It cannot bear contact with gross particles without pain and uneasiness, hence its component elements must be vastly finer than those of other organs, because such contact would produce no pain upon other parts of the system. It is one of the most remarkable mechanical contrivances of which we have any knowledge; without its aid, humanity would be perfectly powerless, they could not supply their own wants, and would consequently cease to exist in a short period. The lenses are so remarkably formed that we see through them, without any re-adjustment, at all distances from a few inches to the farthest visible star, and all visible objects at those various distances are alike reflected upon the retina, and the impression carried to the brain through the same lenses by nature's own adjustment. If we use any artificial lens we must adjust them to suit the eye and the greater or lesser distance of the object. However penetrating the human vision may be, there is a limit beyond which it cannot reach, either out into the broad expanse, or down into the infinitesimal realms.

We understand that telescopic and microscopic lenses have revealed to our astonished vision worlds upon worlds hitherto unknown, both in the far-off regions of space entirely beyond the range of the natural eye, and also down in the infinitesimal realms where objects are so diminutive as to escape our most piercing glances, and we readily perceive, there must be still unlimited fields of unexplored territory upon which this department of science may exercise its increasing accumulations of knowledge. Without doubt, vast undiscovered wonders may yet be found beyond the reach of the best fashioned, most powerful lenses now in use. There are inconceivable unsurveyed regions out in the immensity of the universe, as well as in the infinitesimal depths where dwell the animalculæ and the most sublimated particles of matter. Can we suppose that human skill and genius in this department, have culminated in the attainments of the present age, and that the most powerful lenses have already been manufactured? That cannot be. Instruments of greater and still greater power will no doubt be produced extending further and still further in both directions. Generations to come must continue to enjoy as adequate room for the active exercise of all their organs as those of the past who have revealed such astounding facts in this field of research; or, for the want of the needed activity, organs of this character would cease to perform their proper functions, and this portion of human nature would evidently cease to exist.

But, there is a spiritual telescopic and microscopic vision which goes beyond the material, that reaches inconceivably further than comes within the view of the finest and most powerful glasses human ingenuity has ever yet produced; and, it is not too much to think, that many individuals possess, to a greater or less extent, this spiritual vision. In fact, we may safely say, the germs of this vision are found in all persons. We may almost as well doubt our own senses as to doubt the fact of clairvoyant vision, which is simply bringing into activity the interior organs, or those we shall use when we have passed the boundaries of mortal life. It is simply that vision which appertains to the spirit within us, that is more powerful and sees under different conditions, and at greater distances than the material eye; it is that vision which comes to the aid of the somnambulist, and enables him to perform such astonishing feats in the darkness, with eyes closed to all external objects.

Books of travel, history, and descriptive scenery, would be of little interest, were there no interior vision to be opened to the scenes described, and did they not make a sort of living impression upon those organs, we certainly could receive no particular benefit from such works. If they are well and properly written, they convey mind-pictures, and transfer us back to the time and place of the transactions, and give us a view of the surroundings. What can a Livingstone or a Du Chaillu give us but the spirit of the stirring scenes they encounter, and describe so graphically as existing in the various portions of Africa. What could a Rubens or a Vandyke transfer to the canvas but the spirit of scenes they portray so vividly, which command so much admiration? And, but for the spirit they have discovered, and are, by their genius, enabled to place upon the canvas, their works would possess no value. Thus, all works of art, and much of literature, would be worthless, unless there was a spirit in them, and we have, within ourselves, a power of vision by which we can discover that spirit. This is one method by which we can appreciate their true value. So, we discover that in spirit we may travel to the remote corners of the world, and visit the renowned cities and countries, not only of modern but of ancient times.

We do not propose to write a philosophical treatise upon the eye. Such may be found already in profusion; and we could not improve upon them if we wished. We are to take an entirely different view of this matter. We observe that human vision no doubt has quite a uniform range, and that the size and form of objects are very similar, or present very similar impressions to different minds, beheld by various eyes. There is little doubt but the house, the tree, the man, or any other object, may appear to one individual vision very nearly the same, as to size, form and color, as they do to other persons who possess the organs in a normal condition. But, we discover that, all through the whole range of animated nature, almost every living being, from the smallest to the greatest, are endowed with this power of vision, and that it must of necessity be adapted to the various conditions and surroundings in which this great variety of living organisms are placed. For instance, the eagle that soars aloft and looks down from the aerial regions upon its destined prey, requires a very differently constructed eye, and a different range of vision, from the ox that feeds in the pasture, and whose eye is always in close proximity to his food, and naturalists inform us that each one has an eye suited to their widely different conditions. The eye of the eagle is so constructed as to see from afar; it takes in a long range, while that of the ox is very short in its range, and he may be considered somewhat near-sighted. Change these visions, snd place the eye of the ox in the head of the eagle, and the bird would starve to death; for, it could not see its natural food until it had approached within a very few feet, and most probably the hare or other prey, in that case would not remain to be devoured. Upon the other hand, the ox could with difficulty discern whether the food he was cropping was suited to his necessities.

We have remarked that tbere was a limit to human vision; that there was a point down in the realms of the infinitesimal, beyond which the unaided eye could not penetrate. However, we find within the limits of nature's boundaries, materials from which may be manufactured lenses that entirely change and modify this power, so that objects when observed through such lenses, are apparently enlarged or magnified, and by this means we are enabled to penetrate further into those realms, and behold what was unknown to us before. It will appear evident, then, when this fact first became known to the world, a great principle was established, that may have been overlooked by scientific men, even up to the present time,—and that is, size and distance are relative terms, and are measured and computed upon a fixed standard, which is made to accord precisely to that of the human vision. For, we discover at once, if there are materials in this universe out of which we may manufacture lenses that will entirely change and modify our vision, so that objects will appear much larger than when beheld by the natural eye; then, if all eyes had been composed of such materials, and constructed in manner and form like the magnifying lenses, it would follow that the standard of human vision would have been very different from what it now is, and all men would have beheld all objects very much enlarged compared with the size they now behold them.

If we take a glass that magnifies a hundred times, in looking through one end, we find the object to be a hundred times larger then when beheld by the natural eye, but when we turn the other end, we behold the object proportionately smaller. We find, then, materials in this world, which, when placed in proper form, produce these two different results, and we discover, that if all men, from all time, had been compelled to have beheld all things through one or the other end of this glass, they would have formed a very different estimate of the size of the objects beheld, from that recognized by the ordinary human vision. Again, suppose one-half the human family were compelled to look through one end of the glass, and to see objects magnified a hundred times, while the other half were compelled to behold them through the other, and see them proportionately diminished, what vast differences of opinion would necessarily result between the two parties; in relation to the size of all the objects beheld? We think, then, we shall be compelled to admit, that it is very much if not "all in the eye," in relation to many things that we behold here upon the earth.

There can be no doubt but the human eye, as a mechanical structure, approximates as near perfection as any other thing of a material character that has ever been executed in the great work-shop of the natural universe, but, it is quite evident that the skill and wisdom brought to bear in its construction could have produced an eye with a somewhat different range of vision; one that might have beheld objects either larger or smaller than our general standard. Because, it is very evident that, within the realms of animated nature, eyes must exist, in which may be found very different lenses, and perhaps formed of somewhat different materials from those used in the human race. Ours are admirably adapted to our condition, but our conditions and circumstances are widely different from that of the owl, who seeks its natural aliment in the darkness of night, or the mole, that has its habitation and employment under the earth's surface, or the animalcule, that requires to be magnified a thousand diameters before it can be recognized by human vision. All these conditions are widely different, and doubtless widely different lenses are required to meet their various wants, and to subserve all their different purposes. The animalcule is said by naturalists to possess a great variety of organs, among which may be found those of vision, and we discover at once, that the lenses, and most probably the material used, must be vastly different from those introduced into the human eye. As a visual organ, constructed upon a principle well adapted to the human race, would evidently be of very little service to the animalcule, as he would have to be magnified a thousand times his own bulk before he could see himself. Thus we learn that an eye formed and constructed upon that principle would by no means answer the purposes of the little creature. They must be provided with eyes with which they can discern their food, which must be proportionately smaller than themselves, for animals, no matter what their size, seldom swallow anything larger than their own bulk, as they would evidently be quite unable to contain that which exceeds their own dimensions. Then, we learn, that they require lenses that will magnify a thousand diameters beyond ours, and vastly more, that they may be able to discern objects sufficiently minute to serve their purposes as food.

We shall find, then, that microscopic lenses abound in nature's realms, and instead of being an absolute invention, they are simply, like many other things of that character, an imitation of what already exists, and has so existed from all eternity; for, it is clear that all the inhabitants of the infinitesimal worlds that are out of the range of human vision, must be provided with microscopic eyes or lenses in order to subserve any of the purposes of vision. It is by no means probable that artificial glasses have been constructed that will reach down to the most minute forms of organized life, then it will be impossible for us to contemplate the power of those lenses that must be introduced into the delicate eyes of the animalculæ that inhabit the realms entirely beyond the boundaries of our microscopic vision, or that which we have produced at the present period. For the power of the lenses introduced into the minutest animalcule that has been discovered by our microscopic lenses, must, in magnifying properties, go vastly beyond the power of the lens that is barely able to discern the animalcule itself, in order that its vision should subserve any practical purpose. Thus we discover that, if it was possible to place microscopic vision, with such immense magnifying power in the animalculæ that are so vastly below the reach of our eyes—and we must admit the fact, if we admit they have vision that is of any practical benefit to them,—then it would have been quite possible to have constructed larger eyes upon the same plan, with the same material, and the same fashioned lenses; and if such had been the case, then we discover that all material objects would have presented a very different appearance. So we may learn, that the appearance of the object depends entirely upon the character of the eye with which it is beheld. If our vision was like some others—microscopic in its character—then all things would be proportionately larger, and if it was telescopic to a given extent, then all things would seem proportionally nearer; so we shall learn, at some time, that size and distance are relative terms, and that there can be no standard for their computation, except the peculiar vision through which they are discerned.

We say this globe we inhabit, is about 8,000 miles in diameter, and approximates 25,000 miles in circumference, and that a mile is so many rods, and a rod so many feet, and a foot so many inches, and we think we have the thing ciphered down so that it becomes absolute, and, that no intelligence in this wide universe can dispute with any propriety our measurement. For such dimensions are known to be a well-established verity, accepted by all intelligent men; but, we shall ascertain that the standard of this measurement is based entirely upon the peculiar construction of the human vision. Just take out this eye, and substitute a different kind of lens, perhaps composed of a little different material, and formed upon a little different plan, and you would be compelled to measure again, and make another computation, to ascertain the size and dimensions of your world, because you are beholding it with an entirely different vision. If the animalcule, with this powerful microscopic vision, which we discover it must possess, should reside in the smallest flower or find a home upon the leaf of the minutest plant, it would still have a wide world of its own, in which it could carry out all the purposes for which it is designed, by the power and wisdom that directs and governs. It would have as ample scope, to perform all its functions, in that little flower, or upon that leaf, as we have in this world of ours—as we see its world would be enlarged by its power of seeing, and so would ours if we possessed the same character of vision with the animalcule.

"He that formeth the eye, shall he not see?" and it is very generally supposed that a being who was competent to construct such a curious piece of workmanship, must be infinitely wise and powerful, or in other words must possess all the wisdom and power of all beings. But this is not necessarily the case, for we discover that eyes constitute but a small portion of this universe, and that, like other mechanical contrivances, they are formed in endless variety, and adapted to an inconceivable number of different conditions, and used in a great variety of ways. They are of all sizes and colors, and the corneas, the pupils, and the retinas, have a thousand different forms; and it would appear evident, that some of all these endless varieties would require more skill in their construction than others, and that an intelligence might be competent to construct some of the many varieties, that could not possibly produce others that are more complicated in their character. But it must be conceded, that it would require a spiritual intelligence of eminent abilities to construct the simplest form of visual organ, for as yet it is not known that any person in the form — not even Jesus, who is supposed by so many to have possessed supreme power and wisdom,—have ever made the attempt, or have ever produced an imitation that would serve any kind of purpose. Then it will be seen that they must be produced by spiritual beings who possess the requisite mechanical skill, and in order to construct the numerous varieties, they must well understand their adaptation; and suppose it was necessary to go down into the infinitesimal world, and there form microscopic visions, would it not be absolutely necessary that they should possess the microscopic vision in order to accomplish the work properly? It certainly would, for a two-fold reason: first, the artist would require a powerfully microscopic vision in order to distinguish the particles from which the eye of the animalcule must be manufactured; and, secondly, how can they obtain an absolute competent knowledge of the true nature of the particular vision required, unless they are supplied with a far more intensified vision or eye than they wish to produce?

Suppose, now, we should fall back upon the hypothesis that all those realms were peopled with their inconceivable retinues of inhabitants, by the infinite wisdom and power of one self-existent individual, outside and above all nature, who had never come up through the infinitesimal realms himself, or had any experience there, and had never created any offspring who possessed like powers with himself, or abilities to produce any such mechanical structures in accordance with universal laws. This one being, in order to possess infinite knowledge, must have had a microscopic vision to an infinite extent, and this vision must have been required and called into action in the creation of all those minute beings. Now, as all things worth creating by an infinite God, would certainly be worth watching over, caring for and protecting, we see plainly that he must have unremittingly watched over and attended to the wants of all such beings personally, or else he must have produced other intelligences endowed with the same infinite vision, who could have acted in this capacity in his stead, because it is evident that this portion of animated nature is receiving continual attention from some intelligence endowed with the requisite vision. Although this widely received hypothesis of a single, infinite, personal creator of all visible and invisible things, is entirely preposterous and unsupported by evidence derived from a single fact or analogy in the broad universe, yet it would doubtless absolutely require that spiritual beings should be endowed with microscopic vision of an exceedingly powerful character, to enable them to act in the most subordinate capacities in the realms of nature.

But, we do think the day is not far distant, when it will be generally conceded that all the operations of nature are inside the limits of the natural universe, if it has any limits, and that any being that has come into existence outside, if there can be any such being, can by no means get inside, for all that is inside must be subject to, and governed by, the universal laws that predominate within the boundaries of universal nature. There can be no individualized power who can exercise control over, and change and modify eternal laws. We see at a glance, it is utterly impossible, because those laws are fixed, immutable and uncontrollable. There can be no power in this broad universe that can effect any change in a single mathematical or geometrical proposition, or any other principle or law that is unenacted and comes to us from the eternity of the eternities of the past. There could have been no period when the laws of the natural universe were established, or enacted, and hence there could have been no individualized power that brought them into existence, for they are eternal, and did exist without beginning; and there can be no individualized being, unless he has his being in accordance with universal law, except he originated and exists outside the influence and authority of universal law. Is it any more absurd for the materialist to say that all things came into existence by chance, without power or law, than it is for the religionist to say that a God, possessing all power and wisdom, came into existence by chance, and.without law, and then by this chance wisdom and power, produced all law and all things in accordance with its provisions?

We think, then, as we make so little headway in ascertaining what occurred previous to any existence, or outside the boundaries of the natural universe, we had better confine our explorations, and keep within its limits, for no doubt we shall find sufficient to occupy the attention of the most intellectual powers for very many eternal ages, without crossing its confines in any direction. Doubtless, humanity would have made far more advancement, if they had kept nearer home, and not ventured away so far into the depths of the unknown, in pursuit of knowledge; for, in so doing, they have built up huge superstructures that are resting upon mythical lore and imaginary foundations, and which will all be swept away by time's changes, "like the baseless fabric of a vision." We may take our microscopic lenses and descend down into the depths of the infinitesimal realms, and there by a single glance find more of real truth and absolute knowledge, than by an age of research among all the ponderous records of beliefs and opinions which have been accumulated by all the sects and denominations that have existed up to the present. For down in the lower regions of organic life, we find absolute, living, breathing facts, and clustering around those facts and wonderful phenomena, we find eternal laws and principles which lead us to a contemplation of the most exalted themes the human mind can by any possibility entertain. Our minds seem to be carried directly from an examination of the minutest forms of organic life, which can only be recognized by the most powerful lenses, up to that superior intelligence who must be capable of providing himself with an eye possessing almost infinite microscopic power, in order perfectly to comprehend the delicate workmanship necessary to produce one of those living, moving creatures, with all its various organs.

We shall see that spiritual beings must of necessity possess this wonderful ability of changing at will the lenses, or the eye, through which they behold all objects, in order to be able to discern all things, and to act in all the varied capacities, and attend properly to all their numerous callings and duties. As an evidence that this may be the case, we observe that men in the form may do the same thing by using this coarser material that answers our purpose, and produces such marvelous changes in the range and comprehension of human vision. If we can take this gross matter, and mold it into form of lenses that will aid our vision in looking out into the sidereal heavens and discovering such marvels there, and then down into the lower depths of nature, bringing to light wonders of which the human mind could have had no conception, then we may well suppose that spirits possessing abundance of sublimated materials of the same character, must be able to furnish their own lenses at will, to suit their several purposes. We need not indulge the idea that we are ahead of our spirit fathers in any of the arts or sciences, when all we have yet attained came to us directly from them. We may be assured that whatever we can do of such a character, they can also do, in a far more extended and powerful manner.

We have shown in these pages that all matter increases in power and activity by sublimation or spiritualization, or by division of particles; that steam is more powerful and active than water, and electricity superior to steam, because the atomic particles are more sublimated and finer. Hence it is, that spiritual beings may, from the spiritualized or sublimated particles of the same materials of which visual lenses are formed to suit the purposes of physical organisms, and which are used by them with great success,—produce those which are so much more powerful, because composed of the finer essences of the gross matter. The coarser lenses have served the purposes of our savans extremely well, and enabled them to look out into the unknown regions of space very far beyond human vision, and also down deeply into those unseen realms of infinitesimal organic life, what, then may we expect of those lenses formed from the sublimated essences of the same material, refined to the last extreme of spiritualization?

We have endeavored to keep in view the intimate relationship that must exist between the material and spiritual abodes, and also between the organisms of man in this grosser form, and spirits in their higher and more sublimated condition. Were it not so, our highest aspirations formed in this life, could not by any possibility be realized in the next. If we were not, in spirit life, organized from the same kind of materials that we are in this, or materials sublimated and spiritualized out of such as compose our organisms here, then the relationship would cease, and any hope or aspiration formed here could not be experienced there, because, we should not have the same kind of elements as those in which the hopes and aspirations originated. The connection betwen the two different conditions would be severed, and we should be entirely unable to continue the chain of existence, and carry out the great purposes and designs that have been developing within us up to the present time.

Hence, we see, in order to make the connection perfect, we must be constituted and organized in spirit life, with the same identical elements that we are in this, and being so organized, we may experience and realize fully the most exalted aspiration that can possibly originate, or be developed within us in our present condition. Because, the elements of our natures in spirit life, are precisely the same, only of a more sublimated character, and consequently possessing more activity and power, they must of course be more exquisitely sensitive to all emotions and all the varied kinds of enjoyments that enter the inner receptivities of spiritual beings. Not only the vision is increased in power and activity, by being composed of more etherealized materials, but, all the senses must be equally enhanced. The taste, smell, feeling and hearing,—all, must be as much above ours, as would be indicated by the more spiritualized condition of that life.

Spiritual existence, to us, appears, philosophically, entirely intangible and quite incomprehensible; because, we have, in a normal condition, no eye to behold their personalities, nor ear to hear their gentle whispers. We cannot feel the pressure of their hands, neither can we regale our gross olfactories with the aroma so grateful to them, nor taste the ambrosial food that satisfies their appetite; and hence, the whole subject of spirit conscious existence is dark and inexplicable.

But we need take into consideration the great fact that all these sensuous organs in us, are adapted precisely to our conditions as inhabitants of this earth-sphere; they are composed of materials that render them most proper and advantageous to us in this form. We see, that in order to retain their identity and relationship to this state of existence, they must have the very same sensuous organs, composed of the sublimated elements of the same character, which are precisely adapted to that higher condition. We all entertain hopes and yearnings that seem to originate somewhere in the depths of our natures, and they reach out into the beyond. We know that we can have no realization, in this life, of many of the aspirations that we find existing within; for they swell up and outreach all that this world can supply. There are wants known to the human soul, beyond all the provisions appertaining to earth-life, because, earthly things are too gross to supply those needs that originate in the finer sensibilities of a cultivated mentality. And how can we realize a response to those higher aspirations and the supply of the wants of the soul in the future, unless we are provided with sensuous organs of higher and more exalted powers?

How can you grasp the hand of your departed friend or lover, unless you have a hand that is capable of conveying such sensation to the innermost consciousness, or how can you enjoy anything of spirit existence, unless you are possessed of such powers as will enable you to see, hear, feel, smell and taste all that is provided for the gratification of all the different sensuous organs in spirit life? We cannot see spiritual beings because our organs of vision are too gross to discover the etherealized particles of which they are composed,—but, we must conclude that they have a vision which enables them to behold themselves and all other things existing in their sphere, or else it would be a dark place to inhabit, and they would certainly have a dreary kind of existence. They must also be in possession of all the other senses, for it must surely be as great a calamity in that life to be deprived of one of their senses, as in this, and we can all realize, to some extent, the nature of such deprivation during our earthly existence.

It will not be denied that the large portion of our earthly enjoyments depends upon the possession of well and properly developed sensuous organs. Desolate and unhappy indeed, is the condition of that person, who is deprived of the use of any of those organs. Paralysis of any of the functions of sensation is next door to death; in spirit life it must be the same, for no mind upon the earth has yet pictured to his imagination, any idea of spirit existence which is not connected with some or all of the senses. We are either to see, hear, feel, taste or smell something attached to the most exalted conceptions that ever entered the human brain concerning those realms, in which we rest our loftiest and sublimest hopes and aspirations. We are to wander hand in hand with loved ones, over green fields and flower-clad vales, inhale their aroma and behold their beauties. We are to taste the nectar that is gushing from the crystal fountains, and murmuring in the playful rills, and feel upon our brows the soft breezes of those soul-enchanting hills and vales, where none but the purest joys shall be known. The old enthusiastic Christian says, there I shall *see* Jesus, *feel* his fond embrace, *hear* his voice, and *taste* the sweets of redeeming love, and regale the senses upon the aroma rising from his garments, and be satisfied. So, we see, the different classes of human minds can have no conception of existence, separate from the sensuous organs, and as vision has been presented in this chapter, we will confine our attention to that more particularly, simply remarking that whatever is said of vision, may apply to some extent to all the other senses; for, they must all be equally spiritualized, to answer the purpose of spirit intelligences existing in the higher spheres.

It will be seen, then, that enlarged or microscopic vision, is absolutely necessary, in the spiritual abodes, for all purposes of utility and enjoyment, and, that vision must be sufficiently powerful to render their surroundings clearly visible, so that objects will impress themselves clearly upon the retina of the spirit-eye, and that impression must come in contact with their consciousness precisely the same as with us. If they are composed of highly refined particles, they must, in order to understand themselves, and become acquainted with their own physiological construction, be able to scan those sublimated particles by the power of vision, and they must have an eye correspondingly powerful, for, if they cannot see themselves and their surroundings, then they cannot know themselves and their conditions, any more than humanity could, had they been destitute of the physical eye.

We cannot see light, magnetism, electricity or aura, because the particles are too minute to make a visual impression; and yet, all those elements are known to consist of fluid particles, which are material. Suppose, now, those elemental constituents enter into the constitution of the spiritual form, such form would be entirely invisible to us, however tangible and visible it might be to an eye composed of corresponding elements. We at once discover the superiority of such a physical organization, composed of those and still more refined and powerful materials, to one formed from matter of a similar character, in a more gross and unspiritualized condition; and this is substantially the difference between organizations in the earth-life, and those in the spiritual spheres. One is grosser, the other more sublimated, and still more so as they advance from one condition or sphere to another, in the same manner as they pass from this to the next, by a dissolution of the grosser particles, thus permitting the escape or elimination of the more spiritualized body, each time becoming more sublimated, and acquiring superior and more exalted powers. Each change necessarily brings a still more exquisite refinement of every sense and faculty, and of course a corresponding enlargement of the powers of vision.

We may now begin to get some inkling of the inexhaustible resources of spiritual enjoyment; and of the almost infinitely multiplied powers they possess of opening the gates and avenues to all the storehouses and vast reservoirs where knowledge may be found. How little comparatively has the man or woman enjoyed in their best estate, and how little of themselves and their surroundings have they learned during the longest life, and how many thousand problems which are presented to the mind are to them dark and inexplicable? This darkness arises from the fact that all our sensuous organs are formed of gross material, and that all our higher faculties, expressing themselves through these coarse, earthly organs must necessarily be limited in their powers. Our locomotion is slow and toilsome, our physical strength is weakness, our hearing is extremely limited, our vision narrow, and unaided, it has but a single range, our feeling obtuse, our smelling not equal to the dog's, and our unrefined taste permits us to devour millions of living animalculæ, which if we could see in all their ugly proportions would create ineffable disgust.

There is but one remedy for all these seeming imperfections — one door through which we may escape from this groveling condition — and this door is death. There is found the universal gateway that leads to a purification and sublimation of our whole being, that enables us to lay aside this cumbrous load of gross particles which now chain us to the earth. This change will place at our disposal, and give us for our use, those etherealized sensuous organs and faculties that will bring us into harmony with the great spiritual universe, and give us a clear, unclouded vision of things as they really exist, because we shall be endowed with a vision that may scan the spiritual essential elements, instead of the coarse, material, transitional organization, through which the spirit expresses itself. How unspiritualized and gross in his nature must have been the individual mind who conceived the dogma of the resurrection of the body, and how darkly sensuous and opaque must be the minds of those persons, who, at this more advanced age, endorse the same ridiculous doctrine! What do they propose to do with the material organs in a spiritual condition? For what purpose can they use this restored material eye, ear, tongue, nose, or any nerves of touch or feeling? would they bring them in contact with spiritual essences? if so, why do not the same organs make us realize such contact now? If they are ever to require these bodies again, how very foolish to let them die and rot, and dissolve, and disperse in gases, to the four winds of heaven! Why have all the trouble of collecting the materials again and identifying the same body for the same spirit? If the union of the two is necessary to their enjoyment, why were they dissolved? But this dogma is of a piece with all the others that have been handed down, as relics of a darker age, from father to son, and are still adopted by a large number of people.

The light of eternal truth is dawning upon our world, and such distorted, incongruous, unphilosophical notions will ultimately flee to the dark chambers from whence they issued, having had their day.

The fields existing in this universe, that come within the range of human vision, are comparatively extremely limited and narrow. We think we look out a great way, and behold a vast amount that is wonderful, and the eye is never satisfied with seeing new things and objects. But when we take into consideration the vast and inconceivably extended realms in the great domain, that are entirely out of reach of the human eye, we may directly discover the importance of a vision of greatly augmented powers — of one that is not only telescopic and microscopic, but spiritualized in its character,— and probably the latter would embrace the whole, for no doubt a vision that can discern spiritual essences would embrace both those powers. Science travels out and ranges over vast fields of thought, and contemplates an endless variety of subjects beheld only by the interior or spiritual vision. We never saw with the material eye the first problem in geometry or any other branch of mathematics. We may have seen some problem illustrated in material form, as a circle or a triangle, but the problem itself is beyond the reach of external human vision.

We never saw any of the imponderable agents or forces. Very many of the primary elements in nature have never been beheld, yet science presents us lengthy and very learned essays upon all those invisible subjects. Newton did not see the gravity that brought the apple from the tree, yet he ascertained a principle from its effects, and thus he discovered the universal law of attraction.

The chemist pursues his researches in the dark, as far as human vision is concerned—he never saw a chemical affinity, or one of the gases or essential forces, or qualities that exist in the constituent elements from which he produces his combinations. The astronomer never saw a single principle which he may have deduced from his various observations. The statesman wanders out in his studies upon political economy, and dwells in the mazes of abstract principles unseen by the human eye. The attorney applies principles of law to his several cases, that never came in contact with any of his five senses The clergyman roams amidst a labyrinth of abstruse ideas, doctrines and opinions. He never saw, handled, tasted or smelled one of his weapons of offense or defense—not one of the great dogmas that he so earnestly presents to his hearers, have been subjected to any such test. All are based upon an invisible foundation, which he accepts by an act of his mentality that he terms faith or belief. These invisible, intangible ideas or beliefs have poured out such torrents of the blood of earth's children, that the soul sickens with the horror of its contemplation.

We have learned that there must be infinite lengths beyond, and almost equal depths below, the vision of man, and, that with all its power it has only yet discovered the smallest possible portion of the stupendous whole of the illimitable universe, which may be brought within the comprehension of our visions, at some day in the eternities of the future, when the spiritual eye shall be composed of the most sublimated and etherealized material that exists in the higher realms. What are all the invisible things that compose this overwhelmingly large portion of the universe we inhabit, and which attract so much of the attention of enlightened humanity? What are the invisible elements by which we are surrounded, and that are so necessary to us in sustaining human life? Science answers—they are all composed of material, though sublimated particles, and if so, those particles must be subject to the higher orders of vision. Can there be a division of particles down to that infinitesimal fineness, that shall go beyond the reach of all the possibilities of the still increased powers of spiritualized vision. We are compelled to conclude that there must be, somewhere, powers of vision that are able to scan material or spiritualized substances reduced to the last extent of divisibility. For, if the vision increases in power and extent of range by rising one step higher than our materialized condition (and we perceive it must be so, else spiritual beings could not see themselves, as our vision does not behold them), then, it will proportionately increase in power and range by taking another step, and so on until it shall be able to see all things, for all things must become visible to the eye that is constructed of the most spiritualized substances.

And now, we discern this great principle, that, if spiritual essences are but the sublimations of grosser particles, then all such essences must come within the range of spiritual vision, and as all our well-formed ideas and conceptions of things must be real things or real essences, then it follows that spiritual beings may see, and doubtless handle, those things that are merely ideal with us, precisely the same as we see and handle visible objects here in this material world. If electricity and magnetism, light and atmosphere, are composed of real particles, then they must be subject to the microscopic lenses of spiritual beings, and the extent of the magnifying power of their visual lenses will depend entirely upon their refinement, and the comparative exaltation of their condition. We think that spirits in the second sphere, can have no more absolute knowledge of the power of vision enjoyed in the third or fourth, than we have of that possessed by those that are in the second sphere, only we know that the inhabitants of the second are entirely beyond the reach of our vision, and that theirs must be entirely different and more powerful in order to discern themselves and their conditions. But, we must conclude that there is a vision so exalted and powerful as to discern all of which we can have any conception.

We may now notice, that all ideas, all thoughts, all mathematical problems, solved and unsolved, and all other conceptions of the human mind, that can make an impression upon the walls of our mental organs, are really things, for were they not, they would be nothings. As the mentality can take no cognizance of nothing, unless there is something to make the impression, such impression cannot be made upon our mental organizations. Hence we learn that individualized ideas, and conceptions of the human mind which make an inscription upon the walls of our organs, must be real entities composed of particles, and must also come within the range of possible vision,—and not only so, but that these thought-entities must have size, form, extension, and color. Why should the individual appear dark and murky or bright and sunny, unless the spirit within partakes of those different hues? and why should the spirit be tinged by different hues, unless the thoughts by which it is permeated are susceptible of the various colors? There are many human eyes which seem to be so piercing as to detect these peculiar characteristics in men and women.

We may now enquire further in relation to the possible extent of magnifying power. It is said that all particles are microcosms of the whole; that is, they contain all the essential elements within them which are contained in the whole,—that a drop of water, within its narrow limits embraces in miniature, all that is contained in all the waters of the earth. Man, then, being a microcosm, must contain *all* elementary constituents found upon our globe, and if so, we may naturally conclude that somewhere there must be visions that can behold in man or in the drop of water, all that there is in them. In order to do this, they must behold them in size equal to the whole of which they are a part, so that there must be visions which magnify the drop of water to the extent of all the water upon the earth, and discover in that drop, all that can be discovered in all the waters of the globe. Why not, if one part contains within itself all the elements found in the whole? Again, there must of necessity be visions or lenses that will reduce the vast ocean to a single drop, or the globe we inhabit to the dimensions of a grain of sand, and also peer out upon the remotest orb that has come within the range of the most powerful telescope, and bring it within hailing distance, and hold easy converse with its inhabitants.

Such is the faintest possible gleam of the ever increasing sensuous powers of spiritual intelligent beings during their progressive existence, on to higher and still higher conditions in the celestial spheres. It will be discovered that spirits cannot only see and handle the sublimated particles of light, electricity, magnetism, aura and the various gases; but, that by the intensity of their vision, and the power of their lenses, these fluid particles may be magnified to an indefinite extent, until each separate particle shall be as clearly and unmistakably discovered, as we see and discern the separate trees in our orchards, or the buildings upon our premises. If so, then the very thought-particles that line the chambers of our mentalities, must be as distinctly visible to advanced spirit intelligences, as the flowers that adorn our gardens, or the apples that hang pendant upon the branches. Then, how short-sighted is man! How narrow the limits of human vision! How feeble and vain our efforts in arriving at the real facts by which we are surrounded! How deceptive the best evidences we can gather by the unaided human eye, in deciding the thousand different questions that come up before us for adjudication! All is relative,—all is uncertain,—all would be entirely different, if only beheld by a different vision.

Can we suppose, for a moment, the individual with a refined and delicate appetite, would relish the morsel he eats with so much gusto and satisfaction, if he possessed an eye that would magnify a million diameters, and reveal to his astonished gaze the hideous crawling monsters that make his food their dwelling-place? It requires but small power to show us in the vinegar that we use at the table, unsightly animal organizations, and no doubt increased powers of vision would render that article extremely unpalatable. So we perceive that the human eye, deceptive as it may be, is far better for us in this gross, rudimental condition, than the intensified vision that is adapted to the higher realms. Suppose, for instance, we possessed eyes that would increase all objects beheld, a million times; those infusoria and animalculæ which exist in almost all that we eat, and in the atmosphere we breathe, and the fluids we drink, which are but a millionth part of an inch in length or breadth, would approximate a whole inch. Who of us would like to swallow down whole troops of these crawling, hairy monsters with ugly, protruding legs and claws, of any such proportions? We are, of course, entirely unconscious of the presence of an organized living being, that is but 1-1000th of an inch in length, much less of one that is but 1-1000,000th. It is said, however, that human skill has devised and constructed magnifying lenses that increase the object very many million times, and this is done from the gross material found here upon the earth; that would make the little fellows of the size above mentioned, which we are daily devouring in such quantities, enormous in length and proportionate in breadth—and this only a lens produced from gross materials by human ingenuity.

What then must be the inconceivable power of those lenses that may be produced, by using highly sublimated materials in their construction, and such as must be in common use in the spirit spheres? Suppose, now, you could hold a quiet conversation with one of those highly endowed spiritual intelligences, during your hour of repast. Suppose he should inquire what you were eating and drinking with so much apparent relish and enjoymont? You might reply, that this is really a very extraordinary entertainment,—I have here served up, to gratify my appetite, the richest viands, including all the luxuries that the season and the country can afford, in the shape of food and drink. But, my dear sir, says the spirit, who sees this feast, which is so elaborately prepared, through an entirely different eye, which may be so intensified as to enlarge all things a billion of times,—do not by any means partake of that food or those fluids. Why, sir, they are but one mass of animal life—all manner of creeping things, reptiles and four-footed beasts, are in the food, and in the drink. If you could see them as I do, all your refined sensibilities would be shocked, and you would be overwhelmed with horror and disgust. You would turn away from what you consider an excellent repast, with an unparalleled nausea and loathing, such as no man has experienced.

Now, which of these two is the real vision, and which discloses the real facts in the case? Ours, that is narrow and limited in its range, or the one that is more powerful, and sees inexpressibly further into the depths of the infinitesimal? It cannot be denied, that microscopic lenses that enhance objects a million diameters, disclose to us real facts, and real organized existences, which are entirely beyond the reach of the human eye. Through such a lens, the objects must appear a million times larger than the human vision could render them if it had the power to discern them. We may inquire, which is the real, actual size of those organizations, and if the size is not entirely regulated and governed by the character and quality of the lenses through which they are beheld? We must concede that such is the fact, and that the human vision does not govern the size of objects any more than any other, and as visions differ so extensively, we must conclude that all size, as we before remarked, is relative and depends entirely upon the character and powers of the vision which beholds the object. Here, we unavoidably discover the great fact, that a terrible deception has been practiced upon the whole human family. Some powers entirely superior to ourselves, have placed us in this condition where, by the obtuseness and inferiority of our sensuous organs, we are but a living lie to ourselves, existing in the very midst of a huge delusion, that is practiced upon us with impunity, and which, if we could behold with our natural visions, would cause us to curse the hour of our nativity, and any such continuous existence. For, we should see clearly, that in order to subsist, and continue in these earthly forms, it would be absolutely necessary for us to swallow up the life of those disgusting organized forms, which are so far beneath us, and which are so repulsive. And most assuredly, if we had the enhanced vision to discern those ugly forms, as they really exist in nature, we could not possibly submit to the disgusting process. Hence, the controlling powers have kindly practiced upon us this necessary deception, by giving us a range of vision which is only suited to our condition in the earth-sphere, and which entirely prevents the discernment of the real facts in this case.

This view of the subject presents another most indubitable evidence of the continuous progressive existence of spirit entities, through all forms of organization, from the lowest to the highest, for we turn with loathing from the food that is eagerly devoured, and with great relish, by many organized forms of life below us, and look with disgust while the animal is devouring the garbage and carrion that is thrown into the street. So, those who have a spiritualized vision, must look upon us in a similar manner, when they behold us pouring down our immense throats, whole cataracts of fluids teeming with infusoria in all their various crawling and wriggling forms, and great mountains of solid food, filled with regiments of all manner of animal life, existing in every variety of unsymmetrical and repulsive organisms. We have learned, then, that it is sometimes best the truth should not be told, and that deception is good and beneficial, and that it is a part of the arrangement, that it has a place in the great programme, and that without this benevolent deceit which is practiced upon humanity in relation to vision, they could not by any means subsist, for, if they were enabled to see things as they really appear to a higher and more perfected vision, they would not use the requisite means to prolong their existence. Hence, the absolute necessity of deception in this respect, by providing an imperfect vision, which will not permit us to discern the true nature of our surroundings, showing us most conclusively that we are only passing on the great journey which requires the eternity of eternities to perform, that in this condition truth and falsehood are relative terms, and that "whatever is is right," as adapted to the condition in which it exists.

The upright man that would not tell a falsehood or an untruth for his right hand, and that supposes his large stock of knowledge is an accumulation of verities, dwells in the midst of error and uncertainties; simply because of the imperfection of all his sensuous powers. If he appeals to any of his five senses, they can neither of them tell all the truth, because they cannot come in contact with all there is,—they are material, obtuse and imperfect, and liable every moment to deceive him in regard to the absolute nature of facts. They may tell him a story, but that story is only in accordance with their standard, and cannot extend beyond their powers of discernment. Ask the eye, of that beyond its reach, and it cannot respond to our inquiry. Ask the ear, of what it has never heard, and it has no reply to offer; and so of the rest of the senses. Hence there never, in all this progressive history, will be a time when we may arrive at absolute truth, until the sensuous organs are composed of the most refined and spiritualized material essences possible, until they may be able to reach and penetrate into all the essential truths that exist, and discern all facts, and all principles in the most absolute manner, and with the most highly perfected sensuous organs which may come directly in contact with the very soul-essence of all things.

We now see quite plainly, that such organs cannot be perfected so long as there is any chance for improvement, and they cannot take cognizance of, and appreciate, all of truth, until such perfection is attained. We freely express an opinion, that no such condition can be reached,—that no such attainments can be realized, for in that case the end of existence must surely arrive. There could be nothing more beyond; all knowledge would be grasped, all hopes and aspirations realized, all enjoyments experienced. There would be but one thing left for such a being to do, who has traveled the entire length of the road, who has completed his destiny, and conquered all things, and that would be, to turn within himself, procure his own dissolution, and commence his journey anew. However, the human mind can entertain no conception of the attainment of such a condition, during all the eternities of the future.

We have already observed, that all thoughts which may come within the range of scientific research, and also, every possible conception which can be brought within the contemplation of the most extended philosophy, must, in order to make an impress upon human or spirit mentality, be absolute particled entities, or else no such impress could be made by the thoughts or conceptions. Hence they must, as entities, be recognized by the sensuous organs of more etherealized beings. We now perceive, that the more progressed the organization, the more of real truth it may discover, or the nearer to real truth it may arrive, by the use of the sensuous organs connected with the varied faculties that are their concomitants. For we can arrive at nothing through the organs of sense, unless they are enabled to make a sensible impression, through the brain nerves, upon the mentality. We trust, if we commence at the lowest, and range through all the forms of organized life, we shall find a continuous progressive development in this respect. It will be noticed, that all the lower animal organizations seem to be in possession of the five senses, and some of them have remarkable developments of some particular one of those sensuous organs, as the intensified smell of the hound and the piercing glance of the eagle would denote. The minute animalcule must see, hear, feel, taste and smell, and some one or more, if not all, of these sensuous organs is possessed and enjoyed by the whole range, through all the different gradations from the lowest up to the highest, and the five senses, it must be admitted, are, in them, identical with the same senses in man,—there can be no difference in kind, only in degree.

We who live to-day under what we term the broad glare and sunlight of the nineteenth century, and enjoy the benefits of the discoveries of all the past ages, are apt to conclude that our visions and perceptions are clear, and that we are admitted into the great realms of real truth. But we are willing to concede, that our ancestors who saw things so differently, were somewhat blind and mystified in their perceptions, narrow in their ideas, and, in fact, that they dwelt in the midst of hallucination and deception, both as regards science and religion. Are we quite sure that posterity, a thousand years from this, will not discover the same fact in regard to ourselves? May they not be ready to conclude of this favored age, that its inhabitants dwelt under a cloud, and were unable to perceive the truths which may be quite familiar to them, and that we also live in a land of shadows and deceptions?

How many unnumbered ages did this mundane sphere exist, before any material had become sufficiently refined by the processes made use of in the natural realms, to produce a living organization with sensuous powers? and how many millions of periods since then, before those mysterious processes could work over and produce a material sufficiently refined to enter into the organization of human beings? and still how many ages have passed away before those beings could be endowed with sufficiently refined sensuous perceptive organs, to reflect upon the inner consciousness of mind, our present ideas and conceptions of truth? Can we suppose the world is now finished, and that the present generation have acquired all knowledge, or that we have now attained to that perception of all things, which shall endure through all the coming ages; that we have already worked out all the problems for posterity, and, that they will have no researches or discoveries to make, but just to live, and enjoy the advantages of our acquirements? We need not deceive ourselves with any such vain idea. The world is evidently in a very unfinished condition, material is constantly undergoing preparation for still more refined and spiritualized organizations. The atmosphere is being breathed over and over again, the waters of the ocean are constantly passing through changes by entering into the various organisms,—the carbon, oxygen, hydrogen and nitrogen are by constant use becoming refined and purified,—the caloric, vapor, electricity and magnetism are undergoing the same refining processes. Can we not see that when all the constituent elements which enter into the organization of man, become more spiritualized, they must produce a finer and more etherealized being, possessing more powerful sensuous organs which will reflect a clearer and more enlarged conception of his surroundings upon his consciousness? This will certainly bring him more directly in contact with the spiritual realms, where causes that have produced the effects by which we are surrounded, are more easily recognized and comprehended.

Then, it is by no means marvelous that philosophers of the present day, have not entertained a very clear conception of all the causes that have operated in producing the formation of the globe upon which we dwell, and that they should be somewhat mystified in relation to its physical arrangements; that they should also adopt theories which are so very unnatural, and antagonistic to well-defined principles pervading the universal realms, and, that very eminent scientific men have acknowledged the existence of the most active and explosive elements known to man, in the interior of our globe, in sufficient quantities to blow this whole solar system to fragments. It may not be strange, they have not discovered that our globe must be a mechanical structure, in which, of necessity, must be introduced the highest principles of art; that, as a consequence, the utmost economy of materials must be practiced; that those materials must be so arranged that the structure may subserve, to the greatest possible extent, the purposes for which it was designed; and, that it must also possess, within itself inherent, all the powers and capabilities of any other globe or mechanical structure of the kind. For if not, it would certainly be inferior to others—it would be a defective structure, reflecting little credit upon its builders, and indicate at least, that they were deficient in some of the qualifications necessary in order to build worlds in accordance with the most approved plans, or with the highest principles of the art. Certainly a lighter, more buoyant structure, in the form of a spherical shell, as thin as would be consistent with the required strength, with a convex and concave surface, both enveloped with an atmosphere and all the concomitant elements conducive to organized life and enjoyment, as a work of art exhibiting mechanical skill and ingenuity, would be far superior to a globe formed solid, or one filled with raging fire.

We readily discover, that those who recognized the Ptolemaic system of astronomy as being truthful and correct, had no perception of the wonderful mechanical skill and genius brought to light in the more rational system of Copernicus. They did not perceive, that the motions of the heavenly bodies were unnatural and impossible, nor the increased beauty, rationality and harmony of all those motions and revolutions as presented by the latter system. Neither have the philosophers of our time, seen the huge impropriety of making a world forty times heavier than is actually necessary, when one could have been made that would have subserved more than double the purposes, from one-fortieth of the material, and of proportionate weight. We ask if there is not as much relative difference in the mechanical genius necessary to bring to bear, in the construction of globes upon these two different principles, as there is in the two different systems of astronomy to which we have referred?

The one is awkward and clumsy, unsystematic, unduly weighty and unnatural, and impresses the mind when contemplating its interior, with a sort of dismal gloom, if not horror, and engenders a kind of dissatisfaction with the projectors and builders of such unmechanical structures, while the other is comparatively light, airy and pleasant, symmetrical and beautiful. It impresses the mind, upon its contemplation, with most agreeable and pleasurable emotions in view of the wondrous utility and marvelous ingenuity and wisdom displayed in such an admirably arranged superstructure; and, we are impelled to entertain the highest respect and veneration for the intelligences who could project and bring this marvel of perfection into existence in accordance with their design. Intelligent minds, with the clearer perceptive vision, and the purer mechanical taste that must prevail in future ages, will be as much shocked and pained at our present ideas of the physical formation and construction of our globe, as our minds are, at the astronomical construction and movements of the heavenly bodies, recognized by the Ptolemaic system; for both are equally absurd and unnatural, when contrasted with systems and theories that approximate so much nearer to harmonious principles.

We think it will be conceded, that, if the opinions of men concerning these and all kindred subjects, have been changing in the past, and have kept even pace with the advancing intelligence of the age, and the improved perceptives of the people, then such must be the case in the future; and, that there must be quite as much room for change of opinions and theories in the coming time, as there has been in the past, and that future generations will enjoy very great advantages over the present, in arriving at a nearer approximation to truth, not only from their clearer perceptions, but from the benefits derived from the experiences of their ancestors. It is vain, for us to suppose that we have established theories which will answer the purpose of posterity, unless they have been demonstrated beyond a doubt. Then, no one, we trust, will pronounce our idea concerning the physical structure of this globe, wild and visionary, until we have had the opportunity of exploring every square mile of its superficial area,—until the great polar circle that has been so long locked from human research by everlasting barriers of ice and cold, shall open her profound secrets to the children of men, and, until from actual discovery we learn the humiliating fact, that there was no genius brought to bear in the construction of our globe, that could possibly produce a superstructure in accordance with the highest principles of art,—one that would subserve the purposes for which it must have been designed, to the greatest possible extent.

Until these unfortunate facts shall be absolutely made known to the inhabitants of earth, by research and demonstration, let us cherish the hope, that our world was planned and constructed by the very highest order of mechanical skill, and upon principles that can by no means be improved or excelled. So, that in the distant ages of the future, when we may become somewhat familiar with the mechanical genius that has been brought to bear in the construction of other globes, we may enjoy the proud satisfaction of knowing that ours, upon which we had our birth, existence and experience, was no whit behind, in point of symmetry, beauty and grandeur, any other that may be found in the broad universe.. For, whatever may be our history in the future, we must always entertain an affectionate remembrance and regard for that world which was the home of our childhood, and the scene of our more mature reflections and experiences.

www.ingramcontent.com/pod-product-compliance
Lightning Source LLC
LaVergne TN
LVHW021132110826
845150LV00005B/1001